# DYNAMIC DUOS

*Also by Ken Piesse and published by The Five Mile Press*

Great Australian Cricket Stories (2010)

Great Australian Football Stories (2011)

# DYNAMIC DUOS

*Cricket's Finest Pairs and Partnerships*

Ken Piesse

Foreword by
Matthew Hayden

The Five Mile Press

The Five Mile Press Pty Ltd
1 Centre Road, Scoresby
Victoria 3179 Australia
www.fivemile.com.au

Copyright © Ken Piesse, 2012
Foreword © Matthew Hayden
All rights reserved. No part of this book may be reproduced, stored in a retrieval system, or be transmitted by any form or by any means, electronic, mechanical, photocopying, recording or otherwise, without the prior written permission of the publisher.

First published 2012

Printed in Australia at Griffin Press.
Only wood grown from sustainable regrowth forests is used in the manufacture of paper found in this book.

Page design and typesetting by Shaun Jury
Cover design by Luke Causby, Blue Cork
Front cover image: Famous Australian openers Justin Langer (left) with Matthew Hayden, © Newspix
Back cover images: Dynamic Australian batting duos through the ages: 1930s pair Don Bradman and Bill Brown (middle, author collection), 1960s pair Neil Harvey and Norm O'Neill (left, author collection) and 2010s pair Michael Clarke and Ricky Ponting (right, photographer Peter Argent)

National Library of Australia Cataloguing-in-Publication entry
Piesse, Ken.
Dynamic duos : cricket's finest pairs and partnerships / Ken Piesse.
ISBN: 9781743005330 (pbk.)
Cricket players--Australia
Cricket players--Australia--Anecdotes.
Cricket--Australia
Australia--Anecdotes.
796.3580994

# About the Author

As a young boy growing up in the beachside suburbs of Melbourne, Ken Piesse would borrow all 18 cricket books belonging to the Parkdale Library, sit them on a bookshelf at home and imagine they were his. Asked by his father if he cared to borrow any other books, he said, 'No.'

Now President of the Australian Cricket Society, Ken has his own cricketing library and is Australia's most published cricket and football author, whose books have sold in tens of thousands.

Editor of *Cricketer* magazine for 15 years (1978–92), *Australian Cricket* magazine (1996–2003) and now the *Summer Tour Guide* (2004–), he has also co-written more than a dozen autobiographies with leading personalities including Max Walker, Terry Jenner and Brad Hodge.

*Dynamic Duos: Cricket's Finest Pairs and Partnerships* is his sixty-sixth book and follows his best-selling anthology *Great Australian Cricket Stories*.

In 2012, Ken won the major Media Award from Cricket Victoria for his interview with Australia's one-Test leg-spinner Bryce McGain.

Ken is the cricket commentator for *Radio Sport National*, a life member of the Frankston Peninsula Cricket Club and a member of the Melbourne Cricket Club Media Hall of Fame (inducted in 1999) and the Australian Football League's Media Hall of Fame (2011).

# Foreword

*Matthew Hayden*

It's amazing how people can click. Take Justin Langer and me. 'Alfie' and I are so different in so many ways, him on one side of the country and me on the other, yet I'm just about as close to him as my very own brother.

Despite what he may say, there's no way he recognised me when I walked past him at the Gabba in the lead-up to a Shield game in the early 1990s. I'd been to the beach and was in boardies, thongs and a singlet. We nodded and said 'G'day'. I'm sure he thought I was part of the groundstaff. He couldn't believe it when I came out to bat the next day and started taking guard.

We had six wonderful years opening the batting together and when Alfie retired, it was never quite the same. Phil Jaques and 'Kat' (Simon Katich) were fine players and great blokes, but we just didn't have that same feeling of kinship that 'Alfie' and I share.

And of all my achievements in the game, few gave me as much pleasure as pairing with Alfie. He'd take centre and when I got to the striker's end, I'd cross it with a line to form the sign of a cross. When I was at the bowler's end while he was preparing to face the first ball, I would mark centre and he would cross it when we changed ends. It was another anchor for us.

Opposing attacks found it difficult to bowl to us. Alfie loved to play his cut and pull shots. Anything short was meat and drink for him. I preferred the straighter full ones so I could hit the ball down the ground. It all went back to my backyard Tests inside and outside

---

**Century Specialist**: In addition to making 30 Test centuries for Australia, Matthew Hayden shared in 30 century stands with fellow opener Justin Langer and long-time Australian No. 3 Ricky Ponting.

on the farm with my brother Gary. If it had got too dark to play outside, we'd duck inside into the pool room. We even drew white stumps on the wall, Mum's only proviso was that no shots be made square of the wicket into her glass doors! The habits of hitting straight started then and there.

As bowlers looked to negate us, they would get straighter to Justin and wider to me and that brought other shots into play, Justin's cover drive and me with the cut shot I hadn't been allowed to play as a kid.

Funnily enough, probably our most memorable partnership – certainly one of the most important – wasn't even a century. It was Day 1 of the 2006–07 summer against the Poms, the day Steve Harmison started with one so wide it was taken by Andrew Flintoff at second slip. I still remember the lead-up and all the tension that goes with the start of an Ashes series. They'd beaten us in England in 2005 and we were really keen to start well and keep them on the back foot. This day we started with 79 and we ended up making 600-plus. Winning 5-nil was a bonus none of us will ever forget.

That was the summer Warnie, Glenn McGrath and Alfie all retired, ending a fabulous era for Australian and cricket and one in particular for Alfie and me.

Seeing us on the front cover of *Dynamic Duos* brings back so many happy moments for me. Few could celebrate mid-pitch like us! Two grown men hugging each other after a team or individual milestone became a common occurrence – we were best mates and didn't mind showing it!

The night before my 380 against Zimbabwe in Perth, I went around to Justin and Sue's place and sat on the front lawn and we shared a big cigar to mark the start of the summer. We didn't say much. We didn't have to. We toasted absent friends and just stared at the stars.

We're very lucky as the girls, Kellie and Sue, are the greatest of mates, too, which just adds to the mix. Christmases in Melbourne used to be fantastic for us all. One Christmas Eve, we shared mass together at Mazenod College with Father Pat Maroney, who had married Kell and me. If it was possible, it cemented our bond even more. It was a privilege when Justin and Sue asked Kell to be godmother to their youngest daughter, Grace.

We don't catch up quite as often as we'd like, but when we do, the grins are genuine and the stories invariably embellished.

I'd like to again thank Ken Piesse for asking me to do a foreword to another of his books. His service to cricket is truly remarkable. He knows and loves the game like few I know. Alfie and I shared that same sort of passion and that was one of the reasons why we enjoyed so much success. In time another pair of Australian openers may come along and re-write the record books. I hope they do and if they have as much fun as Alfie and I enjoyed along the way, their time will also be unforgettable.

*Matthew Hayden*

# Author's Note

It was while I was pushing the third and heaviest of three crates containing 51 boxes of cricketana up our driveway that my wife Susan questioned my sanity. Again.

'How much of all this do you intend to keep?' she asked, knowing full well that it was all bound for my library. 'Hope there's something new.'

It was September 2011 and my biggest-ever cricket collection purchase included books, *Wisdens*, rare between-the-wars cricket magazines and souvenir brochures, every *ABC Cricket Book* bar one, trade and cigarette cards, scrapbooks and hundreds of original team and action photographs.

The collection was vast and took weeks to sort. 'Please don't throw *anything* out,' I'd asked my friend's family and, true to their word, it all arrived intact. Talk about Christmas coming early.

The collection belonged to northern New South Wales farmer Gordon Vidler, who died at 90 on 27 August 2008, the centenary of Don Bradman's birth. His son Bob said every farm conversation would always include cricket and the Don.

'It didn't matter what we were discussing, tractors, feed, whatever. Dad would always find a way of talking about Bradman,' he said. 'He first wrote to him in 1933 and they corresponded regularly for a good 60 years and more.'

The Don gave Gordon a pair of gloves which are now on display at the Bradman Museum in Bowral. In 1983 Gordon visited the Don and Lady Jessie in Adelaide, fulfilling a lifelong dream to shake the Don's hand. Bob and his wife Sue still have the photo in pride of place at the farm.

Gordon loved anything to do with the game. Seeing a photograph he liked in a newspaper, Gordon would write away for it, to newspapers in Sydney and Melbourne and to many in the UK.

'Dad loved it when the latest envelope or package would arrive with the mail,' his son said. 'He was collecting right up until the end. He just loved it.'

As I sorted through the treasure trove of photographs, some 'specials' caught my eye and immediately I filed them away for a future project. . . this one.

Among the boxes were dozens of precious team and individual photos, all in their original sleeves, many of which I'd never seen before. Several of the action pictures were signed, including one by Bill Brown and his great opening partner Jack Fingleton, which is included in this book. Another was signed by two other between-the-wars champions, the two Bills: Ponsford and Woodfull. There was a whole series from Manuka Oval of Don Bradman's very last game, including one with Sir Robert Menzies, Australia's cricket-loving Prime Minister of the time.

There were dozens of other more contemporary ones, too, like Bobby Simpson and Bill Lawry, Jeff Thomson and Dennis Lillee, and the South Africans Graeme Pollock and Eddie Barlow.

About this time my publisher at The Five Mile Press, Julia Taylor, was in touch, canvassing ideas for a 2012 cricket book.

'Your timing is impeccable,' I said. 'I'm surrounded by photos. There are some beauties among them.'

The result is *Dynamic Duos: Cricket's Finest Pairs and Partnerships*, and I'd like to thank Julia and everyone at The Five Mile Press for their support of my latest project, my third in as many years with FMP.

While Gordon's photographs were an inspiration, having access to the research skills of one of Australia's leading cricket statisticians, Charles Davis, was a huge bonus and many of Charles' fascinating tables are also included here.

Take Matthew Hayden and Justin Langer, for example, who are pictured on the cover. One of Australia's ultimate opening pairs, they did significantly better when they opened up together. The only Australian ground where they failed to average 50-plus was the WACA Ground in Perth. Matty did me the honour of contributing the foreword.

As Charles was able to show, Shane Warne and Glenn McGrath were finer, more effective bowlers operating in tandem, building pressure and reaping the rewards like no other pair in history. Whenever one was absent, the other invariably would not do as well.

I would toss Charles some thoughts and ideas and within 48 hours, back would come the replies with some remarkably detailed charts. He even re-enacted, over by over, the famous Mackay-Kline last-wicket stand which saved a Test match in Adelaide during the incomparable West Indian summer of 1960–61.

Charles' statistics, like Gordon's photos, have helped to add substance, fibre and fun to this book.

My thanks, too, to so many friends and Test cricketers of note who all answered my queries and SOSs. Among them were Ian Brayshaw, Mark Browning, Stephen Chalke, Greg Chappell, Colin Clowes, Bob Cowper, Jamie Cox, Tony Crafter, Cathy and David Cruse, Ross Dundas, Patrick Eagar, Peter French, Sourav Ganguly, Stephen Gibbs, Adam Gilchrist, Ron Harbourd, Neil Harvey, Ian Healy, Mahela Jayawardene, Bill Lawry, Rod Marsh, Colin McDonald, Arthur Morris, Bruce Postle, Glyn Powell, Craig Reece, Trevor Ruddell, Kumar Sangakkara, Greg Shipperd, Bobby Simpson, Clive van Ryneveld, John Ward, Wasim Akram and Bruce Yardley. My sincere thanks to you all.

My family have also been very supportive, especially my wife Susan who continues to allow me to indulge my passion for writing about the game – and for collecting!

Until next time. . . enjoy.

Ken Piesse
Mt Eliza, July 2012

WACA
OKABURRA

**'They've laughed, they've cried, they've shared, building an unbreakable bond . . .'**

## ACCIDENTAL PAIRING

If it wasn't for a brand new Mini Minor van with a stiff gearshift, Bill Lawry's celebrated pairing with Bobby Simpson at the head of the Australian order would have been delayed at least 15 months.

Australia's senior opening batsman Colin McDonald developed such a sore wrist from changing the gears of a new car during the 1961 tour, he could barely hold a bat. Reserve opener Bobby Simpson had played each of the first three Tests down the list and was promoted to the top of the order with McDonald unavailable for both the fourth and fifth Tests. McDonald had bought the car for his wife Lois and young daughter Karen who, with the assistance of Ashes stalwart Alec Bedser, were renting an apartment in Nightingale Lane, Clapham.

'The wives weren't allowed to be in the same hotel as the players back then,' said McDonald. 'Alec organised this apartment for us and, to help ferry Lois and Karen around, I bought this Mini Minor. I was lucky to get it as the demand for vehicles was far greater than the production, but it had this very stiff gear shift which I could only just move, so much so that I developed a repetitive strain in my left wrist, my top hand [which controls the bat]. By the end of

---

**Consistent:** Justin 'Alfie' Langer shared 14 Test century stands and averaged 51 with Matthew Hayden, including back-to-back double centuries in their first two Tests together on Australian soil in 2001. *Stephen Laffer*

the Leeds Test [the third of five, when McDonald made 54 and 1], I could hardly hold a bat and stood down from the last two Tests. I stayed on after the tour to work in the UK and never played another Test. I wish to goodness I'd never got that car! But it was the start of the Simpson-Lawry union and my injury also saw Brian Booth come into the side for the first time. He was to become a very fine player for Australia.'

The McDonald-Lawry stands in the first three Tests in 1961 had been worth just 27 per innings. Lawry and Simpson flourished from their first Test together at Old Trafford, sharing an important second innings stand of 113 before Richie Benaud famously went around the wicket and spun a revitalised Australia to the Ashes.

It was the first of nine century stands by the pair, including five against the old Enemy, their daredevil running between wickets an immediate characteristic.

'It was something we always did. We both thought it safest at the other end!' said Simpson. 'We didn't always call. Often it was just a nod. We'd drop the ball at our feet and off we'd go. It's a lost art now.'

The pair weren't roomies, or particularly great mates. At night on tour, they'd generally dine separately. Yet Simpson felt more comfortable batting with Lawry than anyone else.

'It was always a great comfort to see Bill at the other end,' said Simpson. 'We knew each other's games backwards and sometimes would look to take a particular end to help each other. I tended to play the spinners a little bit better than Bill. He was a great player of fast bowling and if one or the other was struggling just a little against a particular bowler, you'd take the end where you could best help your mate.'

Earlier in 1961, all in touring matches, Simpson had gone in first with Lawry five times for three century stands, including a double century partnership at Oxford. Few were as versatile in adapting from batting from No. 1 to No. 6. All but three of his first dozen Tests had been in the middle order. In his maiden series in South Africa, Simpson had gone in as low as No. 8 and in his first Ashes series the following Australian summer, he'd played only one of the five Tests and had not been selected for the India and Pakistan tour of 1959–60.

In his bid to resurrect his career, Simpson shifted from New South Wales to Western Australia to open the innings regularly. While the internationals were away on the sub-continent, Simpson amassed 902 Sheffield Shield runs at the remarkable average of 300.66. In eight days he made two career-reviving double centuries, both not out. Of particular satisfaction was his 236 against his mates from New South Wales. He and veteran Ken Meuleman added 301 for the fifth wicket, Meuleman continually advising Simpson to 'cash in'.

'He kept saying to me, "Don't throw it away. Keep going. When you get 200, think about 300." I didn't need much convincing, though,' said Simpson. 'Only big scores were going to get me back into the Test side. I wasn't going to set limits on what I made. I just wanted to bat and the more runs I made the better.'

During his monumental double against New South Wales, Simpson gloved a catch behind but survived the appeal. He was only in his 60s at the time. He always regarded it as the most timely reprieve of his career. Big runs against the power states, New South Wales and Victoria, always counted.

His first Tests opening the batting had been with McDonald at his side during the wonderful Calypso summer of 1960–61, his rapid-fire 92 in the deciding Test in Melbourne featured a rare thrashing of West Indian expressman Wes Hall, whose only five overs cost 40, including 18 off the first and nine off the second.

But it was alongside Lawry, the tall, angular, grafting Melburnian, where he was to make most impact.

So prolific had the unheralded Lawry been on arrival in the UK in 1961 that he'd scored three centuries and averaged 80 leading into the first Test, his double of 104 and 84 not out against the MCC at Lord's an Ashes selection clincher. It wasn't coincidental that his first two Ashes centuries, at Lord's and Old Trafford, had seen the Australians win. By the end of his triumphant first tour, Lawry had been dubbed 'William the Conqueror'.

Don Bradman and the Australian selection panel always favoured a left- and a right-hander at the head of the order and the Simpson-

Lawry combine was a pivotal force in Australia's top-order for five consecutive summers, home and away. Their judgment of the short single always seemed impeccable, ladies in the crowd often screaming as the pair stole ever-so-short singles, despite having just tapped the ball a yard or two in front of their feet.

'We'd call, but not always, especially if we defended at our feet,' said Lawry. 'We always reckoned the safest place to be was at the non-striker's end and we'd do everything possible to get there.'

Their highest stand – and certainly their bravest – came at Bridgetown in 1965 when they defied the fire of the two menacing West Indian expresses, Wes Hall and Charlie Griffith, to become the first Australians to bat through an entire day's play on their way to a record stand of 382.

Griffith bowled five bouncers in six balls to Simpson and struck Lawry almost flush on the cheekbone with another short delivery, yards quicker than his 'normal' ball. From his first delivery in the opening Test in Kingston, the Australians had labelled Griffith as a 'chucker'.

'No man can project a ball at 90 miles per hour from almost a standing start without throwing it,' said Simpson.

The series had been billed as an unofficial world championship and in Hall and Griffith, the West Indies had the fieriest pair since Bodyliners Harold Larwood and Bill Voce. The West Indies won two of the first three Tests, Simpson and Lawry failing to share in even one 40-run partnership in their first five innings of the series. It was the first time they'd ever failed three Tests in a row.

In Port-of-Spain, Griffith scored five direct hits on Australian batsmen. The attack was intense, Griffith's in-slanting bouncer and change-up yorker almost impossible to combat. The Australian anger grew as local umpires refused to intervene against someone they felt was blatantly cheating.

With Australia needing to win both of the last Test matches to hold the Frank Worrell Trophy, the Kensington Oval wicket for the fourth Test was a runmaker's paradise, white and flat, the chances remote of either side bowling the other out twice. But Hall and Griffith attacked furiously, Lawry shaken up by the ball

**AUSTRALIA'S TOP TEN OPENING PAIRS**

| | Runs | Highest | Average | 100s |
|---|---|---|---|---|
| Matthew Hayden and Justin Langer | 5655 | 255 | 51 | 14 |
| Bill Lawry and Bobby Simpson | 3596 | 382 | 60 | 9 |
| Mark Taylor and Michael Slater | 3887 | 260 | 51 | 10 |
| Geoff Marsh and Mark Taylor | 1980 | 329 | 45 | 4 |
| David Boon and Geoff Marsh | 1871 | 217 | 46 | 5 |
| Simon Katich and Shane Watson | 1523 | 182 | 54 | 3 |
| Bill Lawry and Keith Stackpole | 1302 | 95* | 44 | - |
| Colin McDonald and Jim Burke | 1144 | 190 | 39 | 3 |
| Matthew Hayden and Michael Slater | 1045 | 156 | 43 | 3 |
| Bill Brown and Jack Fingleton | 1020 | 233 | 63 | 3 |

* unbeaten

from Griffith he wore on the jaw. Umpire Kippins had earlier given Griffith a 'friendly' warning for too many short deliveries, but after the onslaught of five bouncers in an over at Simpson, Kippins told Griffith that he would be banned from the crease for intimidatory bowling if he continued to pitch short. Griffith noticeably slowed and bowled a fuller length.

Simpson and Lawry added 263 on the first day (Simpson 137, Lawry 102) and extended their stand to 382, the pair becoming the first Test openers to both score double centuries.

'We wanted to keep the singles coming and make the most of anything loose,' said Simpson. 'Wes sent down a lot of short stuff and I was able to square cut and back cut him to keep the runs flowing. Bill kept the singles flowing and farmed the strike back to me as much as possible.'

The two Australians received only 10 six-ball overs in the first hour and 81 for the day, shades of Clive Lloyd's tactics with his West Indian fast bowlers almost a generation on. The world record of 413 for the first wicket between Indians Vinoo Mankad and Pankaj Roy was in their sights before Simpson, the first to 200, played onto Hall having batted almost a day and a half. The game was to be drawn in Australia's favour, Simpson's team winning the final Test in Trinidad.

### BOBBY SIMPSON AND BILL LAWRY IN TESTS

| Opponent | Tests | Innings | Not Out | Runs | Highest | Average | 100s |
|---|---|---|---|---|---|---|---|
| England | 13 | 22 | 1 | 1228 | 244 | 58 | 5 |
| South Africa | 9 | 18 | 0 | 873 | 118 | 48 | 1 |
| West Indies | 5 | 9 | 1 | 585 | 382 | 73 | 1 |
| India | 5 | 9 | 0 | 753 | 191 | 83 | 2 |
| Pakistan | 2 | 4 | 0 | 157 | 81 | 39 | 0 |
| **Total** | **34** | **62** | **2** | **3596** | **382** | **60** | **9** |

Fittingly, Simpson and Lawry were at the wicket when victory was completed. It was Australia's only win of the ill-tempered tour.

Back in Australia the Ashes were retained, a 244-run partnership between Simpson and Lawry in Adelaide the highlight of an innings' victory.

They remained at the head of the order until 1967–68 when Simpson told chairman of selectors Don Bradman that he would not be touring England in 1968 and was immediately dropped!

'Given my time again I wouldn't have said a word to the Don,' said Simpson, who'd started the Tests with scores of 55, 103 and 109 against the touring Indians.

In their last match together, in Melbourne at Christmastime in 1967, the pair added 191, passing India's all out score of 173 themselves.

In Simpson's absence, Lawry was to have five different partners in four years. 'Redders [Ian Redpath] wasn't a good judge of a run, Stacky [Keith Stackpole] didn't like running much, but Bobby was such a good judge of angles,' said Lawry. 'Occasionally, though we'd get it wrong. Did Bobby tell you that he ran me out three times!'

## ALFIE AND HAYDOS

Apart than being left-handers, Matthew Hayden and Justin Langer, Australia's most famous set of openers seemed to share little common ground. They'd come from opposite ends of Australia, one from the country, one from the city. Matthew Hayden was tall and intimidating, wide of smile, a late bloomer, advancing at even the quickest of bowlers and launching his shots imperiously wide of mid-on; Justin 'Alfie' Langer was shorter, sensitive, intense, determined, a nudger and a deflecter, an ally, reliable, committed and dependable.

Langer was at the Australian Cricket Academy in Adelaide in 1995 looking to revive his Test career when head coach Rod Marsh organised a weekend camp involving the most promising non-Academy batsmen from around Australia. Hayden was one of the invitees. After a blazing near 1000-run opening season of Shield cricket, Hayden had been part of Australia's Ashes squad in 1993, only to lose form and favour. At a panel discussion one evening he was asked what it was like to be out of form. After a pause, Hayden said: 'You go out to bat and you feel like you've got someone else's dick in your hand. . . your bat just doesn't feel right in your hands.'

If it hadn't been such a serious forum, Langer would have been rolling around the aisles in hysterics. From that moment he knew that 'Haydos', the 'Big Unit', the 'Nature Boy', would be his mate.

They were to become the most-capped and most prolific set of openers in Australian Test history. Their wives also cemented the closest of friendships, which sees Kellie Hayden godmother to Langer's youngest daughter Grace. Hayden says Langer is as dear to him as his own brother. They've laughed, they've cried, they've shared, building an unbreakable bond.

From the time they first opened in England in 2001, sharing the first of 14 century partnerships together, they provided a sure and consistent launching pad for the Australian top-order which hadn't been present since the days of Bobby Simpson and Bill Lawry.

Langer was a central part of Australia's unprecedented 16 Test wins in a row. Hayden's exploits included a new Test record of 380 against Zimbabwe in Perth, a colossal knock featuring thirty-eight 4s and eleven 6s.

They were cornerstones in Australia's extraordinary run of success, broken only by the series loss in England in 2005.

Hayden was to score 24 of his 30 Test centuries with Langer beside him. Langer scored 17 of his 23 centuries with Hayden beside him.

**CENTURY STANDS IN TESTS BY JUSTIN LANGER AND MATTHEW HAYDEN**

| Stand | Details |
|---|---|
| 158 | v England, The Oval, 2001<br>Langer 102 retired hurt, Hayden 68 |
| 224 | v New Zealand, Brisbane, 2001–02<br>Langer 104, Hayden 136 |
| 223 | v New Zealand, Hobart, 2001–02<br>Langer 123, Hayden 91 |
| 202 | v South Africa, Melbourne, 2001–02<br>Langer 85, Hayden 138 |
| 219 | v South Africa, Sydney, 2001–02<br>Langer 126, Hayden 105 |
| 102 | v South Africa, Cape Town, 2001–02<br>Langer 58, Hayden 96 |
| 101 | v England, Adelaide, 2002–03<br>Langer 48, Hayden 46 |
| 195 | v England, Melbourne, 2002–03<br>Langer 250, Hayden 102 |
| 242 | v West Indies, Antigua, 2002–03<br>Langer 111, Hayden 177 |
| 147 | v India, Sydney, 2003–04<br>Langer 117, Hayden 67 |
| 255 | v Sri Lanka, Cairns, 2004<br>Langer 162, Hayden 117 |
| 136 | v India, Chennai, 2004–05<br>Langer 71, Hayden 58 |
| 137 | v New Zealand, Adelaide, 2004–05<br>Langer 215, Hayden 70 |
| 185 | v England, The Oval, 2005<br>Langer 105, Hayden 138 |

In five years they opened Australia's batting 113 times. Four of their first 11 stands resulted in double-centuries, including back-to-back Tests against the South Africans in 2001–02. Their highest stand was 255 against Sri Lanka at Cazaly Stadium, Cairns, and their dearest, 79 in the opening Ashes Test of 2006–07 when the battle lines were being drawn and Steve Harmison's ever-so-nervous first ball was taken at second slip.

The number of hugs, high-fives and back-slaps were never recorded, but they were plentiful. The only two international pairings who stepped out first more often together were the West Indians Gordon Greenidge and Desmond Haynes (with 148 innings together) and the Sri Lankans Marvan Atapattu and Sanath Jayasuriya (118). Neither showed their sheer joy at each other's accomplishments as often or as openly as Hayden and Langer.

Hayden and Langer averaged 51 together as openers. Previously when Langer was coming in at No. 3, their stands were under 40.

Langer liked to take strike and, especially later in his career, was known to crash an immediate drive or two through to the cover fence. In Hobart in 2001, on their way to a stand of 223, Hayden was just 1 when Langer was raising his bat to acknowledge the applause for his 50, a happy snap of the lop-sided scoreboard taking pride of place in the Langer games room in Perth. Hayden may have had the big shots, but Langer invariably kept pace. Looks can be deceiving. Statistician Charles Davis says Langer outpaced Hayden 53 to 47 for every 100 runs they scored.

Hayden's sheer stature and attacking flair encouraged an inner confidence in Langer he'd never experienced with any other partner.

'Batting with one of your best mates is an inspired feeling,' Langer said. 'I felt like I had one of the Greek or Roman warriors like Spartacus or Maximus beside me every time we strode onto a cricket ground. He was the size of a warrior, walked like a warrior and batted like a warrior.'

Hayden said he never ever felt quite the same opening the batting with others after Langer's international retirement in 2007.

'It had absolutely nothing to do with the calibre of his replacements Phil Jaques and Simon Katich, who are terrific blokes and fine players,' he said. 'But when you have a partnership that's right, everything just flows. It's like driving from Brisbane to Cairns at your own pace, just floating along. Having a new partner is like making the same trip with a police car on your tail. You're instantly aware of every little detail. Should I be indicating? Am I going too fast? Alfie and I never tried to analyse our connection too much. It was what it was.'

### MATTHEW HAYDEN'S OPENING TEST PARTNERS

| | Innings | Runs | Average for partnership |
|---|---|---|---|
| Justin Langer | 113 | 5655 | 51 |
| Michael Slater | 25 | 1045 | 43 |
| Phil Jaques | 11 | 784 | 71 |
| Simon Katich | 17 | 557 | 34 |
| Michael Hussey | 7 | 458 | 65 |
| Mark Taylor | 10 | 132 | 13 |
| Adam Gilchrist | 1 | 30 | 30 |

### JUSTIN LANGER'S OPENING TEST PARTNERS

| | Innings | Runs | Average for partnership |
|---|---|---|---|
| David Boon | 2 | 40 | 20 |
| Matthew Hayden | 113 | 5655 | 51 |

### MATTHEW HAYDEN AND JUSTIN LANGER IN TESTS IN AUSTRALIA

| | Innings | Runs | Average for partnership |
|---|---|---|---|
| Hobart | 1 | 223 | 223 |
| Brisbane | 8 | 563 | 70 |
| Sydney | 16 | 810 | 57 |
| Melbourne | 9 | 519 | 57 |
| Adelaide | 11 | 621 | 56 |
| Perth | 10 | 196 | 19 |

## AMBY AND CUDDY

For a decade and more in the 1980s and early 1990s, the West Indies were undisputed champions of the cricket world thanks to Clive Lloyd, King Viv and an arsenal of imposing fast bowlers who continued to beat up and intimidate the best batsmen in the world, series after series. Some teams were beaten even before they started, such was the aura and sense of invincibility surrounding the all-stars from the Caribbean.

There were signs in Australia in 1992–93, however, that the Windies had become a little vulnerable – until the final decisive Test in Perth when the tall, imposing Antiguan Curtly Ambrose went into overdrive, ending the match before lunch on the third day, the earliest finish to a Test down under since 1931.

Twelve months later, England had hopes of recovering the Wisden Trophy until confronted by the combined hostility of Ambrose and the almost-as-tall Jamaican Courtney Walsh, who shared 18 wickets between them in runaway West Indian victories at Sabina Park and Bourda.

The English hit back and controlled the pivotal third Test at Queens Park, Port-of-Spain, until the final eventful hour on the penultimate night when they were blown away by a fast-bowling onslaught of rare venom and quality.

Eyeing a target of just 194, England's captain Mike Atherton succumbed to Ambrose's high-speed first ball, a wicked delivery which nipped back and trapped him in front. Mark Ramprakash was run out off his fifth and Robin Smith castled by his eighth as England went to stumps at 8–40 on its way to a humiliating 46 all out – surpassing by just one run its lowest Test score in 699 Tests. Even gritty Graham Thorpe, top scorer in the first innings with a Barrington-like 86, was to succumb in the final hour as Ambrose and Walsh tore into the visitors, Ambrose taking six for 24 from 10 high-octane overs and Walsh three for 16 from 9.1. Only one Englishman made double figures, opener Alec Stewart with 18.

'They had 15 overs at us before the close,' said Stewart, 'and Ambrose and Walsh came out with guns blazing and really slipped themselves. When the bowlers have only seven or eight overs each before the close, they can bend their backs and for a batsman with close fielders breathing down his neck, all that adds to the pressure.'

Both West Indians kept the ball full and rarely allowed a loose ball, Atherton rating the onslaught as one of the best he'd ever seen.

'Ambrose, in particular, was simply astonishing,' he said. 'He sensed there was a match to win and a wearing pitch to exploit.'

Having seen a nervy Ramprakash run himself out, Atherton retired to the showers and when he re-emerged, England was six down. Game over. England's room was deathly silent that night.

'We couldn't believe it,' said Stewart. 'The game had been taken away from us in just over an hour. If we had been four down overnight, there might have been a chance for us, but not at 40 for eight.'

Cementing their standing in the Caribbean's fast-bowling Hall of Fame, 30-year-old Ambrose claimed 11 wickets for the game and 31-year-old Walsh five.

Until those two memorable late March days in 1994, two West Indians had never before bowled unchanged through an innings.

The pair were to play 95 Tests together, the most by any pair of fast bowlers and second only behind the Australians Shane Warne and McGrath (with 104) and equal to the Sri Lankans Muthiah Muralidaran and Chaminda Vaas.

The West Indies has boasted faster new ball combinations: Wes Hall and Charlie Griffith, Andy Roberts and Michael Holding, and Holding and Malcolm Marshall. But none were as consistently intimidating, lethal or as enduring as 'Amby' and 'Cuddy'. They opened the bowling together 86 times, the majority later in their careers when they defied advancing years to keep West Indian cricket competitive.

'We knew what was best for each other,' said Walsh, 'and we knew what was best for the team.'

Committed, dedicated and passionate, few were prouder of their maroon West Indian cap than Walsh. He moved the new ball into the right-handers at high pace and sometimes followed with a second spell of searing short deliveries, zeroing in directly at the throats of opposing right-handers. Most of the time, though, he bowled within himself, fulfilling into-the-wind team roles, maintaining peak pressure. He revelled in responsibility and once sent down 26 overs unchanged in a home Test.

At 200 cm (6 ft 7 in) Ambrose was taller, more athletic and consistently faster, his change-up deliveries being near-express. Rarely would he allow batsmen the opportunity to move onto the front foot, his trampolining bounce an intimidating constant, even on flat wickets.

'He projected the ball from such a great height,' said Thorpe. 'He didn't like conceding runs and bowled just short of a good length. It made it almost impossible to drive him down the ground. Walsh was very different. He varied things a lot, bowled a fuller length and could swing the ball. He had a good bouncer and later also developed a hard-to-detect slower ball that made him an absolute nightmare to face.'

Walsh had originally been the silent partner behind the more glamorous 'pacers' Holding, Marshall, Joel Garner and Colin Croft, before opening regularly with Ambrose, their combination becoming as feared and potent as any in the game.

The pair didn't share the new ball at all in the first 28 matches they played together, but once they were given centre stage, they provided a winning edge to the West Indian attack which enabled the team to stay at the top even into the mid-1990s after the retirements of Viv Richards and co.

Walsh was at his best when opening the bowling alongside Ambrose, who fretted when even a single was conceded. The pair built pressure at both ends, Walsh averaging 22.4 runs per wicket and 4.54 wickets per match in 52 games with Ambrose at the other end, against his career statistics of 24.4 and 3.93. Ambrose took slightly fewer wickets per match when he opened with Walsh than over his whole career (3.85 versus 4.13); his bowling average, however, was largely unchanged (21 versus 21.2).

No opening partnership consistently prospered against the high-speed duo. English pair Atherton and Stewart had their moments but still averaged less than 50.

In the Barbados Test of 1994, just a week after the humiliation of Trinidad, more than 6000 English fans were at Kensington Oval and started cheering when Atherton and Stewart advanced the score to 47, one more than the infamous all-out for 46 at Port-of-Spain! Stewart regards the twin centuries he made in that game against such high-class opposition as among the very best of a distinguished career.

**AMBROSE AND WALSH IN INTERNATIONAL CRICKET**

| | Span | Test Matches | Wickets | Average | BB | 5wI | 10wM |
|---|---|---|---|---|---|---|---|
| Courtney Walsh | 1984–2000 | 132 | 519 | 24.44 | 7-37 | 22 | 3 |
| Curtly Ambrose | 1987–2000 | 98 | 405 | 20.99 | 8-45 | 22 | 3 |

BB denotes Best Bowling, 5wI denotes 5 wickets in an innings, 10wM denotes 10 wickets in a match
Walsh also took 227 wickets in 205 One-Day Internationals. Ambrose took 225 in 176 ODIs.

A highpoint in their careers together came in Adelaide in 1992–93 when the West Indies won by a single run, the narrowest winning margin in Test history. Ambrose took 10 wickets and Walsh three, including the lucky last, Australia's No. 11 Craig McDermott, caught off his helmet just as a famous upset beckoned. A week later Ambrose took seven for 1 as the Australians were humbled at the pacy WACA Ground.

Walsh's remarkable Test involvements included 28 series without defeat. In the third and final Test at Chandigarh in 1994–95, with the Windies trailing 1–0, Walsh told his teammates pre-match how he had never played in a losing series and 'would rather lose 2–0 than go home 1–0 losers'. He took five wickets for the game as the Windies triumphed by 243 runs. When his right to a place in the side was being questioned, he proudly wore a t-shirt around which said: 'FORM IS TEMPORARY, CLASS IS PERMANENT'.

## AND 'AB' DIDN'T SEE EVEN ONE BALL LIVE!

Never before in an Ashes Test in England had an opening pair batted through an entire day. And never before had a captain not seen even one ball of the massive partnership live.

In scoring 301 runs on the opening day of the 1989 Ashes Test at Trent Bridge, Mark Taylor and Geoff Marsh consigned England to playing 'catch-up' status, home captain David Gower even sending a message upstairs to the press box to see if anyone had any ideas!

Continuing the series of his career, Taylor made 141 not out and Marsh 125, the pair scoring 88 in the first session, 104 in the second and 109 in the last. They had their slices of luck, but to bat 102 overs takes remarkable focus and concentration and the Trent Bridge crowd were generous in their applause as the two unconquered Australians wearily walked off. Marsh later quipped that Australia's No. 3 David Boon was probably just as tired as he was, having had his pads on all day!

The bowling was willing and resolute but lacking inspiration. Having withstood the early fire from expressman Devon Malcolm, Marsh used his feet with gusto to the finger spin of Eddie Hemmings and Nick Cook. Taylor, too, was in superb touch, continuing his remarkable summer. Records tumbled as the pair crushed the Englishmen. At 245, they passed Bobby Simpson and Bill Lawry's previous highest Ashes partnership of 244, and early on Day 2, they toppled Jack Hobbs and Wilfred Rhodes' monumental 323, the all-time highest first-wicket stand in Anglo-Australian cricket. It was a red letter day for Marsh, one of Australian cricket's most team-oriented players.

Ironically, captain Allan Border didn't see even one ball of the stand from his normal vantage spot on the viewing balcony. He'd watched the early action on television while finishing off some correspondence. Duties completed and with lunchtime approaching, he went to join the players, only to be told by Terry Alderman that the team was 'none-for' and he should stay where he was in case he broke the good luck spell. So for the rest of the day, bar the breaks, Border had to stay in the same seat, glued to the TV monitor!

'Everyone was rapt for "Swampy" [Marsh],' said Border. 'The press had been on his back, talking about dropping him, and he knew he could have played a bit better. But of course there was never a thought of dropping him. The fact was that only once, at Lord's, did we not get off to a reasonable start. Usually Swampy and "Tubby" [Taylor] got through the first dozen of 20 overs with the new ball.'

In the preceding two Tests at Edgbaston and Old Trafford they'd started with 88, 81, 135 and 62.

**Flawless:** South Australian Greg Blewett batted five sessions with Steve Waugh to amass a record 385 run stand against the South Africans in Johannesburg in 1996–97. Only two other Australian pairs had also gone undefeated for an entire day's play at Test match level, Bill Lawry and Bobby Simpson in the West Indies in 1965 and Geoff Marsh and Mark Taylor in England in 1989. *David Munden/Sportsline*

As was his habit, most of Marsh's runs came through gully and point. He could easily have been adjudged lbw to Malcolm early on, but umpire Nigel Plews rejected the unanimous appeal.

'He was plumb,' said Malcolm, playing his first Test match. 'I just couldn't believe that decision. I watched the ball again on TV that night and it was still out. I agreed the ball was missing off stump and indeed leg stump – but not middle! The Aussies just batted us out of the game over the next two days. It was demoralising. They were so hard-nosed. When Terry Alderman took five wickets in our first innings, I was walking back to the pavilion and said to him: "Well bowled." I was astonished when he snarled and swore at me!'

It wasn't until the eighth hour of the innings and ball No. 744, shortly after noon on the second day, that Marsh finally succumbed, caught at slip trying to lift Cook out of the ground. His share of the

**AUSTRALIANS TO BAT THROUGH A DAY'S PLAY IN TESTS**

| Year | Players | Runs in day | Overs | Run-rate |
|---|---|---|---|---|
| 1964–65 Bridgetown | Bobby Simpson (137) and Bill Lawry (102) | 263 | 81 | 3.2 |
| 1989 Trent Bridge | Geoff Marsh (125) and Mark Taylor (141) | 301 | 102 | 2.9 |
| 1996–97 Johannesburg | Greg Blewett (156) and Steve Waugh (137) | 288 | 93 | 3.0 |
| **The first to do it:** | | | | |
| 1924–25 Melbourne | Jack Hobbs (154) and Herbert Sutcliffe (123) | 283 | 83 (eight-ball overs) | 3.3 |

329-run stand was 138. At lunchtime Gower celebrated England's only wicket with a glass of champagne.

Taylor was to carry on to 219 as the Australians reached 6–602 declared, before bowling England out twice in less than five sessions to cruise to their fourth Test win from five. Other than a half-chance into the slips at 3, his innings had been peerless, the tough-as Border later telling him that he had fluffed a rare opportunity at a triple-century!

Only two other Australian pairs had batted through an entire day's play: Bobby Simpson and Bill Lawry against the West Indies in Bridgetown in 1964–65; and Steve Waugh and Greg Blewett who went unbeaten all day against the South Africans at Johannesburg in 1996–97.

Marsh was to share some other tall opening stands, most notably with long-time West Australian partner Mike Veletta. Against the South Australians in Perth in 1989–90 they started with 431, Marsh's share 355 not out and Veletta's 150.

Taylor's union with Michael Slater was to become one of the best of all time, the pair amassing 10 Test century stands in 78 innings together. Now they are co-commentators with Channel Nine.

**Invincible:** The unveiling of the Bradman statue in Melbourne in May 2003 brought three of his old 'Invincibles' teammates to town. From left: Arthur Morris, Sam Loxton and Neil Harvey. 'Arr,' said Sam, taking centre stage, 'the rose amongst the thorns!' *Bruce Postle*

# B

**'Tell your little mate,' said Bradman, 'that you can't get out if you hit the ball along the ground . . .'**

## BATTING ROYALTY

They ruled peerlessly for almost two decades, beacons in a top six as distinguished and prolific as any in history: Rahul Dravid from Karnataka and Sachin Tendulkar, Mumbai. They cornered the No. 3 and No. 4 positions in India's batting order for 15 years, sharing in a record 20 Test and 11 One-Day International century stands.

The pivotal pair in India's charge to No. 1 in the Test rankings in 2009, they pillaged and pummelled opposing attacks worldwide. Dravid, 'The Wall', seemingly impregnable, the grand master of crease occupation, and Tendulkar, the best since Bradman, imperious, inspired, wristy, formidable.

Along with fellow batting 'Dons', VVS Laxman and Virender Sehwag, they provided Indian bowlers with a consistent springboard of runs from which to defend. No other pair in the history of Test cricket has amassed more runs and only a few had their average of 50 runs per partnership.

In the Christmas Test in Melbourne in 2011–12, their twentieth Test century stand momentarily threatened Australia's superiority. On their dismissal, India capitulated, never to recover. Tendulkar's 73 was a masterly cameo that few of us wanted to see finish. To the first ball after an interval from expressman Peter Siddle, he deliberately deflected a lifter over the top of the slips cordon all the way and over the third man rope for a miraculous 6. It was a shot of genius, a reminder of the Little Master's halcyon best. He played with all his flowing precision before being castled late in the day by Siddle – arguably the most important ball bowled all summer.

The applause accorded Tendulkar Australia-wide, stretching into the one-dayers, was loud and generous. His place only just behind Don Bradman as cricket's finest batsman was simply indisputable.

Dravid, too, was admired for his mental toughness and unflappable ways, a rock every other Test nation would have loved to have had at No. 3. Even as a 38-year-old in 2011, he amassed five centuries in a calendar year, including three against the No. 1 ranked team in the world, England.

When Dravid and Tendulkar shared in century stands, India invariably won. No pair seemed as certain or as composed. It was as if their bats were broader than everyone else's. Their most prolific period together came in the late 1990s and early 2000s, when they combined in four century stands, including three doubles in two home seasons. In back-to-back Tests, Heath Streak's 2000–01 Zimbabweans conceded 525 runs to the pair in three innings.

Their ODI partnerships in this period were also significant and featured a triple-century for the second wicket against the visiting New Zealanders at Hyderabad.

The pair always seemed at ease with each other, Dravid satisfied to play a back-seat role when Tendulkar was on song, which was most of the time. He always marvelled at Tendulkar's passion for practice, his balance and unerring focus, believing Tendulkar's success as a teenager had quickened the advancement of several of India's other champions, especially Sourav Ganguly. India was fortunate to have so many of the great stars of the game.

Dravid also had a massively successful pairing with Laxman, the two averaging 51 and sharing 12 century stands in Tests. Tendulkar and Ganguly also teamed together brilliantly at one day level.

## TEST CENTURY STANDS BETWEEN RAHUL DRAVID AND SACHIN TENDULKAR

| Stand | Result |
|---|---|
| 170 v West Indies, Bridgetown, 1996–97 | Lost |
| 163 v West Indies, Georgetown, 1996–97 | Drawn |
| 113 v Australia, Chennai (Chepauk), 1997–98 | Won |
| 140 v Australia, Calcutta, 1997–98 | Won |
| 109 v New Zealand, Hamilton, 1998–99 | Drawn |
| 229 v New Zealand, Mohali, 1999–00 | Drawn |
| 213 v Zimbabwe, Delhi (FSK), 2000–01 | Won |
| 249 v Zimbabwe, Nagpur, 2000–01 | Drawn |
| 169 v Australia, Chennai (Chepauk), 2000–01 | Won |
| 124 v West Indies, Port-of-Spain, 2001–02 | Won |
| 163 v England, Nottingham, 2002 | Drawn |
| 150 v England, Leeds, 2002 | Won |
| 138 v Australia, Sydney, 2003–04 | Drawn |
| 122 v Pakistan, Kolkata, 2004–05 | Won |
| 127 v Bangladesh, Mirpur , 2007 | Won |
| 139 v Australia, Perth, 2007–08 | Won |
| 222 v Bangladesh, Mirpur, 2009–10 | Won |
| 119 v Sri Lanka, Galle, 2010 | Lost |
| 104 v New Zealand, Nagpur, 2010–11 | Won |
| 117 v Australia, Melbourne, 2011–12 | Won |
| **And their most memorable ODI stands:** | |
| 331 v New Zealand, Hyderabad, 1999 (in 46 overs) | Won |
| 237* v Kenya, Bristol, 1999 World Cup (29 overs) | Won |

*unfinished

## MOST CENTURY PARTNERSHIPS IN TESTS

| | |
|---|---|
| 20 | Rahul Dravid and Sachin Tendulkar (India) |
| 16 | Gordon Greenidge and Desmond Haynes (West Indies)<br>Matthew Hayden and Ricky Ponting (Australia) |
| 15 | Herbert Sutcliffe and Jack Hobbs (England) |
| 14 | Mahela Sangakkara and Mahela Jayawardene (Sri Lanka)<br>Justin Langer and Matthew Hayden (Australia)<br>Justin Langer and Ricky Ponting (Australia) |

| | |
|---|---|
| 13 | Andrew Strauss and Alastair Cook (England) |
| 12 | Brian Lara and Ramnaresh Sarwan (West Indies)<br>Sourav Ganguly and Sachin Tendulkar (India) |
| 11 | Arjuna Ranatunga and Aravinda de Silva (Sri Lanka)<br>Jacques Kallis and AB de Villiers (South Africa)<br>Alastair Cook and Kevin Pietersen (England)<br>David Boon and Mark Waugh (Australia)<br>Desmond Haynes and Richie Richardson (West Indies) |
| 10 | Sunil Gavaskar and Chetan Chauhan (India)<br>Gautam Gambhir and Virender Sehwag (India)<br>Rahul Dravid and Virender Sehwag (India)<br>Rahul Dravid and Sourav Ganguly (India)<br>Sunil Gavaskar and Mohinder Amarnath (India)<br>Mahela Jayawardene and Thilan Samaraweera (Sri Lanka)<br>Inzamam-ul-Haq and Mohammad Yousuf (Pakistan)<br>Javed Miandad and Mudassar Nazar (Pakistan)<br>Mark Taylor and Michael Slater (Australia)<br>Marcus Trescothick and Michael Vaughan (England) |

## BOSOM BUDDIES

Spencer Street railway station, Melbourne, January 1947: the Victorian team is assembling for its northern tour to Brisbane and Sydney. Captain Lindsay Hassett calls Sam Loxton over and points in the direction of the team's teen star, Neil Harvey, and says: 'You'd betta take care of the little bloke.'

And so began a happy 65 years together, which saw Loxton and Harvey become regular teammates at interstate and Australian level. They roomed together on two tours and later served as national selectors. They even linked up on the after-dinner speaking circuit, telling tall tales and true of life with Don Bradman's fabled 1948 Invincibles.

They'd come from opposite sides of the Yarra, Loxton from prestigious Wesley College, where he was a champion cricketer and footballer; Harvey from the more humble backstreets of working-class Fitzroy. Sam was bold and opinionated and larger than life. He would have been the one in the wild west show to theatrically fling open the saloon doors to announce his arrival in town. Harv's entrance would have been deliberately less dramatic. He always preferred to let his bat do the talking. Whereas Loxton would often bludgeon the ball to the fence, Harvey would caress it, relying on his footwork and exquisite timing.

Loxton had already celebrated his twenty-first birthday when he first opposed a 15-year-old Harvey at Brunswick Street. The kid caught him, after Sammy had made 66.

'Even back then I was looking after him!' said Sam, breaking into trademark gusts of laughter. There may have been seven years between them but they shared a chemistry, and remained inseparable right up until Sam's death in 2011.

In Loxton's debut Test, a virtual touring trial game against the Indians in Melbourne in 1948, he made 80 and shared a fourth-wicket stand of 159 with Harvey, who top-scored with 153 in only his second Test.

Loxton always thanked his lucky stars to have been included on the most famous tour of all, to England in 1948. He and Harvey were the two youngest in the chosen 17.

In the privacy of their room, Loxton said to Harvey: 'How are we going to get a game in this [star-studded] side?'

Years later he told me: 'I thought I was along for the ride, to pull the roller if the horse broke down.'

Circumstances were to conspire in both their favours. Keith Miller's troublesome back saw the Australians one short in the pace bowling department, giving Loxton the break he needed from mid-tour. When Sid Barnes, fielding at short leg, was cleaned up by English tailender Dick Pollard, Harvey took his place and promptly made a fairytale century on debut.

Ironically, after a barren first month, Harvey asked Loxton to approach the Don and ask him what he was doing wrong. He was too shy to go himself.

'Tell your little mate,' said Bradman, 'that you can't get out if you hit the ball along the ground.'

In the epic fourth Test at Leeds, where Harvey made 112 and Loxton 93, sharing a century stand for the fifth wicket, the pair were batting together when Harvey stole his one hundredth run into the covers and had to shield his face to avoid being struck as the throw at the stumps came to his end. Loxton had sprinted through and doubled back almost as quickly to offer his congratulations. He was just as excited as Harvey.

Given that England had started with almost 500 and the Australians were 4–189 when Loxton joined his mate, their 105-run partnership was pivotal in Australia's recovery. Loxton made 54 of the runs and Harvey 51.

'It was always great batting with Nin [Harvey],' Loxton said, 'we have always been the greatest of pals. We roomed together for Victoria [from 1946] and on two tours for Australia [to England in 1948] and South Africa [1949–50]. He could do anything on the cricket field. He was a magnificent bat and I never saw him fall over in the field. He was magnificent. He had perfect balance whatever he did.'

On a crumbling Durban dustbowl in the first weeks of 1950, they shared their most significant stand, 145 for the fifth wicket after the Australians had slumped to 4–95 chasing 336 for an unlikely victory. The ball spun wickedly from the second day, South Africa's Hugh 'Toey' Tayfield taking nine wickets for the game, including seven for 23 in the first innings.

Harvey mixed soft-handed defence with vicious square cuts and pull shots when it was safe. He'd never previously batted three sessions of a Test. In a wonderful career, this was to be his stellar five-and-a-half hours, his unbeaten 151 lifting Australia to an unforgettable victory.

'The wicket was badly pock-marked. There were holes all over it,' he said. 'Their spinners, Tayfield and Tufty Mann [an orthodox left-arm bowler] were turning it a couple of feet and you never knew if the ball was going to stand up or shoot after hitting one of the crumbling holes. Sam's 54 was so important for us. It was the innings of his life. We had to work for every run as Tayfield and Mann were so accurate [bowling more than 100 eight-ball overs between them].'

Loxton succumbed to Mann at 230 before Harvey combined with Colin McCool for another century stand to ensure the win.

'We won a game we had no right to win, not on that wicket,' said McCool.

The pair played the last of their 11 Tests together in 1951 and remained ever-so-close as Victorian Sheffield Shield teammates.

On the eve of one important state game in Sydney, the Victorians practised before deciding where to have lunch. Loxton was about to take off his boots in readiness to join them when Harvey interrupted: 'No, Slox,' he said. 'You're not playing well. We'll get a pie [for lunch] and then I'll bowl to you in the nets.'

'And he did,' said Loxton, 'for two hours non-stop. That's mateship for you. It was just wonderful. It was the way it happened in those days.'

Another time, at the Melbourne Cricket Ground, Loxton was batting with Harvey and was well set. One of his superstitions was never to look at his score on the scoreboard, so this day he asked Harvey how many he was.

'Don't ask me,' said Harvey, who was short-sighted and struggled to see anything beyond 22 yards away. 'Let's wait to lunchtime and we get closer to the board.'

Their liaison continued in 1959–60 with Loxton as team manager and Harvey as player on Australia's tour of India and Pakistan. Later, throughout the 1970s, they were national selectors and along with Sir Donald Bradman, responsible for the fast-tracking of icons including Rod Marsh and Dennis Lillee into Australia's Test team during the 1970–71 summer.

'We were running out of fast bowlers like nobody's business in 1970 and we sat down for a meeting and the master [Bradman] said: "Seen any fast bowlers around the place? We seem to be getting frightfully short of them."

'Almost simultaneously Harv and I said: "As a matter of fact we have. There's a kid in Perth called Lillee."

'"I haven't seen him. Does he know where it's going?"

'"No, I don't think so," said Loxton. "But that shouldn't worry us."

'"Why?"

'"Because if he doesn't know where it's going, the batsman certainly won't!"'

Dennis Lillee was chosen, took a 'five-for' on debut, the start of one of the great careers which was to net more than 400 Test and Supertest wickets.

In the early 2000s, Loxton and Harvey teamed up again, this time as professional storytellers, delighting audiences with their reminiscences from the 1948 tour. They told stories about the memorable boat trip to Dover, the shipboard games and antics, and having to buy dinner suits to dress up for dinner.

'The only night you were allowed to appear [for dinner] in a lounge suit was Sundays,' said Harvey.

Opening batsman Sid Barnes, one of only four survivors from the 1938 tour, had paid a kid a fiver to rubber stamp his signature on hundreds of team autograph sheets and sat back and enjoyed the view as the others developed writer's cramp signing the sheets.

The Don spent much of his time downstairs composing his speeches for the many functions at London's swishest addresses from the Savoy and the Dorchester to the House of Commons.

'Don knew how good this team could be,' said Loxton. 'He put all this time into his speeches and never repeated himself even once. Not only was he the world's greatest cricketer, he was one of the greatest after-dinner speakers as well.'

The Australians' county game against Surrey at The Oval was a favourite moment. Harvey and Loxton opened the innings on the final afternoon and struck 122 in less than an hour to lift their team to a 10-wicket victory.

The RW Crockett bat with which Harvey had made his 112 on his memorable Ashes debut shortly afterwards had been borrowed from the Fitzroy Cricket Club, the only bat he owned having been broken during his Test debut in Adelaide.

'I'd saved up some money and went into the Melbourne Sports Depot and bought this brand new cricket bat only for the handle to break within two overs [on debut],' Harvey said. 'I had to borrow one out of the kit after that.'

Following Harvey's grand entry, one of the most pivotal in Australia's magnificent seven-wicket win, Loxton took his mate's bat to Bradman, saying: 'This is the kid's bat. Would you like to sign it?'

Bradman not only signed it but also inscribed it: 'This bat is a symbol of a great innings by my friend Neil Harvey in Australia's greatest victory, Leeds, 1948. . . Don Bradman.'

After a lifetime in the game, it remains Harvey's most treasured possession. 'I never thought I'd meet Don Bradman, let alone play with him,' he said.

Their nostalgia shows were invariably sell-outs and often stretched into the wee hours. Invariably they'd leave us all laughing.

'Just one more Nin. . . before we hit the road,' Sam would say. 'Can I tell this one?' An hour later they'd still be talking, with everyone hanging on every word.

## BOWLED SHANE

Without the mesmeric, compelling powers of Shane Warne, Ian Healy says he would never have been able to truly showcase his wicketkeeping talents.

'It was always intriguing, challenging and good fun keeping to Shane,' he said. 'There was no batsman alive Shane didn't think he couldn't dismiss.'

As a young child from the Melbourne bayside, Warne developed extraordinary power in his wrists and fingers after breaking both legs. For 12 months he used a billycart to propel himself from room to room.

From the time one of the seniors at East Sandringham CC showed him how to flick a leg-spinner, he was soon astonishing them all with his talent to immediately implement what he'd been shown. The Warne leg-break, even then, would curve in the air and hum at the opposing batsman before biting and spinning wickedly towards slip. Mind you, that was only one in six and the all-weather wickets were much worn, encouraging extravagant spin. After he'd experimented for a while, he'd go back to his long run and pretend he was Dennis Lillee running through the Poms at the Centenary Test.

Having survived many a low point – one of his first captains at Brighton suggested he'd be better off concentrating on his batting as he didn't think much of his bowling – Warne was identified as a teenager of uncommon promise and 702 Test wickets later – plus six more if you count an Exhibition 'test' in Sydney – he stands alone as Australia's finest-ever bowler, ahead of Lillee, Lindwall, O'Reilly, Grimmett and even Glenn McGrath.

Healy, his first wicketkeeper, was also to become a world-beater. From tiny Biloela in central Queensland, he was five years older than Warne and had already been central in two Ashes campaigns before they first played in the same XI. He'd also survived rocky beginnings, when in his debut Test he dropped local hero Javed Miandad and watched with increasing despair as Javed made 210 and Pakistan batted into a third day at its cricketing citadel, Karachi. The rookie Queenslander also grassed a chance from Salim Malik and was certain his first Test would be his last. He was a very much the baby of the team and had served a remarkably short apprenticeship. Greg Chappell had warned him that Pakistan would be the hardest tour of his life and, on return to Brisbane, Healy worked himself to a standstill, sharpening his footwork, glovework and fitness reserves with exhausting daily routines. Slowly his inner confidence returned, as did his form on the faster, bouncier, more-familiar Australian wickets. A chat with his hero Rod Marsh reinforced that he was heading in the right direction. Marsh liked the way Healy was staying on his feet and taking the ball on the inside of his body.

Healy had righted his career and was the unanimous choice as Australia's No. 1 wicketkeeper when Warne was similarly fast-tracked, giving Healy the opportunity to excel standing up to the stumps, a true test of a wicketkeeper's ability. They were to become a noted combination, Healy's shouts of 'Bowled Shane' being picked up with the use of the stump microphones at the base of the wickets. It was to become one of Australian cricket's best-known catch-cries.

With his wide smile, ample waistline and love of fags and fun, Warne had reminded Healy of an old bush player who didn't care if he was hit for a six or two, as long as he eventually got the wicket he wanted. Even at 22, Healy regarded Warne as a champion, 'And you can't say that about most young blokes, no matter how gifted they are.'

Fifteen per cent of Warne's Test wickets were the result of stumpings or catches behind, including 49 to Healy.

Other notable wrist spinners from Arthur Mailey and Clarrie Grimmett through to Bill O'Reilly and Richie Benaud all had a great reliance on their wicketkeepers. As good as they all were, none possessed Warne's sublime talent and extraordinary accuracy.

The Healy-Warne combo tended to strike twice every three games. Healy's predecessor Adam Gilchrist was to share in 59 dismissals with a percentage closer to one a match. Like Healy, he was a world record holder, whose wicketkeeping abilities were often underrated because of the majesty and power of his batting.

Even though Gilchrist's percentages were superior, Healy was rated the more-rounded gloveman, especially the skills he displayed standing up. He loved Warne's array of leg-spinners, flippers, sliders and zootas. Sometimes he'd even bowl a traditional googly – just to show he had one. In Bermuda one afternoon, one of the locals was floundering with Warne's variety and whispered to Healy: 'This bloke's a lot easier to read on spin vision!'

Warne loved it when batsmen would engage with him and return some of his banter. In Sydney in 1994, South African tailender Pat Symcox kept padding Warne away.

'You'll never get through there, boy!' he called.

Warne paused at the top of his approach, smiled, and continuing around the wicket, sent a leg-break *in between* Symcox's legs which struck his middle and leg stumps. 'People watching the dismissal on television couldn't understand why the boys celebrated as if we had just dismissed Brian Lara for a duck,' said Healy.

Healy kept to Warne for his first 1440 overs and 3450 overs overall in international cricket and said he could pick each of his deliveries in his sleep. Yet when he batted against Warne in a Sheffield Shield match in Melbourne in the mid-1990s, he wondered how he could possibly score, before Warne lobbed some higher-than-normal leggies which Healy was able to hit over the infield. It reinforced to Healy just how menacing Warne was, especially when it counted most.

Two of Healy's all-time favourite dismissals were from Warne's bowling, both in 1993 when he established himself as the leading slow bowler in the world.

'We went to New Zealand before England and Shane hardly bowled a loose one, even in the nets, all tour,' he said. 'He was getting some extraordinary side spin and at Christchurch late in the first Test, he pitched one so far outside Ken Rutherford's leg stump that I was unsighted. It bit and bounced and he nicked it and I managed to hang onto it. Kenny had made a 100 and that was a big wicket for us. [Australia won by an innings.]

'The other one was a stumping from Graham Thorpe at Edgbaston [in the fifth and final Test]. He'd made 60 or so and they were fighting to save the game. He charged at him, it bounced and spun, one of Shane's classic leg-breaks, and he was stranded. He was their last recognised batsman and we were able to go on and win by eight or nine wickets, our fourth win in five. You don't forget moments like that.'

One delivery, however, still haunts Healy, a difficult, low-down stumping chance at Karachi in 1994 which went for the winning four byes as Inzamam-el-Haq and Mushtaq Ahmed added 57 in eight overs, the highest last-wicket partnership to win a Test match.

Having already taken eight wickets in the game, Warne bowled a leg-break pitching outside leg stump. Inzamam initially thought he could lift it to the vacant deep mid-wicket before changing his mind in mid-stroke and missing it completely. He thought he'd been bowled. So did Healy and, momentarily distracted, he lost focus and the ball scuttled through low, just missing the off stump *and* Healy's gloves.

'How I would have loved to have made that stumping,' Healy said. 'It was a chance a career could have been built on.' It was a blimp – a big one at the time as Australia had never before won at Karachi. Healy kicked the stumps down in his frustration. Even the champions are human.

## BRADMAN'S BEST

It wasn't Ponsford, McCabe, Barnes or Morris: the greatest partner in Sir Donald Bradman's life was his wife of 65 years, Lady Jessie Bradman.

The pair were inseparable, Bradman writing of the 'comfort and encouragement' and 'sound judgement and counsel' he received from his wife. 'I would never have achieved what I achieved without Jessie,' he said.

They first met in 1921, when Jessie Menzies, the daughter of a Glenquarry dairy farmer, came to board with the Bradmans during her first year of secondary school. She and the young Don would walk together across the local oval to school, Bradman carrying her books. She was 15 months younger than the Don. For him it was 'love at first sight'.

'I well remember the day [we met] as I'd been sent down the street to buy some groceries,' Bradman said in an interview with Channel Nine's Ray Martin in the mid-1990s. 'I ran into the doctor's car on my bike and had an accident. He had to take me home. My nose was all cut and there were scratches all over my face. And when I got home she [Jessie] was there at the door, having just been delivered by her father. She was going to stay with us and go to school [in Bowral] for 12 months. And we went to school every day for the rest of the year. That was when I fell in love with her, that very first day. . . [but] I don't think she fell in love with me until much later because I was a terrible sight the day she saw me!'

Jessie was a grand beauty with wavy auburn hair and deep blue eyes. She was warm, outgoing and intelligent.

Bradman had wanted to become engaged on the eve of the 1930 Ashes tour of England but Jessie told Don he should go to England with his cricket as a free man and see if he felt the same way about her on his return. Their engagement was formalised in 1931. Six months later they were married and enjoyed an extended honeymoon in the USA and Canada where Bradman was the star attraction in a private tour arranged by the ex-Australian leg-spinner Arthur Mailey.

Fifty-two games were scheduled, Bradman playing all but two. After his epic Ashes summer of 1930, he was a magnetic drawcard everywhere. Americans used to seeing the hulking figure of baseball hero Babe Ruth marvelled at the Don's slender frame and wondered how he could 'whack 'em' so far. On his way to amassing almost 4000 runs at an average of 99.45, Bradman notched 18 centuries including a highest score of 260 on a matting pitch laid over turf at the Ontario Reformatory in Guelph, the highest score ever made in Canada. He also took 24 wickets including six wickets in one eight-ball over against a Vancouver XV at Mt Tomie in Victoria. The team visited Yankee Stadium where Bradman met the Babe and other baseball legends. They also were shown around Hollywood and introduced to leading screen actors and actresses including Jean Harlow, Clark Gable, Mary Astor and Myrna Loy. On Broadway, the young honeymooners saw Paul Robeson sing his stirring 'Ol' Man River' from the hit musical *Showboat*. It remained one of their all-time favourites.

With the Great Depression biting, the Bradmans moved to Adelaide, the prospect of a regular job with stockbroker and local cricket administrator Harry Hodgetts an irresistible lure in tough times. Cricket was only a leisure activity. Even record breakers needed to have Monday-to-Friday employment.

When Bradman became critically ill with peritonitis at the conclusion of the 1934 Ashes tour, Jessie took a train from Sydney to Melbourne and on to Perth to meet the *Maloja*, which was sailing to London. Reports circulated that Bradman had died, but Jessie continued her journey having telephoned the London hospital and being told her husband, while seriously ill, was still very much alive thanks to the expertise of the Australian surgeon Sir Douglas Shields. Peritonitis was a very serious and often fatal condition in those days before sulfa drugs and penicillin were available.

The *Maloja* arrived in London the day before Bradman was released, and the couple spent time in Scotland, London and the south of France before arriving back in Australia in early 1935.

The first of their three children, Ross, was to die within 48 hours of his birth in October 1936. Another son, John, was born in 1939 and daughter, Shirley, in 1941. Both had health issues and challenges. When John, a promising athlete, contracted polio in 1951 and spent most of the year in a steel frame, Bradman temporarily resigned all of his cricket administrative roles to share the caring duties with Jessie. At the launch of my Boys' Own centenary book, *Our Don Bradman*, honouring Bradman in 2008, John said the months his Dad spent at home were among the happiest of his life.

While John was to make a full recovery and play first-grade cricket at Kensington, his father's old club, he found the glare of being Don Bradman's son so stifling that he was to change his name to Bradsen. Jessie was heartbroken. John reverted back to the Bradman name only months before his father's death.

The Bradmans had built a two-storey brick house in Holden Street, Kensington Park, soon after their arrival in Adelaide and were to live there for the rest of their lives.

Jessie was not only a wife and a mother, she helped Bradman write some of his speeches and worked part-time as a bookkeeper when he was establishing his stockbroking business, Don Bradman and Co. During the Second World War, when Bradman was discharged with fibrositis, she nursed him and even shaved him.

Jessie was also instrumental in Bradman returning to cricket for the 1946–47 Ashes summer, saying to her husband it would be a pity if young John never got to see him play.

The Don's passion for cricket saw him involved in numerous committees at both state and national level and cricket meetings took him away from home two and three nights a week for 30 years. After his extraordinary contributions on and off the field, he was to retreat from public view, refusing all interviews, until the mid-1990s when Channel Nine paid a seven-figure sum towards the Bradman Museum in Bowral, opening the door for the Don's last major public interview.

Previously Jessie had often been pivotal in the Don agreeing to speak to journalists. Melbourne *Herald* photographer Ken Rainsbury famously captured the Don in his pyjamas and robe sipping a cup of tea one morning in Melbourne while he was still chairman of the Australian Cricket Board. The Don hadn't been keen to do the interview, until Jessie persuaded him.

For some, she was the ultimate cricket widow, but the pair were extraordinarily close. On her death from cancer in 1997, Bradman said he'd never known an Adelaide winter to be so cold. He never truly recovered from her passing. His partnership with Jessie was by far the best of his life. She was the finest woman he ever met.

# C

**'Dennis was such a strong-willed beggar and such a good bowler that you had to accept occasionally he was going to get pig-headed. . .'**

## CAUGHT MARSH, BOWLED LILLEE

Even 30 years on, they remain the most revered wicketkeeper-bowler combination of all. The entry 'caught Marsh, bowled Lillee' has appeared in more Test scorebooks than any other.

The two cricket royals combined in more than 200 dismissals, almost half in Tests – yet it took them years to truly 'engage' and become bosom buddies. Dennis Lillee had originally thought a teenage Rod Marsh to be everything he wasn't.

'He was a scruffy, overweight, beer-swilling intellectual,' said Lillee, 'not my sort of person at all. And I wasn't his choice of friend because I was too straight and didn't drink.'

From being 'different people' and 'not hitting it off', Lillee was to warm to his chunky mate. He admired Marsh's ability and respected his tactical acumen. In particular he loved the comradeship he built in the West Australian and Australian dressing rooms. The union was cemented when he also happened to start taking some truly spectacular catches.

Marsh had a share in three of Lillee's extraordinary haul of eight wickets, all caught, in the memorable Saturday morning session against the Rest of the World in 1971–72. From 7.1 overs,

---

**Christmas Cheer:** Alan Kippax and his workmate Hal Hooker batted all Christmas Day against the Victorians in 1928 to help New South Wales force an unlikely draw.

Lillee claimed eight for 29, including five for 0 from his final 15 balls.

'That morning Dennis bowled as fast and as dangerously and as well as I could imagine a bowler bring able to,' said Marsh. 'True, he had a helping pitch – the WACA Ground strip was black and lightning fast that day – but he was just so fast and so hostile that the term "unplayable", which is often abused, could fairly and honestly be applied. It was great fun behind the stumps even though there were times when I needed a stepladder to reach him!'

Marsh said it was 'a dream' to keep wickets to Lillee and one of his few disappointments in his international career was that slipsman Greg Chappell, rather than he, took the wicket with which Lillee broke the world record for most Test wickets in Melbourne in the 1981 Christmas Test.

The sight of Marsh propelling himself left or right to accept catches from Lillee was an ongoing signature in Australia's world champion teams of the 1970s and early 1980s. They plotted and planned, Marsh's great ability to sum up opposing batsmen a huge boon for both bowler and captain. Lillee would deny a free-driving batsman room by angling three or four into him, just short of a length, allowing him no width in which to free his arms, before delivering his signature outswinger, a little faster, a little wider and fuller, encouraging the drive and Marsh was often the beneficiary of the resultant edge.

Lillee played all but one of his 70 Tests beside Marsh, the only exception being the one-off Test against the Sri Lankans in Kandy in 1983 when Tasmania's Roger Woolley kept wickets.

One of their most memorable dismissals was in the 1976–77 Gillette Cup final in Perth, the 'Miracle Match' in which Western Australia successfully defended 77 thanks to an extraordinary Lillee onslaught which saw Viv Richards and David Ogilvie dismissed immediately, followed by Greg Chappell caught wide down the leg side by Marsh. 'King Viv' was bounced four times in a row before Lillee hit the top of his off stump. Ogilvie also succumbed straight away. Enter Chappell, Queensland's captain and the outstanding batsman in the world.

'I was at the top of my mark, about to bowl to Greg, when I saw Rod standing down the leg side signalling for a high ball on that line,' said Lillee. 'We couldn't afford to give away a boundary to a player of Greg's calibre, but I did as Rod had called and sent down a wide leg-side bouncer. Greg went for it, got the finest of edges and there was Rod, standing yards and yards wide, waiting for it. He'd moved into that position even before I'd let the ball go. Greg just stood there absolutely nonplussed. He couldn't believe that Rod could be out so wide to catch him.'

Lillee said he'd 'gone for broke' that day, bowling as fast as he could, ignoring his doctor's advice who feared he risked another breakdown if he went at full throttle in between Tests. Soon afterwards, Lillee took 12 wickets in the Centenary Test before withdrawing from the Ashes tour of England to rest.

He was to average five wickets per Test and Supertest on his return to international ranks and continued playing first-class cricket until 1988. Even at the age of 50 he was still taking wickets at international level at the annual season opener at Lilac Hill.

Lillee always reckoned he would have died on the pitch for his country and it so often showed as he bowled through pain, his superhuman efforts in the Centenary Test a never-to-be-forgotten high in the greatest fast-bowling career of all.

Marsh loved everything about Lillee's on-field persona: his spirit, skill, stamina and particularly the pride he took in his and Australia's performances. Just occasionally, though, Lillee overstepped the mark, like in the first 'reconciliation' Test match of 1979–80 when Greg Chappell preferred Jeff Thomson and Rodney Hogg with the new ball in the final hour of a game meandering to a draw. Spinner Ray Bright even bowled first change ahead of Lillee and when he was finally given a turn, he bowled a slow off-break from just three or four paces.

'What are you bowling, Dennis?' called Chappell from slip. 'Fast or spin?'

'Spin!'

Chappell adjusted the field accordingly and Marsh stood over the stumps, only for Lillee to deliver a searing bouncer which ripped past the nose of an astonished Collis King and thumped into Marsh's gloves, causing him to swear and curse. There wasn't a hint of an apology from Lillee, who merely turned and marched back to his mark, muttering obscenities. Chappell jogged 50 yards to the top of Lillee's mark to deliver an admonishment. The confrontation overshadowed the match-saving centuries earlier that day from Chappell and Kim Hughes.

'Dennis was such a strong-willed beggar and such a good bowler that you had to accept occasionally he was going to get pig-headed,' said Chappell. 'The adrenalin would pump so fast he'd go over the top.'

At Leeds in 1972, an uneven run-up saw Lillee bowl three or four accidental beaners which Marsh only just stopped, the welts on his arms and upper body proof of the velocity of Lillee at his tear-away best. That summer he consistently produced express deliveries to rival those of England's 1950s speed king Frank 'Typhoon' Tyson.

Marsh would consistently stand a cricket pitch back, sometimes more on the bouncy WACA, when Lillee was at his quickest. Even then, like in Sydney in 1974–75, he couldn't always intercept the Lillee bouncers which whistled over his and the batsman's heads and cannoned first bounce into the sightscreen!

Their record-breaking ways had begun in an otherwise nondescript Sheffield Shield game at the Gabba in 1969–70 when Queenslander Keith Dudgeon was caught behind. It was Lillee's second major wicket on his representative debut and Marsh's first match as West Australia's specialist wicketkeeper.

That was the summer WA's captain Tony Lock, a hard-bitten, no-nonsense English professional, called Lillee a 'Flippin' Old Tart' (or something like that) after he reckoned Lillee had been daydreaming in the outfield. John Inverarity shortened it to 'FOT', a nickname which stuck.

In addition to their share in 95 Test wickets, Marsh and Lillee also combined in 17 dismissals in 15 World Series Supertests and almost 100 for Western Australia. All-up, including minor games, they shared in 288 dismissals. Their best match haul was six dismissals for WA against Victoria on the bouncy WACA wicket in 1975–76. At Ashes level their most successful series was in 1972 when they combined in 10 wickets in five Tests. They took 11 in both the 1979–80 and 1980–81 Australian seasons when six Tests were played. Six times they claimed three dismissals in a Test innings and five times claimed four wickets in a match.

Marsh also formed wonderful alliances with Max Walker and Geoff Lawson, but none were as fabled as his work with Lillee. It was fitting that after 14 years they retired from international cricket on the same day.

In one of their farewell games, Dean Jones' testimonial match at the MCG in the early 1990s, a still-fit Lillee took the new ball at his favourite Southern Stand end and watched in astonishment as 18-year-old local Brad Hodge ran at him and swatted his first delivery over cover point to the foot of the Ponsford Stand. The next one was two yards quicker and aimed directly at Hodge, brushing his armpit on the way through to Marsh, who burst into laughter.

'No-one charges the great "DK" [and gets away with it],' said Marsh.

A brilliant catch made by diving outstretched to his right to dismiss Clive Lloyd one day at the WACA remains one of Marsh's favourite wickets – aside from those with a Lillee connection. Another came when he captained Australia for a day and a bit in Adelaide in 1981–82. Kim Hughes, Chappell and Lillee were all off the field as the West Indies completed a hard-fought five-wicket victory to retain the Frank Worrell Trophy.

Joel 'Big Bird' Garner had just struck Bruce Yardley for a tremendous six over long-on. It was a 'seven' at any other ground in the country. Marsh immediately motioned for Graeme Wood to take long-on, only to call him back inside the ring again, Garner top-edging the next one ever-so-high to be caught by Wood to end the West Indian innings.

'How's that for captaincy!' winked Marsh to Yardley as they walked off. 'I should have this job all the time!'

'Waddaya mean?' said Yardley

'Bird told me, "Marshy if you leave him on the fence I'm not trying again maarn," so I said, "If I bring him in, will you go for it again?"'

Marsh did and so did Garner – and Marshy had his man. Again.

### CAUGHT MARSH, BOWLED LILLEE

| | Total dismissals | In Australia |
|---|---|---|
| **TRADITIONAL CRICKET** | | |
| All Tests | 95 | 65 |
| Sheffield Shield | 95 | 95 |
| Other Australian first-class | 15 | 15 |
| Other English first-class | 12 | 0 |
| Other New Zealand first-class | 1 | 0 |
| **Total first-class dismissals** | **218** | **175** |
| | | |
| ODIs | 22 | 13 |
| List A interstate | 10 | 10 |
| List A other | 2 | 2 |
| Other misc one-day | 2 | 1 |

### WORLD SERIES CRICKET

| | | | |
|---|---|---|---|
| WSC in Australia | 19 | 19 | (8 × 5-day, 11 × 1-day) |
| WSC in New Zealand | 3 | 0 | (1 × 4-day, 2 × 1-day) |
| WSC in West Indies | 12 | 0 | (9 × 5-day, 3 × 1-day) |

### BATSMEN MOST DISMISSED c MARSH, b LILLEE

| | |
|---|---|
| **Tests** | |
| Five times | Tony Greig (England) |
| Four | Ian Botham (England), Deryck Murray (West Indies), Viv Richards (West Indies) |
| Three | Alan Knott (England), Majid Khan (Pakistan), Mudassar Nazar (Pakistan) |
| **World Series Supertests** | |
| Four times | Viv Richards (West Indies) |
| Two | Clive Lloyd (West Indies), Gordon Greenidge (West Indies) |

## LEADING WICKETKEEPER-BOWLER PARTNERSHIPS

| Dismissals | Combination/country | Matches | Dismissals per match |
|---|---|---|---|
| 95 | Rod Marsh-Dennis Lillee (Australia) | 69 | 1.38 |
| 90 | Adam Gilchrist-Glenn McGrath (Australia) | 71 | 1.27 |
| 84 | Mark Boucher-Makhaya Ntini (South Africa) | 96 | 0.88 |
| 81 | Adam Gilchrist-Brett Lee (Australia) | 65 | 1.25 |
| 79 | Mark Boucher-Shaun Pollock (South Africa) | 88 | 0.90 |
| 71 | Jeff Dujon-Malcolm Marshall (West Indies) | 68 | 1.04 |
| 68 | Mark Boucher-Jacques Kallis (South Africa) | 134 | 0.51 |
| 60 | Bob Taylor-Ian Botham (England) | 51 | 1.18 |
| 59 | Adam Gilchrist-Shane Warne (Australia) (39 catches, 20 stumpings) | 70 | 0.84 |
| 58 | Adam Gilchrist-Jason Gillespie (Australia) | 57 | 1.02 |
| 58 | Ian Healy-Glenn McGrath (Australia) | 52 | 1.12 |
| 57 | Mark Boucher-Dale Steyn (South Africa) | 49 | 1.16 |
| 55 | Ian Healy-Craig McDrmott (Australia) | 48 | 1.15 |
| 53 | Mark Boucher-Allan Donald (South Africa) | 35 | 1.51 |
| 51 | Syed Kirmani-Kapil Dev (India) | 67 | 0.76 |
| 50 | Kumar Sangakkara-Muthiah Muralidaran (Sri Lanka) (35 catches, 15 stumpings) | 77 | 0.65 |
| **Other pairs:** | | | |
| 47 | Brad Haddin-Mitchell Johnson (Australia) | 36 | 1.31 |
| 45 | Wally Grout-Alan Davidson (Australia) (44 catches, 1 stumping) | 28 | 1.61 |

| Dismissals | Combination/country | Matches | Dismissals per match |
|---|---|---|---|
| 37 | Bert Oldfield-Clarrie Grimmett (Australia) (9 catches, 28 stumpings) | 37 | 1.00 |
| 30 | Gerry Alexander-Wes Hall (West Indies) | 18 | 1.67 |

## A CHRISTMAS TO REMEMBER

Arthur Mailey called it cricket's greatest ever partnership. Certainly it was the most extraordinary and, more than 80 years on, it remains the game's all-time highest tenth-wicket stand.

Alan Kippax and Hal Hooker were close mates and were responsible for enlivening Melbourne's Christmas week with a record 307 last-wicket stand when New South Wales was heading for a follow-on and seemingly certain defeat in 1928–29. For the first time, the Sheffield Shield clash between the two arch rivals had included play on Christmas Day, and the pro-Victorian crowd was in a jovial mood as New South Wales lost two more pre-lunch wickets on a near-perfect wicket to be 9–113 chasing Victoria's 376.

Kippax, 1 not out overnight, had advanced his score to only 20 when joined at the wicket by Hooker, who worked for Kippax at his New South Wales Sports Store in Martin Place. With just 17 runs in four previous innings that summer and an all-time high of just 28, Hooker batted after the ferrets even at club level. He was never one to hang around for long. But this day, with New South Wales in such dire straits, urged on by his partner and boss, he protected his wicket like never before.

In searing heat, Hooker made just 14 in the period between lunch and tea while Kippax added 85. Hearing of the great stand, the crowd doubled to more than 15,000 and marvelled at Kippax's expert 'farming' of the strike, which often denied the Victorians even one ball at Hooker.

Ninety-seven more runs came in the final session, neither batsman giving even a half-chance. Every time Hooker was on strike, the Victorians crowded around him – 'like detectives seeking a confession' according to historian Geoff Armstrong. He responded by driving Reg Ellis past the close-in fielders for four to register the 200-run partnership. 'I think we can get them,' Kippax had told Hooker just minutes earlier. Writing in the daily *Argus* and the *Australasian*, published Saturdays, Ernie Wilmot marvelled at Hooker's defiance and Kippax's polish and placement.

'Miraculously, Kippax was so often able to score off the last ball of an over and keep the strike,' he wrote.

The pair exceeded the tenth-wicket Australian record of 211 and the English record of 235, the scoring rate continuing to accelerate when 'Stork' Hendry reverted to leg theory, the pair finding gaps in a stacked leg-side and lifting the stumps scoreline to 9–367, just nine runs behind Victoria's first innings of 376. Of the stand of 254, Kippax's share was 201 and Hooker's 51. The reception for Hooker's 50 was long and generous. And both men were again roundly cheered from the MCG, both touched by the crowd's sportsmanship, especially given the intense rivalry between the two champion cricketing states. At lunch the following day, after the pair had extended their stand to 307, ensuring the first innings points for New South Wales, the Victorian Cricket Association's president Donald Mackinnon asked his guests to remain standing after the toast to the King while he also congratulated Kippax and Hooker 'on their wonderful achievement'. There was loud applause all round the room. Later, the two balls used during their unforgettable stand were mounted and presented to the pair in recognition of one of cricket's most unlikely feats.

Kippax finished with 260 not out, including 240 of the 307-run stand. Hooker made 62, finally holing out to Victoria's captain Jack Ryder at mid-off from the bowling of Ted a'Beckett. Having batted five hours and four minutes, he said he was stiff for days.

Kippax told him afterwards he'd been riding his mate to score a century. Years later Hooker could still recall his keen disappointment at his best-ever chance of making a first-class hundred.

'I hadn't missed a ball over the two days,' he said. 'More than 50 years later I still regret it. But I don't regret being at the other end watching Alan bat. The shots he made were just amazing. It was all

## THE SCOREBOARD: VICTORIA v NEW SOUTH WALES

**Sheffield Shield**

Melbourne Cricket Ground, 24–27 December, 1928

**Toss:** Victoria

Victoria 376 (Ryder 175, a'Beckett 113, Hooker 3–100) and 6–251 declared (a'Beckett 95, Hendry 69 not out, Fairfax 3–45)

**VICTORIA**

FA Baring, HSTL Hendry, J Ryder (captain), KE Rigg, RN Ellis, JW Scaife, EL a'Beckett, JL Ellis+, HI Ebeling, WJ Rayson, H Ironmonger

**NEW SOUTH WALES first innings**

| | | |
|---|---|---|
| AG Fairfax | c Ironmonger, b a'Beckett | 2 |
| A Jackson | c JL Ellis, b Ironmonger | 19 |
| TJE Andrews | b Hendry | 33 |
| AK Kippax (c) | not out | 260 |
| DG Bradman | b Hendry | 1 |
| C Kelleway | b Hendry | 0 |
| CD Seddon | lbw b Ironmonger | 0 |
| HSB Love+ | lbw b Ebeling | 0 |
| CO Nicholls | b Ebeling | 10 |
| SC Everett | lbw b Ironmonger | 20 |
| JEH Hooker | c Ryder, b a'Beckett | 62 |
| Extras | | 13 |
| **Total** | | **420** |

**Fall:** 2, 46, 54, 55, 55, 57, 58, 74, 113, 420

**Bowling:** a'Beckett 29.1–2–92–2, Ebeling 25–1–81–2, Ironmonger 33–4–95–3, Hendry 18–5–58–3, Rayson 7–0–42–0, RN Ellis 10–1–31–0, Baring 5–1–8–0

**New South Wales second innings:** 2–156 (Bradman 71 not out)

**Umpires:** J Richards, PE Smith

**Close of play scores:**

**First day:** Victoria 5–162 (Ryder 95, a'Beckett 17)

**Second day:** New South Wales 7–58 (Kippax 1)

**Third day:** New South Wales 9–367 (Kippax 221, Hooker 51)

**Fourth day:** Victoria 6–251 (Hendry 69, Rayson 4)

**Match drawn1**

**+ denotes wicketkeeper**

**SIX MORE EPIC TENTH-WICKET STANDS**

| | | | |
|---|---|---|---|
| 289* | EH Kekwick (227*) and JGF Matthews (141*) | North Adelaide v Sturt | Adelaide, 1901–02 |
| 245 | CSC Cochrane (317) and AG Burgoyne (28*) | Brush Farm Reformatory, Carpentaria v Waratah | Eastwood, New South Wales, 1902–03 |
| 244* | D White (70*) and W McGregor (146*) | South Melbourne v Melbourne | Melbourne, 1899–1900 |
| 226 | WW Armstrong (166) and TG Armstrong (89*) | Melbourne v Waikato | Hamilton, New Zealand, 1926–27 |
| 220 | J Kyle (153*) and WR Robertson (82) | South Melbourne jnrs v East Brunswick | Melbourne, 1906–07 |
| 197 | S Kingwell (171) and M Walsh (45*) | Kingston Saints v Brunswick | Brunswick, Melbourne, 2007–08 |

* unbeaten

right for me. I could just stick out a straight bat – that's if it was in line with the stumps – and leave anything that was off them. Alan had to get the runs and he did it so magnificently well.'

The five-day game was to finish in a draw. Don Bradman, having been dropped from the Australian team, scored a quickfire 71 not out in the second innings to regain his place for the third Test beginning almost immediately in Melbourne, where the in-form Kippax made his first Ashes century.

In the return clash against the Victorians, Hooker was to take four wickets in four balls, an unprecedented feat in Sheffield Shield cricket, but he remained more renowned for his triple century stand with Kippax, which was the talk of the cricket world that Christmas.

Later, at Kippax's request, Hooker headed north to set up a sports store in Newcastle on behalf of his old friend. He later became a popular ABC cricket commentator and never tired of telling about the time he and Kippax had spoiled Christmas for 15,000 Victorians!

**He Loved Cricket:** Long-time Australian Prime Minister Sir Robert Menzies (*left*) with a veteran Bert Ironmonger, who flicked his testing slow-medium spinners off the butt of an index finger damaged in a childhood accident.

# D

**'The old Bradman would of course have kept it out of his stumps by one of those quick reactions of his. . .'**

## DIPLOMACY AND THE DON

Australia's longest-serving Prime Minister Sir Robert Menzies loved cricket. On summer Saturdays he'd often have his driver run past Glenferrie Oval, Hawthorn, to see if Bob Cowper was batting. He was a regular at the Melbourne Cricket Ground and it was amazing how the affairs of the nation would find him in London every four years around the time of the Lord's Test!

He built a strong friendship with Sir Donald Bradman and it was at his urgings that the Don, 55, agreed to come out of retirement and play in Sir Robert's annual Prime Minister's XI match against Ted Dexter's visiting MCC in 1963.

Bradman's presence ensured a stellar crowd of more than 11,000 at Manuka Oval and a healthy injection of monies for Legacy. The ground's brand new pavilion was named in the Don's honour on the day.

Menzies was in his element, walking beside the Don. Arguably they were Australia's two most famous men; certainly they were among the most photographed.

'It was a most dramatic moment,' said Menzies, decked out in an immaculate morning suit, 'when before a record crowd, the well-known figure [of Bradman] was seen walking to the wickets [at No. 5].

'He began in style by playing an off-drive to the boundary in his most characteristic manner [from the part-time bowling of Tom Graveney]. Brian Statham came on the other end and, calling on

**The Last Hurrah:** Cajoled out of retirement at the age of 55, Don Bradman captained the Prime Minister XI against the touring MCC in Canberra in February, 1963. Flanked by ex-teammate and politician Sam Loxton (*above*), he led his side onto Manuka Oval to a wonderful reception after England's captain Ted Dexter had won the toss (*opposite, right*) and elected to bat. Later, going in at No.5, with Don Chipp as his partner, the Don made 4 from five balls (*opposite, left*). It was his last game. The proceeds from the match went to Legacy.

his very considerable powers, he bowled a ball to Bradman which Bradman just came down on, the ball spinning back towards the stumps. The old Bradman would of course have kept it out of his stumps by one of those quick reactions of his. But his reactions were slower and the bails just fell. Poor Brian Statham was most dejected. The umpire [Alan Davidson] should have no-balled him for the

common good. Still there must be some limit to illegibility, even in a Prime Minister's match!'

So the Don was out for 4 in his last 'big' game. He'd lasted just five balls, but it was still a triumph, not only for cricket, but for the persuasive diplomatic skills of his old friend, Sir Robert Menzies.

# E

**'Australia's manager Steve Bernard put a stop to anyone getting naked in public, saying the team was in Muslim country. . .'**

## AN EXTRAORDINARY FAREWELL

Like most fast bowlers, Jason Gillespie always fancied his batting. His philosophy was simple: block the straight ones and attack anything wide. Trouble was, he was only averaging 12. In a team of champions he was required to bowl, not bat.

There was genuine delight when he broke through for an against-the-odds maiden Test half-century in his seventy-seventh innings against New Zealand in Brisbane in 2004–05 and celebrated by riding his cricket bat down the wicket *à la* Adam Sandler in *Happy Gilmore.*

Rarely did he ever bat higher than No. 10, but occasional night-watchman opportunities arose, including one extraordinary time against Bangladesh at Chittagong in 2005–06 when he was elevated to No. 3 after the late dismissal of Matthew Hayden.

In the most unlikely of partnerships, Gillespie and the more-rated Mike Hussey shared a remarkable stand of 320 in what proved to be a farewell to remember for the tall South Australian, who for years had formed a mega bowling partnership with Glenn McGrath.

Gillespie's share was a career-best 201 not out!

'I'd never got a 100 before in any form of cricket, so to make one

---

**'Gelignite Jack':** Three-in-one cricketer Jack Gregory from Sydney formed one of Australia's mightiest Ashes new ball combinations with the Tasmanian-born EA 'Ted' McDonald.

**One-off wonders:** Len Hutton (*left*) and Maurice Leyland only ever batted once together, adding 380 against Australia at The Oval in 1938.

## ONE-OFF 'SUPER' PARTNERSHIPS*

| | | |
|---|---|---|
| 382 | Len Hutton and Maurice Leyland (England) | v Australia, The Oval, 1938 |
| 320 | Jason Gillespie and Mike Hussey (Australia) | v Bangladesh, Chittagong, 2005–06 |
| 245 | Frank Woolley and Bob Wyatt (England) | v South Africa, Old Trafford, 1929 |
| 243 | Clem Hill and Roger Hartigan (Australia) | v England, Adelaide Oval, 1907–08 |
| 233 | Paul Sheahan and John Benaud (Australia) | v Pakistan, Melbourne, 1972–73 |
| 207 | HJH 'Tup' Scott and Billy Murdoch (Australia) | v England, The Oval, 1884 |
| 206 | Dave Nourse and Charlie Frank (South Africa) | v Australia, Johannesburg, 1921–22 |
| **Other Australian one-off stands of note:** | | |
| 198 | Doug Walters and Peter Burge | v England, Melbourne, 1965–66 |
| 185 | Graham Yallop and Greg Matthews | v Pakistan, Melbourne, 1983–84 |

*** The largest partnerships between batsmen who only ever had one partnership in Tests**

and then turn it into two was something beyond all comprehension,' he said.

Having batted through the second day on a wicket he rated as an absolute 'road', he was having a massage afterwards when the Australian physiotherapist Lucy Frostick suggested how good it would be if he could go on and make 200. Gillespie scoffed at the idea and said if he did that he'd celebrate by running around the oval nude.

Having only just won the opening Test of the series, the Australians were dominating the second. The Bangladeshi bowling and the fielding fell away dramatically as the Gillespie-Hussey partnership prospered. Finding himself in the 170s, Gillespie momentarily lost concentration and played a poor shot, earning an immediate rebuke from Hussey.

'Huss urged me not to throw it away and said I'd never ever get another opportunity to make a Test double ton,' said Gillespie, 'so I put my head down again and pushed on.'

Having tucked a single around the corner for his double-century, he raised his bat in triumph, the wide smiles in the Australian dressing room reflecting one of the most bizarre feats of all.

Australia's manager Steve Bernard put a stop to anyone getting naked in public, saying the team was in a Muslim country and should obey local protocol. Gillespie kept his clobber on. It was some farewell Test.

**STATS FACT:** Gillespie and Pakistan's Wasim Akram are the only two batsmen to have a top score more than 10 times their career batting average.

## ELEVEN MONTHS OF MAYHEM

Jack Gregory and Ted McDonald reigned together for less than a calendar year but struck as much apprehension into the minds of batsmen of the early 1920s as post-war expresses Lindwall and Miller and 1970s 'demons' Lillee and Thomson.

'They were the sternest challenges to manhood,' said historian David Frith.

**JACK GREGORY AND TED McDONALD TOGETHER**

| | Matches | Wickets | Average | BB | 5wI |
|---|---|---|---|---|---|
| **1920–21 (in Australia)** | | | | | |
| Jack Gregory | 5 | 23 | 24.17 | 7–69 | 1 |
| Ted McDonald | 3 | 6 | 65.33 | 2–95 | – |
| **1921 (England)** | | | | | |
| Jack Gregory | 5 | 19 | 29.05 | 6–58 | 1 |
| Ted McDonald | 5 | 27 | 24.74 | 5–32 | 2 |
| **1921–22 (South Africa)** | | | | | |
| Jack Gregory | 3 | 15 | 18.93 | 6–77 | 1 |
| Ted McDonald | 3 | 10 | 37.10 | 3–53 | – |

With his bounding 15-yard run, kangaroo leap and intimidating pace, 'Gelignite Jack' Gregory made batsmen dance when they didn't want to, backing his express bowling with cavalier batting and brilliant slips fielding.

Ted McDonald complemented him perfectly with his remarkable stamina, silky-smooth approach – which was longer than Gregory's – deadly command of line and length and a breakback so vicious that it often bowled the unaware shouldering arms.

In the 11 Tests they played together immediately after World War I, Australia won seven and drew four, the pair amassing 100 wickets at an average of nine a match.

They claimed five or more wickets in an innings on five occasions, England playing all 16 of its tourists against them in 1920–21 and a record 30 in the five home Tests of 1921.

Gregory's violent pace was responsible for more direct hits on English batsmen than any Australian in the first 75 years of Test cricket. In 1921 at Trent Bridge, Gregory struck debutant Ernest Tyldesley on the side of the face, the batsman all but passing out as the ball was breaking his wicket. At Lord's, Gregory collected Frank Woolley on the back and the wrist just as he'd come in, and at Old Trafford, hit Phil Mead on the shoulder. All up, Gregory was responsible for 20 'hits' on Englishmen, not that far behind the record of menacing Bodyliner Harold Larwood, with 33 hits on Australians, including two dozen in 1932–33.

Gregory had caused a sensation in the 1919 English season, taking more than 100 wickets and making almost 1000 runs for the Australian Imperial Forces team, despite having played only down the grades back home in Sydney. He said 'the family name' had triggered his initial Services team selection ahead of others. A right-arm fast bowler and a left-handed batsman educated at Shore school, he was the pivotal force in Australia building its unprecedented record of eight Ashes wins in a row.

His opening partner at the start of that record run in 1920–21 was the more leisurely paced Sydney-sider Charles Kelleway, before journeyman McDonald was included in the New Year of 1921, having taken nine wickets for Victoria against South Australia, eight either bowled or caught by wicketkeeper Jack Ellis. His returns in his opening Tests were modest, but in 1921, he stepped up and bowled at a sharp pace, his line perfect and his bouncer a genuine weapon, as Tyldesley found at The Oval when struck on the neck, one of McDonald's six 'direct hits' in Ashes matches.

The pair created havoc all summer and mowed through English county and representative teams, amassing 270 wickets between them: McDonald 150 at 15.97 and Gregory 120 at 16.53.

'He [McDonald] is that greatest asset any team can have,' said *Wisden*, 'a bowler difficult to play on the most perfect wickets.' When the wickets were in favour of bowlers as they were at Liverpool, he took eight Lancastrian wickets for 62 and 10 for the match in a rain-ruined draw.

Originally from Launceston, McDonald had first represented Tasmania just a month after his nineteenth birthday and moved to the mainland to enhance both his cricket and football careers. Before playing his first Tests for Australia, aged 30, he appeared in a premiership team for Fitzroy.

His success in England led to a Lancashire League contract and regular county cricket with Lancashire, where he became one of the ultimate champions of the game. Gregory continued to harass and hurry batsmen until the opening Ashes Test of 1928–29, when he broke down with a knee injury and declared: 'That's it.'

# F

**'Haven't you got a watch, Wal?' asked the Don.<br>'Every man should have a watch.<br>How do you expect to keep appointments?'**

## FIVE FIVE FIVE

It may not have been 'Obbs and Sutcliffe, but it was a partnership of remarkable quality and substance. Eighty years on, the feats of Percy Holmes and Herbert Sutcliffe remain an integral part of the records of *Wisden*, their understanding when stealing short singles 'positively telepathic'.

For sheer dimension and consistency, no set of openers has equalled their deeds of sharing in 74 three-figure first-wicket stands, including their astonishing 555 for Yorkshire against Essex at Leyton in 1932, still the highest stand for any wicket in a match played in England.

Holmes, from Huddersfield, and Sutcliffe, from Pudsey, were a rare combination who looked entrenched from the time they took guard. However, bar the opening Ashes match in 1921, when he top-scored on a fiery Trent Bridge wicket against Jack Gregory and Ted McDonald, Holmes never appeared against Australia, and in all was to play just seven Tests; Jack Hobbs' long-term stature as England's first-chosen professional, a perennial roadblock.

Despite the selection injustices – Holmes could have slotted anywhere into the top six – he maintained good humour and a

---

**Percy:** Affable Yorkshireman Percy Holmes shared one of the epic English county championship partnerships of all, 555 with Herbert Sutcliffe in 1932.

## A CELEBRATION POEM TO SUTCLIFFE AND HOLMES

*There's a sportsmanlike couple more famous I guess,*
*For excellent teamwork than Gilbert and S,*
*More mighty than emperors, storied in tomes. . .*
*Of course, I'm referring to Sutcliffe and Holmes*

*So keen is old Yorkshire on cricket today*
*That a duo so striking as Bryant and May,*
*Or Sankey and Moody must suffer eclipse*
*When 'Sutcliffe' and 'Holmes' are the words on our lips.*

*Yes even the Dares (namely Zena and Phyllis),*
*Or a trio like Freeman and Hardy and Willis,*
*Are put in the shade, where the Yorkshireman roams,*
*By the millions of mentions of Sutcliffe and Holmes.*

*As egg is to bacon or knife is to fork*
*As ale is to Burton or ham is to York;*
*As peach is to Melba or Persian to cat,*
*So is Sutcliffe and Holmes when they've started to bat.*

*You cannot divide them whatever you do;*
*Men link them together from Leeds to Peru,*
*Till even in fairyland, cricketing gnomes*
*Breathe the magical formula – 'Sutcliffe and Holmes'.*

– Mercurious

perky disposition, his 40-plus county average including a triple-ton at Lord's.

Holmes was 45 and increasingly suffering from lumbago the year of the famous 555 stand. At 0–423, Yorkshire could readily have declared overnight at this mid-June fixture and Holmes, who

## HIGHEST PARTNERSHIPS FOR THE FIRST WICKET

| | |
|---|---|
| 561 | Waheed Mirza and Mansoor Akhtar, Karachi Whites v Quetta, Karachi, 1976–77 |
| 555 | Percy Holmes and Herbert Sutcliffe, Yorkshire v Essex, Leyton, 1932 |
| 554 | Jack Brown and John Tunnicliffe, Yorkshire v Derbyshire, Chesterfield, 1898 |
| **Best by Australians:** | |
| 456 | Edgar Mayne and Bill Ponsford, Victoria v Queensland, Melbourne, 1923–24 |
| 431 | Mike Veletta and Geoff Marsh, Western Australia v South Australia, Perth, 1989–90 |

## HERBERT SUTCLIFFE'S 100-PARTNERSHIPS HABIT

- Herbert Sutcliffe was involved in 145 first wicket century stands, of which 98 were with Yorkshire: 69 with Percy Holmes as his partner, 15 with Len Hutton, six with Arthur Mitchell, four with Maurice Leyland, two with Wilfred Barber and one each with Paul Gibb and Emmott Robinson.
- Thirteen of these 18 partnerships with Holmes were of 250 and over.
- He and Jack Hobbs shared 26 century stands for the first wicket, including 15 in Tests, seven of which exceeded 200.

was sore, would have been perfectly happy to take his usual place at slip.

But captain Brian Sellers, new to the role, opted for his star opening pair to bat on, no doubt fortified by seeing the crowd numbers swell in anticipation of a new world record, eclipsing the 554 held by two other Yorkies, Jack Brown and 'Long John' Tunnicliffe, for almost a generation.

With the prospect of the second new ball being taken immediately, Holmes and Sutcliffe opted to play as carefully as possible in the first 20 minutes before opening up again, trusting their tired muscles would be sufficiently warmed to accelerate the run-rate. The 500 was raised to great cheering, but at 522, Holmes was all but caught at slip and an anxious Sutcliffe called down the wicket: 'Percy, do you or do you *not* want to go for this record?'

Having reached his first-ever triple century, Sutcliffe hit two 4s in three balls from the medium-paced Lawrie Eastman to bring up the magical 555. Years later he wrote: 'I remember my first four in Test cricket and I remember very well the impudently desperate six with which I completed my first hundred in county cricket, but I don't think I ever hit a ball with such joy as that delivered by Eastman that Thursday morning at Leyton.'

According to eye-witnesses, the cheering was rapturous. There were few more popular sportsmen in all England than the two long-time Yorkshire openers: Holmes, all jauntiness, combining a thumping hook shot with deft late cuts; and Sutcliffe, imperious, unhurried and fiercely determined, a man to bat for your life.

Having reached the 555, Sutcliffe's famed focus was broken and he was bowled the very next ball, causing a minor commotion as the Yorkshire scorer did some recalculations and reckoned the stand was 554 and that the pair had only equalled the previous record, rather than surpassing it! But it was found a no-ball hadn't been allowed for, so the 555 stood, much to everyone's relief.

For 15 seasons Holmes and Sutcliffe averaged almost five century stands a year, including 11 in 1928. Biographer Leslie Duckworth dubbed them the ultimate run stealers. Yet they were to open together in only one Test in England – just a fortnight after their new world record.

Had Holmes possessed the same resilience as his unflappable partner, he would have played more often.

'If only I had his patience,' he once said.

## FOR CLUB, STATE AND COUNTRY

George Thoms and Colin McDonald are unique among Australian pairs, being the only duo to open up at club, interstate and national level in the *same* summer. The pair were teammates at Melbourne University and were averaging almost 65 runs per partnership with Victoria in 1951–52 when both were called into the Australian team for the first time in the New Year of 1952. It was to be Thoms'

**Lifelong mates:** George Thoms and Colin McDonald went from club to country within weeks in 1951–52, both playing their debut Tests in Sydney against the West Indies. Australia's team, back row, left to right: Ian Johnson (12th man), Graeme Hole, Doug Ring, Bill Johnston, Richie Benaud, Alan Barnes (manager). Front: Thoms, Gil Langley, Keith Miller, Lindsay Hassett (captain), Neil Harvey, McDonald, Ray Lindwall.

**One Test Wonder:** Melbourne University's George Thoms in 1951. He retired prematurely to concentrate on his work as a gynaecologist.

only Test. A gynaecologist, he said he couldn't afford to have his fingers injured, so retired. McDonald carried on, and in 1958–59 made more than 500 Ashes runs to be among the most-rated batsmen in the world.

## FUN WITH WAL

Sir Donald Bradman had the healthiest regard for the silky skills of Wally Grout, Australia's late blooming wicketkeeper of the late 1950s and early 1960s. He liked his knockabout ways, his good humour and his passion for the game.

The Don was having lunch at the Cricketers' Club in Sydney with Grout and noted cricket writer Ray Robinson when Grout asked him the time.

'Haven't you got a watch, Wal?' asked the Don. 'Every man should have a watch. How do you expect to keep appointments?'

Grout replied that he'd never owned a watch but would like to afford a really good one.

A week later he was involved in a Shield game in Adelaide and was handed a package during a break by the roomie. It was a gold

**Buddies:** Wally Grout (*right*) and his great ally Don Bradman, who on retirement, became Australia's frontline selector for two decades.

watch from Bradman with an accompanying note thanking Grout for his contributions to Australian cricket.

In his final years in particular, Grout was very sensitive about his place in the Australian side and the form of South Australia's wicketkeeper, the younger Barry Jarman, who would have been a Test regular virtually anywhere else in the world.

The Don had agreed to write the foreword to Grout's soon-to-be-published autobiography *My Country's Keeper*. Grout told the Don of his intention to include a few chapters about the forthcoming Australian tour of the Caribbean, to which the Don replied, 'That's too bad, Wal. The manager's job has been filled and we're not going to send a baggageman!'

The Don was well aware of Grout's rivalry with Jarman and liked to have some fun at Grout's expense.

In the lead-up to the selection, Grout was a guest of the Don and Lady Jessie at their Kensington home for dinner one night. Shirley Bradman asked her father had he seen Wally's 'wonderful catch' to dismiss the South Australian Brian Hurn?

'No,' said her Dad, grinning. 'I was in the rooms with Barry Jarman at the time!'

Grout toured as the senior keeper, Jarman again as bridesmaid.

**Heroes:** Lindsay Kline and Ken Mackay saved Australia from defeat in one of the most gripping finishes to a Test down under in Adelaide during the fabulous West Indian summer of 1960–61. The team was, back row, left to right: Les Favell, Kline, Frank Misson, Des Hoare, Peter Burge, Bobby Simpson, Johnny Martin (twelfth man). Front: Wally Grout, Colin McDonald, Richie Benaud, Mackay, Norm O'Neill.

# G

**'Do you think we should get Malinga on?'**
**'Do you want to be alive after this Test match?'**

## GELIGNITE JACK'S ADELAIDE MIRACLE

Slipsmen love quality leg-spinners. When Australia's long-limbed post-war superstar 'Gelignite Jack' Gregory took an Ashes-record 15 catches against England in 1920–21, seven were from the bowling of Arthur Mailey and another three from fellow leg-spinner Warwick Armstrong.

Mailey's lofty hard-spun leg-breaks and googlies were often of such extravagant height that batsmen felt compelled to attack, with stumper Bert Oldfield and first-slipsman Gregory regular beneficiaries.

On one famous occasion in Adelaide in the New Year of 1925, Mailey and Gregory schemed to dismiss the English master Jack Hobbs, scorer of three 100s in as many Tests. The plan was for Mailey to bowl his wrong-'un third ball of an over with Gregory quietly shifting himself to leg slip for the catch. The only trouble was that Mailey forgot the plan and ripped a big leg-break which bit and spun so much that it caught the edge of Hobbs' ever-so-broad bat and veered towards first slip. Gregory scrambled back to the off-side just in time to take a spectacular catch. Afterwards, asked what had happened, Hobbs said: 'I'm not sure, but there was a helluva lotta noise behind me!'

Years later, Mark Taylor took some equally telling catches at slip from the bowling of Shane Warne, who ripped his signature leg-break *à la* Mailey. One of the best was his diving one-hander from the South African Dave Richardson during the New Year Test in Sydney in 1994 when Warne claimed seven-for on the opening day. An even better catch came in Melbourne on the final day of the Christmas Test of 1997 when another Protea, Adam Bacher, was dismissed. Taylor was slightly 'blinded' by wicketkeeper Ian Healy and took it one-handed just a centimetre from the turf, diving wide to his left. It was a screamer.

The Taylor-Warne pair is among the top three fielder-bowler combinations in Test history. In 66 Tests, they shared 51 wickets, the best strike-rate of any of the 'moderns'.

The most distinguished slipsman-bowler combination is Sri Lanka's Mahela Jayawardene and Muthiah Muralidaran who shared a record 64 dismissals in 96 Tests. Murali's mid-career mastery of his doosra gave the close-in fieldsmen unparalleled extra opportunity.

Jayawardene, one of the great first slipsmen, says he was always too scared to drop any chances from Murali's bowling.

'Have you seen his face if someone drops a catch off him? His eyes go so wide! Of all the catches I took, the most difficult one was the last one, his eight-hundredth [at Galle].We'd wanted him to play the entire Test series [against the Indians in 2010] and take the eight wickets he wanted but he insisted, "No, this is my last Test. I'm retiring. This is it." We tried to talk him around. "Think about it," we said. "In 10, 12 or 15 years you might have 799 Test wickets. You have the opportunity to play all three matches. . ."

'"No, if I can't take 800 that's it."

'He got five-for in the first innings and was on 799 with India's last pair in the second innings. At the other end Ragana Herath was bowling and we were hoping that he wouldn't take the last wicket. Kumar [Sangakkara] had swapped Murali from end to end. He was alternating from over and around the wicket and was into his 40-something over. We had fielders all around the bat, everyone willing him to get his eight-hundredth.

'There was a little bit of a cloud cover around and they had extended the lead close to 100 when Kumar said to me: "Do you think we should get Malinga on?" [from Murali's end].

'"Do you want to be alive after this Test match?"

'Everyone was gathering around the batsmen [Murali bowling

**TEST CRICKET'S ELITE FIELDER-BOWLER PARTNERSHIPS**

| Dismissals | Combination/country | Matches | Dismissals per match |
|---|---|---|---|
| 64 | Mahela Jayawardene–Muthiah Muralidaran (Sri Lanka) | 96 | 0.67 |
| 55 | Rahul Dravid–Anil Kumble (India) | 107 | 0.51 |
| 51 | Mark Taylor–Shane Warne (Australia) | 66 | 0.77 |
| 51 | Rahul Dravid–Harbhajan Singh (India) | 95 | 0.54 |
| 39 | Garry Sobers–Lance Gibbs (West Indies) | 60 | 0.65 |
| 39 | Mark Waugh–Shane Warne (Australia) | 103 | 0.38 |
| 39 | Matthew Hayden–Shane Warne (Australia) | 69 | 0.57 |
| 36 | Ricky Ponting–Shane Warne (Australia) | 85 | 0.42 |
| 35 | Jacques Kallis–Makhaya Ntini (South Africa) | 93 | 0.38 |

with two slips, a gully and a silly mid-off]. The youngsters wanted to take that last catch. "Imagine if any of them dropped it!" I thought to myself. "The entire Sri Lankan community would never forgive them." Then the Indian No. 11 [Pragyan Ojha] didn't quite cover Murali's off-break. The edge came to me and I clasped both hands around it. It was a wonderful feeling to be a part of all that, one of the highlights of my time representing Sri Lanka.'

Another of the best performed combinations, strike-rate wise, was the West Indian pair of Garry Sobers and Lance Gibbs, who shared 39 dismissals in 60 games together.

In one inspired hour-and-a-half at Bridgetown in 1962, Sobers took three catches from Gibbs' bowling as India slumped from 2–158 to 187 all out and a big defeat. Sobers was a magnificent fieldsman anywhere, at slip or at short-leg where his reputation for taking reflex catches rivalled the great Englishman Tony Lock.

Gibbs' analysis in that action-packed final session was a best-ever 15.3–14–6–8!

## THE GREAT ESCAPE

It was an immortal moment. In engineering the greatest last wicket escape in Test history, Australians Ken Mackay and Lindsay Kline ensured their places in any 'Great Moments' cavalcade by batting out the last 110 minutes against Frank Worrell's 1960–61 West Indians in Adelaide.

Thinking the game was all but over, Wally Grout was among several of the Australians who began to pack their bags or head for the showers as Kline joined Mackay at the wicket. Grout's grandson and biographer, Wally Wright, said Grout even poured himself a beer in anticipation of the early ending. Having seen Kline successfully negotiate his first overs, looking as comfortable as a No. 11 can, Grout playfully announced to the dressing room that he would down a beer every additional over that Kline lasted.

'"You'll be tanked," said a teammate.

'"I hope you have to carry me out," said Wal.

'While Wally didn't keep his word and down a beer at *every* change of ends, he had a fair crack,' Wright says. 'As Mackay faced out the final over of the match from Wes Hall, my grandfather's teammates recall Wally being engulfed in a thick cloud of cigarette smoke with half a dozen empty West End beer bottles strewn around him. If it wasn't for the fact that Wally, like most cricketers, was superstitious about leaving his seat [to get another beer] when the game was on a knife's edge, he may well have needed a few teammates to "carry him out" after the match!'

The Australians' scepticism of Kline's ability to be able to withstand the pace of Wes Hall and the spin of Garry Sobers and co. was well founded. The Victorian wrist spinner had a highest Test score of just 14 and an average of 6. But he could be hard to shift, and according to statistician Charles Davis had a surprisingly high average innings time of 45 minutes. As a teenager, he'd opened the innings for Melbourne's second XI in District cricket ranks.

During the tea break Kline had ducked out to the practice nets for an impromptu hit against spinners Johnnie Martin and Norman O'Neill, only to be dismissed nine or 10 times in quick time.

As Kline fumbled around his crease, mis-hitting and miscalculating and regularly losing his castle, a woman standing behind the nets said: 'Well, we can't rely on you, can we?'

Kline grinned and replied: 'No, I'll have to do a bit better, won't I? But if I get rid of all my outs now, perhaps I won't have them when I get out in the centre!'

Against all odds, Kline stayed with Mackay throughout the final session to force Test cricket's most famous draw.

The two had little in common other than being left-handers, though they had batted together before, in back-to-back Tests in South Africa in 1957–58.

Immediately after the interval, Mackay began playing shots off the spinners, scoring at almost a run a minute for the first half an hour. He had no serious thoughts, then, of looking to last until 6 pm. But Kline was middling virtually everything and members of the crowd, who had been contemplating an early exit, stayed riveted to their seats hoping against hope that the two left-handers could continue to hold the West Indians at bay.

Adelaide's police force didn't share their optimism. From tea-time about 30 boys in blue positioned themselves in a ring around the entire boundary edge.

Early on, Mackay played a ball from Worrell firmly into the ground straight to Garry Sobers at silly mid-off who took the ball and began to walk off as if it was a clear catch. Mackay knew it was a bump ball. Importantly, so did umpire Col Egar who rejected a belated appeal. There were still 75 minutes to play.

'Right,' said Mackay to himself. 'You'll have to dig me out now.' He hated being railroaded. It was only then that he decided to play for time.

Worrell took the new ball, adding further dimension to the drama but not producing the wicket the Windies needed. Both Mackay and

Kline were well set. When spin returned only six overs later, the intensity levels rose again with both batsmen surrounded by a brace of close-in fielders, Sobers' bouncy wrong-'un a particular danger.

'The batsmen settled into total defence,' said Davis, 'and there was almost no scoring and the batsmen didn't change ends even once.'

Kline was more comfortable opposing the medium pace of Worrell than the spin of Sobers, Lance Gibbs and Alf Valentine. So he batted one end and Mackay the other, every defensive shot being cheered.

'That was a first for me!' quipped Mackay, one of the most noted defensive players in the world.

The bowlers rushed through their overs, the West Indians showing growing concern at their inability to finish the match. Worrell even used tiny Joe Solomon to help break Mackay's concentration. Mackay had never seen him bowl even in the nets.

West Indies had declared their second innings on the fourth day at 6–432, setting Australia 460 to win in 400 minutes. At 3–31 at stumps on the penultimate night, it seemed inevitable that the tourists would win and square the series. From 3–116 at lunch on the final day, Australia slid to 6–144 but Mackay and Grout, who were both part of Gibbs' hat-trick in the first innings, held on for 76 minutes before Grout was dismissed on the point of tea. Tailenders Des Hoare and Frank Misson followed immediately afterwards.

As Kline walked through the member's onto the ground, one said: 'Last out, ho, ho, ho. . . it's all up to you now,' and everyone around him started to laugh. But within the hour, as noted author Mike Coward reported, 'as news of the extraordinary partnership reached the city, offices and shops emptied and a small gathering resigned to defeat was soon swollen to a crowd of 13,691 that dared to consider an improbable draw.'

As the overs were ticked off, the pair said little to each other in the centre other than a 'Keep your head down' from Mackay to Kline, who responded with a nod and a mumbled 'yes'.

Their partnership was to stretch to 283 balls, not including no-balls, the longest tenth-wicket stand, per balls bowled, for which records have been found, exceeding the 280 balls by Peter Willey and Bob Willis against the West Indies at The Oval in 1980 and 278 balls for two more Englishmen, John Snow and Ken Higgs, against the West Indies at The Oval in 1966. (In Melbourne in the Ashes Test of 1901–02 there was a 148-minute tenth-wicket stand of 120 by specialist Australian batsmen Warwick Armstrong and Reg Duff that in all probability lasted longer than 300 balls, but the exact figure is unknown.)

Mackay said the old clock at The Oval must have stopped '10 or 12 times'. He tried to stall for time, but Worrell was able to give his trump card Hall one last over with just 15 seconds to go before 6 pm, a never-to-be-forgotten over Mackay was able to negotiate – just.

Hurrying through their overs, the Windies were to bowl a record 905 balls for the day, including 39.3 overs after tea.

'It was a probably million-to-one chance that I got through,' said Kline years later. 'It was wonderful to do something so special for the team.'

## GREAT ESCAPE TIMELINE

The following timeline, by Charles Davis – without the assistance of the official scorebook which has been lost – begins with the last over before tea:

Over 81, 3.39 pm: Worrell's third over of the innings. Grout (42) lbw to the fifth ball, a contentious decision – Worrell was bowling around the wicket. Tea called immediately. Australia 7–203, Mackay 14 not out in 94 minutes.

4.00: Play re-commences. Worrell completes over, bowling to Des Hoare.

Over 85, 4.13: Hoare (1) c Joe Solomon, b Worrell at leg slip, second ball of the over. Frank Misson (0) b Worrell, fifth ball of the over. Kline comes to the crease at 4.19, with 101 minutes to play. 9–207, Mackay 16.

Over 86: Sobers bowling (wrist) spin. Single to Mackay.

Over 87: Mackay (on 17) given not out to a disputed catch by Sobers off Worrell. 9–208.

Overs 90–100: Mackay and Kline score relatively freely. New ball available but not taken.

Over 95: Mackay hits eight runs off Worrell (4+2+2).

Over 97: Worrell off, Gibbs on; Gibbs hit for four by Kline.

Over 98: Sobers off, Valentine on.

Over 100, 4.55: With two 4s in an over off Valentine, Mackay reaches 50 in 150 minutes (with five 4s).

Over 101, 4.58: New ball taken at 249 by Hall, bowling to Kline. A no-ball brings up Australia's 250 (in 340 minutes). Kline then hits Hall to the cover-point boundary.

Over 102: Sobers (replacing Valentine), medium pace.

Over 104, 5.10: Kline hits Sobers for three to register 50 partnership in even time. 9–258.

5.19: Partnership 59 in an hour (9–266). Kline half-chance off Sobers at 13 (Gibbs).

Over 107, 5.27: Hall off, Worrell on; maiden.

Over 108: Sobers switches to spin and sends down an over in just two minutes. Scoring ceases.

5.40: 9–270, Mackay 60, Kline 15. Sobers off, Gibbs bowls to Mackay.

5.45 or 5.50 (over 114 or 116): Gibbs off, Valentine on; maiden. Signs of desperation, WI rushing through overs: 'They're bowling too fast,' says the reporter from the *Times*.

5.54: Two runs to Mackay off Valentine. Worrell sixteenth over a maiden.

Over 119, 5.57: Worrell bowls his seventeenth and last over, a maiden to Kline, with nine close-in fielders.

## THEY ALSO SAVED A TEST MATCH

| |
|---|
| 2009, Centurion: England's No. 11 Graham Onions plays out a maiden over from Makhaya Ntini to force a draw after England had caved on the final afternoon against the South Africans. His senior partner Paul Collingwood is criticised for agreeing to a single from the fourth ball of the penultimate over, exposing Onions for the last six deliveries of an 11-ball partnership. |
| 2009, Cardiff: English tailenders Monty Panesar, one of the ultimate No. 11s of them all, and James Anderson hold out for 40 minutes and 69 balls to force an improbable Ashes draw after Australia had controlled the game throughout. |
| 2009, St John's: Daren Powell and Fidel Edwards survive 36 minutes and 10 overs to force a draw in the third of five West Indian-English Tests for the Wisden Trophy. |
| 2003, Harare: West Indian last pair Ridley Jacobs and Fidel Edwards bat 32 minutes and 71 balls to deny Zimbabwe a rare Test win. |
| 1997, Hobart: Kiwi tailenders Simon Doull and Shayne O'Connor bat 38 minutes and 64 balls to avert an Australian clean-sweep in the third of three Tests. |
| 1963: Lord's: England's Colin Cowdrey, batting at No. 11 with a broken arm, helps David Allen to force a draw. Any of the four results are possible as the final ball from West Indian speedster Wes Hall is bowled. |

Over 120, 5.59: Hall, the last over to Mackay, a maiden taking almost 10 minutes. Balls 1 and 4 played by Mackay, the latter almost a boundary but no run taken. Balls 2, 3 and 5 pass down leg side. Balls 6 and 7 bowled round the wicket. The last ball (with Hall back over the wicket) takes three attempts – an aborted run up, an interruption from a spectator on the ground, then a no-ball followed by a crowd invasion of the ground, and finally, excruciating minutes later, a short ball that Mackay deliberately takes on the chest.

6.09: Stumps: Australia 9–273 (408 minutes), Mackay 62 in 223 minutes, Kline 15 in 110 minutes. Draw!

**Debonair:** Ray Lindwall (right) with his fast-bowler partner Keith Miller at the height of their fame in the early 1950s. They opened the Australian bowling in six Ashes campaigns.

# H

**‘Give us Keith Miller and we’ll beat the world. . .’**

## HUNTING IN PAIRS

The greatest fast bowlers have always hunted in pairs. Few were more explosive, or as enduring, as Australia’s post-war dynamos Ray Lindwall and Keith Miller, responsible for more than 40 per cent of Australia’s wickets in the first decade of post-war Test cricket.

With his graceful, accelerating run-up, classic side-on action and signature outswing, Lindwall was the Rolls-Royce of fast bowlers and for a decade and more the most admired and threatening expressman in the world. No two Lindwall balls in a row were ever alike, and with his low action, his bouncer would skid straight at the throat. Handsome, charismatic Miller, the game’s Errol Flynn, was a three-in-one cricketer, bowling devilishly fast, batting in the top four or five and taking astonishing reflex catches in the slips as if he was nonchalantly rolling a cigarette. Had the war not delayed his debut until his late 20s, his record would have been even more impressive.

The pair were central in Australia’s remarkable run of success in the first decade after the war, smashing through top-orders from Birmingham to Brisbane, and with ‘Big Bill’ Johnston, the multi-gifted Victorian, were a formidable fast-bowling trinity on the 1948 tour when Australia remained unbeaten over five months and 34 matches.

Despite disparate backgrounds and differing cities of origin – one was from Sydney, the other from Melbourne – they were the closest of mates, hooking up originally in New Zealand in 1946 and became inseparable, rooming together, sharing beers and banter like two long-lost brothers.

One of their habits each night on tour was to empty out their pockets and leave their change in a mounting heap on the dressing table, Lindwall, a staunch Catholic, taking it to the church on Sundays. Miller would prefer to snooze in but would always say as Lindwall was leaving: 'Say a few Hail Marys for me, too, Jack [his nickname for Lindwall].'

Together they took almost 400 Test wickets, Lindwall being the first Australian fast bowler to a double-century. Stockier and broader of chest, Lindwall was consistently faster than his mate and hooped the ball away from the right-handers at near express speed. His captains, from Don Bradman to Richie Benaud, always gave him the choice of ends. In sweltering summer heat in Melbourne one day, Victoria's one-Test opener George Thoms had the temerity to question Lindwall's pace and was immediately subjected to the two fastest overs of his life. In South Africa in 1949–50, Lindwall threatened to flatten captain Lindsay Hassett when told he was being dropped from the fifth Test team. He had a fast bowler's temper.

Miller, taller, bouncier and more unpredictable, was just as lethal and even more volatile. Working into the wind gave him more scope for his in-swinger and he could still a pin a batsman onto his back foot with a throat-high bouncer. Once he did it to Don Bradman in his Sydney testimonial. It was no coincidence that within weeks he'd been sensationally omitted from Australia's next tour. He blamed Bradman for his failure to be appointed Australia's captain and died still harbouring grudges against the Don, who he believed played the game too ruthlessly.

He had no such reservations about pace partner Lindwall, believing him to be in a class of his own, on and off the field.

'No one could touch Ray,' he told me. 'He was a great man, a church-goer, and it was a privilege to play with him. As a fast bowler there was daylight between him and the rest. He'd bowl his first ball as fast as his last. One morning at Lord's [in 1953], he yorked Tom Graveney first-ball and Tom was in good touch, too. He'd told me in the rooms that morning: "Let's limber up here, Nug. Get into him flat out straight away. He looks a bit sluggish when he starts." And

**Partners in Pace:** Keith Miller and Ray Lindwall took eight wickets against England in a high scoring draw in Adelaide in 1946–47. The team was: back row, left to right: Fred Freer (12th man), Don Tallon, Bruce Dooland, Ernie Toshack, Keith Miller, Ray Lindwall, Arthur Morris. Front: Colin McCool, Lindsay Hassett, Don Bradman (captain), Merv Harvey, Ian Johnson.

before most of the members had had a chance to even take their seats, he went straight through him. It was a cracker. That set Ray apart from every other fast bowler. He thought about what he was doing and always bowled it exactly where he wanted.'

Lindwall's extraordinary burst of six for 20 in the final Test at The Oval in 1948 saw England bowled out in two and a half hours for just 52. A decade earlier at the same ground it had batted into a third day and made 7–903 declared!

Lindwall and Miller captured 40 wickets for the series, Lindwall a career-best 27 and Miller 13, a lingering back injury from his war years not allowing him to bowl as often as he and Bradman wanted.

The Don carried the scars of Australia's 1938 drubbing at The Oval into his farewell tour in 1948 and, looking for revenge, wanted Lindwall and Miller to bowl short and intimidate the English top-order at every opportunity. A new ball was allowed every 55 overs

**Post-War Destroyers:** Few top-orders could repel the duel menace of Ray Lindwall (*left*) and Keith Miller.

### RAY LINDWALL AND KEITH MILLER'S BEST TESTS TOGETHER

| |
|---|
| Fifth Test v West Indies, 1951–52:<br>Fourteen wickets (for 155) – Lindwall 2–20 and 5–52, Miller 5–26 and 2–57 |
| Fourth Test v England, Leeds, 1953:<br>Fourteen wickets (for 260) – Lindwall 5–54 and 3–104, Miller 2–39 and 4–63 |

that summer and rarely were Lindwall, Miller or Johnston required to bowl with anything that wasn't shiny or near new.

Having played their debut Test together, an eight-hour affair against the New Zealanders in Wellington in autumn, 1946, the Lindwall-Miller combine had shifted into top gear against Wally Hammond's visiting Englishmen with the resumption of Ashes cricket at the Gabba in 1946–47. In a sensational start to his Ashes career, Miller took seven for 60 and two for 17 to go with his 79 from No. 5. He even knocked the cap of tough-as-teak Lancastrian Cyril Washbrook from his head. Lindwall was ill and able to bowl just 12 overs for the game. Returning in mid-summer he took three wickets in Melbourne, six in Adelaide and nine in Sydney.

The following summer, Miller was having a drink with his mate after a tough day of leather-chasing in Adelaide when told by an administrator Bill Jeanes to 'finish up' as he had taxis waiting downstairs. The heat was sweltering, and the champion Indian Vijay Hazare had made a second century in the match of his life. He kept whipping Miller through square leg and Miller had asked Bradman for reinforcement, but was told 'no'. Miller finished his over with two off-breaks and was immediately taken off.

Given the 35-degree heat, Jeanes was as frazzled as the two fast bowlers and sharp words were exchanged. Bradman was notified. He asked Miller to see him at his stockbroking office the following day. Miller felt like an errant schoolboy being summoned into the Head's study. In Melbourne he'd grabbed a souvenir stump at the match-end only to again be admonished. Administrators felt him intolerably extrovert. Miller knew he was lucky to be alive and like Arthur Morris and others who had seen active duty during the seven dark years of war, it felt surreal to be playing cricket again. He didn't like Bradman treating it like a war.

During the 1948 tour, Miller took exception when Bradman asked him to pepper fellow serviceman Bill Edrich with bumpers. Edrich was a family man who Miller liked. All England was on rations after the War. Almost everyone was doing it hard. Not for the first time, he tossed the ball back to Bradman, suggesting someone else do his 'dirty work'.

Throughout his career Miller bowled less often than most front-liners, Lindwall averaging 20 per cent more overs. Fifty-one of Miller's 55 Tests were alongside Lindwall. In the four matches he played without his mate, he shouldered more responsibility, including at Lord's in 1956 when he took the only 10-wicket match haul of his career.

The pair remained Australia's first choice opening pair through six Ashes series in a row, their spirited duels with England's champion Len Hutton always a highlight. Twice they took 14 wickets in Tests and three times shared 40 wickets for the series. The showdown for world supremacy against the West Indies in 1951–52 was a fizzer after Lindwall and Miller worked over the Windies' three batting stars – Everton Weekes, Frank Worrell and Clyde Walcott – with the greatest bumper assault seen since Bodyline. Having shocked

**RAY LINDWALL AND KEITH MILLER IN TEST CRICKET**

| | | Ray Lindwall | | Keith Miller | |
|---|---|---|---|---|---|
| Season | Opponent | Wickets | Average | Wickets | Average |
| 1945–46 | New Zealand (a) | 2 | 14.50 | 2 | 3.00 |
| 1946–47 | England (h) | 18 | 20.38 | 16 | 20.87 |
| 1947–48 | India (h) | 18 | 16.89 | 9 | 24.78 |
| 1948 | England (a) | 27 | 19.62 | 13 | 23.15 |
| 1949–50 | South Africa (a) | 12 | 20.66 | 17 | 22.94 |
| 1950–51 | England (h) | 15 | 22.93 | 17 | 17.70 |
| 1951–52 | West Indies (h) | 21 | 23.05 | 20 | 19.90 |
| 1952–53 | South Africa (h) | 19 | 20.16 | 13 | 18.54 |
| 1953 | England (a) | 26 | 18.84 | 10 | 30.30 |
| 1954–55 | England (h) | 14 | 27.21 | 10 | 24.30 |
| 1955 | West Indies (a) | 20 | 31.85 | 20 | 32.05 |
| 1956 | England (a) | 7 | 34.00 | 21 | 22.23 |
| 1956–57 | Pakistan (a) | 1 | 64.00 | 2 | 29.00 |
| 1956–57 | India (a) | 12 | 16.58 | – | – |
| 1958–59 | England (h) | 7 | 29.85 | – | – |
| 1959–60 | Pakistan (a) | 3 | 40.67 | – | – |
| 1959–60 | India (a) | 6 | 37.00 | – | – |
| **Totals** | | **228** | **23.03** | **170** | **22.97** |

England with a 3–1 victory in 1950, the Windies were beaten 4–1, Lindwall taking 21 wickets and Miller 20. The peppering began in Brisbane, Miller being warned after bowling three bouncers before finishing the over with a slow off-break. 'Any objections to that?' he asked the umpire.

In 1955 in the Caribbean, the locals howled with excitement when Lindwall and Miller unleashed their bumpers, one even penning a ditty to Lindwall: 'Bowl Lindwall,' he said. 'Don't be 'fraid, if da can't bat, break der shoulder blade.'

With his war record, charisma and matinee-idol looks, Miller was hero-worshipped everywhere he went. He was the ultimate sports hero for tens of thousands of Australians, young and old, male and female in the 1950s. If the Australian team visited a country centre, captain Lindsay Hassett would always invite Miller on stage with him as part of the welcome.

'Never before,' Miller would invariably begin, 'have I ever seen such a motley mob of men. . . or. . . such a beautiful array of gorgeous gals!'

During a wartime services match in India, a swarm of insects surrounded Miller, Hassett immediately quipping: 'Must be female!'

Miller was 27 and Lindwall 25 when Ashes cricket resumed after the war. While Lindwall was a comparative unknown, Miller already had a profile in England, having been based in London throughout much of the war. Representing the Dominions at Lord's in 1943, he came on to bowl at second change. Denis Compton was on strike and turning to the wicketkeeper Stan Sismey, asked, 'What does this chap do?'

'He doesn't really bowl,' replied Sismey. 'Just turns his arm over. Probably just wants a bit of exercise. But he can be a bit quick.' Miller was quick all right, the fastest Compton had faced since Ernie McCormick in 1938.

In 1945 at Lord's, he made 185 for the Dominions, his greatest ever innings. When he wasn't playing cricket, he'd be charming the members at Ascot in top hat and tails. He was the classiest of all wild colonial boys.

Even into his mid-30s Miller had the ability to swing matches. Bowling unchanged before lunch in the Melbourne Test of 1954–55, Miller took three for 8 in one of the great opening spells. Later that memorable summer, in Adelaide when England was set just 94 to win the Ashes, a supercharged Miller dismissed captain Hutton, Edrich and Colin Cowdrey in 20 balls and took a low-down, disputed catch on the offside to dismiss Peter May, at which a despairing Hutton exclaimed, 'the boogers have doon us!' England was to win by five wickets but it had been an inspired effort from Miller, whose best was always extraordinary.

'Give us Keith Miller,' West Indian captain John Goddard once said, 'and we'll beat the world.'

# I

**‘Haynes told him he should be back in school, before yelling back up the wicket in deep West Indian: “KILL HIM BISHY”.’**

## IN A LEAGUE OF THEIR OWN

The tiny pear-shaped island of Barbados has long been Caribbean cricket’s Shangri-La. There are more turf wickets per square metre in Barbados than anywhere else in the world. Vacant street corners will have a goat or two grazing, plus a 22-yard wicket.

It is extraordinary that an island easily circumnavigated in half a day has been so cricket-rich. Of the West Indies’ first 200 Test cricketers, 25 per cent were from Barbados. Among them were the game’s outstanding all-rounder Garry Sobers; the Three W’s Everton Weekes, Frank Worrell and Clyde Walcott; pacemen Wes Hall, Charlie Griffith, Malcolm Marshall and Joel Garner; and opening batting supremos Gordon Greenidge and Desmond Haynes.

It was in this elite cricketing environment that Greenidge, from Black Bess, and Haynes, from tough-as Holder’s Hill, were first introduced to the game. Like most cricket-mad Bajan kids, they played from dawn to dusk most months of the year on sun-drenched vacant fields, roads and beaches, developing an eagle-eye and a sure confidence so characteristic of their play at international grounds around the world.

‘We used to brag and say if you wanted to learn cricket, come into Holder’s Hill,’ said Haynes. ‘We not only played, we talked

---

**Ferocious:** Gordon Greenidge was the aggressor in a magnificent opening combine with fellow Bajan Desmond Haynes. *Patrick Eagar*

about it. As a young boy I could listen and hear all sorts of stories and learn.'

Greenidge joined his mother in England from his early teens, beginning his apprenticeship with the assistance of John Arlott at Hampshire before returning to Barbados where he was to become an integral part of one of the great all-time teams which ruled the cricket world for 15 years.

Greenidge hooked up with Haynes from 1978, the pair becoming the most enduring, prolific and intimidating in the history of Test cricket, opening a record 148 times and amassing almost 6500 runs at an average only a touch below 50. Ten of their 16 century stands came on home wickets in the Caribbean, where they averaged 65 and were truly in a league of their own.

'They were an opening bowler's nightmare come true,' said long-time opponent, Australian Geoff Lawson. 'Both had superb defensive techniques that had them well equipped to keep out the best you could serve up. After repelling the early stuff, they would carry the attack to the bowlers. Most of your energy would then be spent trying to save runs.'

Their longevity was extraordinary, and over their 13 years and 89 Tests at the head of the order, the West Indies won 48 and lost only eight games. No team had a higher quality battery of fast bowlers to rank with the seemingly endless line of the Caribbean's flamethrowers, but with Greenidge and Haynes at the head of the order and King Viv in at three, they invariably had lots of runs to play with.

From being out-and-out dashers, Greenidge and Haynes learned to temper their aggression – but not always their volatility. They were invariably among the most 'chatty' of the West Indian short catchers. Haynes at short leg was always keen to remind a new batsman of the physical danger confronting him. As a wide-eyed first-gamer, Justin Langer was taking guard against Ian Bishop in Adelaide in 1992–93. Haynes told him he should be back in school, before yelling back up the wicket in deep West Indian: 'KILL HIM BISHY.'

Despite his wide, engaging smile, Haynes could be easily upset – and confrontational. In 1984, as the Windies rolled to an easy win against Kim Hughes' Australians in Brisbane, he was dismissed by the hard-line Lawson and took umbrage at the throwaway line 'On ya bike champ' (or something like that).

As he was walking off he turned and, using his bat like a gun, pointed it straight at Lawson and 'fired'. The game ended within minutes and a still-angry Haynes grabbed a stump and went to charge into the Australian room only to be held back by teammates. I was in a corner chatting with Michael Holding at the time. He just shook his head.

'Greenidge and Haynes didn't always appreciate having their arrogance thrown back in their faces,' said Lawson in explanation, 'and often reacted childishly.'

In 1991 when Australian wicketkeeper Ian Healy claimed a low catch Haynes felt had bounced at his home ground Kensington Oval, Haynes called him a cheat, triggering more on-field drama. An incensed Healy told Haynes to 'let the effing umpire do his effing job'. Haynes responded by inviting Healy to meet him after the game. It was distasteful and unnecessary.

Greenidge was five years Haynes' senior and given his experience of playing county cricket in England and opening up with the fabled South African Barry Richards, he was a father figure for Haynes and many of the other younger West Indians, quietly offering advice and encouragement when asked.

In Haynes he recognised a young, committed, very emotional champion in the making. He had rough edges, but he also possessed a rare drive to improve and hated it when he felt he'd let the team down.

'Even if I got our first,' said Greenidge, 'he'd be the one who screamed, threw tantrums, just trying to release that sense of disappointment and frustration.'

Greenidge had overcome a pair on debut against the Australians in 1975–76 to become one of world cricket's most complete batsmen, equally at home against the pace as he was against the spinners. He could be introverted, even sullen. Haynes was more flamboyant. The gold chain around his neck summed up his attitude to life: 'Live, Love, Laugh'.

As running partners they had a fine understanding and were involved in only four run-outs in their 148 innings. They'd regularly run singles with just a nod of the head, rather than a call. Haynes became used to senior pro Greenidge farming the strike by taking a single from the last ball of an over.

'The better his form was, the more eager he was to get the strike, the further he backed up. "Let me get the strike man," he would say to me,' said Haynes. 'So I played second fiddle. I fed him. I knew if someone was going to be dropped, it wasn't going to be him. There was a greater onus on me to maintain the partnership. Just watching him from the other end was a lesson. I was perfectly happy and proud to be second fiddle to him.'

They built an air of impregnability from the time they started with 87 in the opening Test against Jeff Thomson and the 1978 Australians at Port-of-Spain. A fortnight later they shared their first century stand, 131, in front of an adoring home crowd at Kensington Oval, Bridgetown. Included were sixteen 4s and three 6s.

'They worked as a wonderful partnership. . . rarely was there a dull moment,' said Bruce Yardley, who opposed them in that 1978 series. 'They applied the basics of cricket, defended the good stuff, and boy, didn't they attack anything they fancied!'

Haynes' whirlwind maiden Test knocks of 61, 66 and 55 against the Australians earned him the nickname of 'Hammer' Haynes. A great entertainer, he was rarely out of form for too long.

Their golden period came in the early to mid-1980s when, in the space of 30 Tests, they amassed two 250-run opening stands, the highpoints in five century stands. Additionally, they were responsible for 16 half-century starts.

At St John's in 1990, they began with a career-best 298 against England, Greenidge in his one hundredth Test making 149 and Haynes 167, the Windies winning by an innings.

They established record stands against four countries: England, Australia, New Zealand and India. In eight series they averaged 50 or more and in 1983–84 against the Australians, their average ballooned to 136. The partnerships that golden summer were: 29 and 250 unfinished (Georgetown), 35 (Port-of-Spain), 132 and 21 unfinished

**GREENIDGE AND HAYNES'S 100-RUN TEST STANDS**

| | |
|---|---|
| 298 | v England, St John's, 1989–90 |
| 296* | v Australia, St John's, 1983–84 |
| 296 | v India, St John's, 1982–83 |
| 250* | v Australia, Georgetown, 1983–84 |
| 225 | v New Zealand, Christchurch, 1980 |
| 168 | v England Port-of-Spain, 1980–81 |
| 162 | v Australia, Kingston, 1983–84 |
| 150 | v New Zealand, Wellington, 1986–87 |
| 135 | v Australia, Brisbane 1988–89 |
| 132 | v Australia, Bridgetown, 1983–84 |
| 131 | v Australia, Bridgetown, 1977–78 |
| 129 | v Australia, Bridgetown, 1990–91 |
| 118 | v Australia, Kingston, 1990–91 |
| 116 | v England, Kingston, 1981–82 |
| 114 | v India, Calcutta, 1987–88 |
| 106 | v England, Leeds, 1984 |

* unfinished

(Bridgetown), 0 (St John's) and 162 and 55 unfinished (Kingston). Greenidge averaged 78 and Haynes 93, the Windies winning 3–0.

The pair 'played for each other', said long-time teammate Courtney Walsh. 'When they were both in their prime, to watch them was to see perfection in the science of opening an innings,' he said.

Greenidge struck the ball straight with such brutal power that at practice the West Indian fast bowlers dared not turn their backs on him as they walked back to the top of their marks. Viv Richards was the only other player accorded similar respect.

Australian fast bowler Rodney Hogg reckoned you almost needed to bowl in a helmet, as Greenidge smoked his on-the-up drives straight back up the wicket. Even when Dennis Lillee and Jeff Thomson were at their fieriest, Greenidge would belligerently launch onto the front foot, looking to power the ball straight through the covers. If it was short, he'd pull and cut with equal savagery. He had massive biceps and forearms. Like Everton Weekes, when he hit a ball, it stayed hit, even with the wafer-thin bats then in use.

With his English experience, he was technically tighter than Haynes and often just as dangerous when he was limping as when he seemed to be 100 per cent fit.

Haynes was a wonderfully rhythmic stroke-maker who learnt to convert his starts into bigger scores. A deep thinker, he opened his stance in mid-career with considerable success. Few played Dennis Lillee with as much assurance – or were as consistently combative, one of the offshoots of coming from the highly competitive atmosphere of cricket at Holder's Hill.

'He always had the drive to succeed,' said Greenidge, 'but it took time for him to build up the technical side of his game. The mental capacity was always there, it was just a matter of bringing it out. I could not have asked for a better partner. He kept going, kept growing, not just in batting terms but also in his all-round cricketing knowledge.'

Greenidge and Haynes were also masters of the one-day game and together they were the first to 15 ODI century stands and remain among the few limited-over pairs to have averaged 50 or more. With their trademark aggression the Windies would invariably score their

**Spanning Sixteen Years:** Ashes openers Len Hutton (*left*) with Bill Edrich. They opened first in 1938 and for the last time in 1954–55.

**Barbados Masters:** Desmond Haynes (*left*) with fellow Bajan Gordon Greenidge. They brutalised opposing attacks.

first 60 runs at four an over, setting the scene for King Viv, Richie Richardson and co., and this in an era before the advent of Twenty20 cricket, big bats and shorter boundaries.

On his West Indian debut against the 1978 Australians, Haynes slammed a memorable 148 from 136 balls, the first of his 17 ODI centuries.

'It was a one-dayer at Antigua,' said Yardley. 'Roy Fredericks had retired and Dessie tore our attack apart, including "Two-up" [Jeff Thomson]. Dessie actually went down on one knee and cover drove him for four. [Captain] Bob Simpson played as our spinner that day and Dessie propped forward, rocked back and off the back foot and

### MOST PARTNERSHIPS IN TESTS

| | |
|---|---|
| 148 | Gordon Greenidge and Desmond Haynes (West Indies) |
| 143 | Rahul Dravid and Sachin Tendulkar (India) |
| 122 | Justin Langer and Matthew Hayden (Australia)<br>Marvan Atapattu and Sanath Jayasuriya (Sri Lanka) |
| 117 | Andrew Strauss and Alastair Cook (England) |
| 95 | Mahela Jayawardene and Kumar Sangakkara (Sri Lanka) |
| 88 | Alec Stewart and Mike Atherton (England) |
| 85 | David Boon and Mark Taylor (Australia)<br>Rahul Dravid and VVS Laxman (India) |
| **Other Australian pairs:** | |
| 78 | Mark Taylor and Michael Slater |
| 76 | Matthew Hayden and Ricky Ponting |
| 73 | Mark Waugh and Steve Waugh |
| 64 | Bobby Simpson and Bill Lawry |
| 61 | Steve Waugh and Ian Healy |

### THEY OPENED IN TESTS SPANNING 10 YEARS AND MORE

| Span in years | | Innings | Last Test |
|---|---|---|---|
| 16 | Len Hutton and Bill Edrich (England) | 10 | 1954–55 |
| 13 | Bruce Mitchell and Eric Rowan (South Africa) | 6 | 1948–49 |
| 13 | Gordon Greenidge and Desmond Haynes (WI) | 148 | 1990–91 |

| Span in years | | Innings | Last Test |
|---|---|---|---|
| 11 | Jack Hobbs and Wilfred Rhodes (England) | 36 | 1920–21 |
| 10 | Sid Gregory and Victor Trumper (Australia) | 3 | 1911–12 |
| 10 | Charles Macartney and Warren Bardsley (Australia) | 2 | 1921 |
| 10 | Mushtaq Ali and Vijay Merchant (India) | 7 | 1946 |
| 10 | Marvan Atapattu and Sanath Jayasuriya (Sri Lanka) | 118 | 2007–08 |
| **Other Australian pairs:** | | | |
| 7 | Bill Ponsford and Bill Woodfull | 22 | 1934 |
| 7 | Michael Slater and Matthew Hayden | 25 | 2001 |
| 6 | Bobby Simpson and Bill Lawry | 62 | 1967–68 |
| 6 | Andrew Hilditch and Graeme Wood | 18 | 1985 |
| 5 | Mark Taylor and Michael Slater | 78 | 1998–99 |
| 5 | Matthew Hayden and Justin Langer | 113 | 2006–07 |

put it over long on, into the street. "Holy smoke," we wondered, "Who is this guy?"

'And Gordon smacked them even harder. In Sydney in 1982, "DK" [Lillee] bowled a bouncer and Gordon absolutely smashed it into the square leg fence. I don't think I've ever seen a ball hit harder. I wondered when DK would test him again but he made him wait for several overs. It was shrewd and brilliant. Having bowled a series of good length deliveries, giving Gordon no room to swing, Dennis sensed the moment and bowled one shorter and faster. Gordon was seeing it like a watermelon but this one was onto him quicker, he got the pull shot high on the bat and "Stumpy" [Bruce Laird] racing in from mid-on, took an amazing diving catch at the bowler's end stumps. It was some contest whenever those two were opposed.'

## INSPIRED

On song, they were as inspired and exhilarating as any Australian pair and often reserved their best for the most pivotal moments.

Bars emptied when Norman O'Neill and Neil Harvey were in occupation in the late 1950s and early 1960s. No wanted to miss a ball, so joyous and effortless was their strokeplay.

Five times they shared century stands in Tests – and often when runs were at a premium and high-profiled teammates out cheaply.

On a spinner's wicket against the West Indians in Sydney in 1960–61, they added 108 in even time before Harvey hurt his leg, halting Australia's advance on the final morning.

Their highest and most important partnership was their 207 out of 387 in ferocious heat at Bombay in 1959–60. Harvey was the in-form player in the world and delighted with his twinkling footwork and eagle eye. O'Neill's driving was supreme and for almost five hours he and Harvey defied the Indians, Harvey scoring 102 and O'Neill 163. No-one else made 40.

As he was leaving the dressing room, O'Neill was stopped by captain Richie Benaud. 'You are one of the best players in the world. Go out and thrash 'em.'

The Indians bowled immaculate lines, their left-arm spinner Bapu Nadkarni defying the heat to deliver more than 50 overs.

Hour after hour the pair batted, defying the bowling and the firecrackers which were part of the general commotion, even when bowlers were about to deliver.

As was the Indian custom, on reaching their hundreds, they each received a garland of flowers and a handful of lemons from fans who jumped the fence and ran onto the pitch.

In their last stand together, against Ted Dexter's 1962–63 Englishmen in Adelaide, they added 194 in less than three hours against the might of Trueman, Statham and co.

As Test partners, they averaged 70 together, their displays truly majestic, as if each was inspired by the other.

Harvey was almost 10 years older than O'Neill – not that it showed. Even into his 30s, he would scamper up and down the wicket like a teenager and it wasn't until his final Ashes summer in 1962–63 that he vacated the No. 3 position in favour of his gifted New South Wales teammate.

**Graceful:** Mark Waugh helped form one of the great Australian top-orders with his twin brother Steve. Their mega moment came at Sabina Park, Kingston, Jamaica, in 1995 when they added 231 in even time as Australia won the world Test championship.

# J

**'They peppered him and looked to intimidate him, but Steve is one person you just don't pick a scrap with...'**

## JAMAICAN GEM

Of all Steve and Mark Waugh's colossal achievements, this was the most stirring and crucial. A double-century partnership in a Test match is special at any time, but when it decides the world championship, it's truly monumental.

For 15 years the West Indies had enjoyed top-of-the-tree status among the elite Test nations, their magnificent, never-ending battery of intimidating fast bowlers pivotal in humbling countless world-rated top 6s. Come 1995, Australia felt it had its best chance of toppling the champs. Having won the opening Test at Kensington Oval and drawn the second at St John's, the Australians were dismayed to find a greentop at Queen's Park and were comfortably beaten inside three days, the two West Indian expresses Curtly Ambrose and Courtney Walsh sharing 15 wickets.

The showdown match a week later was on a glistening, marble-like surface at Sabina Park in Kingston, Jamaica, the West Indies starting with 265, having been 1–100 just before lunch. In reply, however, the Australians lost three key wickets in the first hour and a half. The game was very much in the balance.

Steve Waugh joined twin brother Mark at the wicket with the scoreline a precarious 3–73. Steve was full of confidence having made 63 and 21 in an incredibly brave double in the previous Test in Trinidad. Along the way he so enraged Ambrose that the West Indian captain Richie Richardson had to forcibly pull his fast bowler away after two short and sharp abusive words from the Australian.

Waugh, about to become the No. 1 ranked batsman in the world, was primed for another almighty scrap.

His twin brother, however, wasn't as certain. He'd failed in three of his four previous innings. His net form hadn't been overly special. Yet from the first ball, which he middled, he played his greatest innings, sharing a 231-run stand which turned the match, triggering an innings victory and the return of the Frank Worrell Trophy.

It was the highest of their nine Test century partnerships together. Mark tended to outscore Steve – but was the first out in these stands eight times out of nine.

Captain Mark Taylor said Mark appeared so assured this day that he looked capable of making 500 before being out to a bat-pad catch to straight-breaker Carl Hooper. Most in the Australian dressing room agreed that there had been no finer partnership in their time, especially given the enormity of the stakes.

Ambrose, Walsh and the two Benjamins, Kenny and Winston, bowled three and four throat-high deliveries most overs. It was an incredibly hostile attack, Bodyline revisited, yet both Waughs stood firm, Mark playing one out-of-this-world pull shot against Walsh followed by a deliberate glide over the top of second slip which also flew to the boundary. They were the strokes of a maestro at the very top of his game. Mark was to admit later that he'd found himself in a rare zone.

'Leading into it, though, I certainly wasn't confident,' he said. 'I didn't have any great practice [sessions]. I hadn't been hitting the ball well and wasn't confident just watching the bowling before I went out to bat, and yet I went out and batted the best I ever have. And yet there have been other times when I've felt I'm going really well, but don't. It's one of the things which is really attractive about cricket, the uncertainty of it all.'

Despite the diet of never-ending short balls, the twins scored at four runs an over in as exhilarating a display of batsmanship as seen from an Australian pair overseas since Don Bradman and Arthur Morris at Leeds in 1948.

Steve Waugh wasn't as fluent, but he was near-flawless, parrying and side-stepping the short ones and going after anything pitched in his half.

Ever since forfeiting his place to his brother in the Australian team in the New Year of 1991, Steve had rationalised his game, keeping what worked and shunning any strokes he considered high-risk, including the hook. Fast bowlers interpreted the changes in his game to a new vulnerability and, while at times his evasions appeared ungainly, rarely, if ever, was he dismissed by a bouncer.

'Steve was relentless,' said Ian Healy. 'He just refused to get out. It was a tremendous effort. . . the best innings I witnessed in my time in Test cricket. They peppered him and looked to intimidate him, but Steve is one person you just don't pick a scrap with. His stand with Junior [Mark Waugh] meant everything to us.'

Once Steve was struck a stunning blow on the elbow by Walsh, but hardly even rubbed it, so intent was he on maintaining his psychological edge.

The two Benjamins bowled at near-express pace, too, and, like Ambrose and Walsh, regularly steepled the ball on a bouncy wicket not unlike the WACA in Perth.

To help break up the West Indian field, the twins ran a succession of daring short singles, much to the irritation of the home team. Twice in a 15-minute period four overthrows were conceded and gradually the West Indian menace diminished and Hooper's skidding slows introduced.

'Mark and I realised that our partnership was the key to the outcome,' said Steve. 'His hand was among the best two or three digs of his career in terms of influencing the outcome and the crispness of his strokeplay.'

Mark said, 'To have that sort of stand with Stephen made it particularly special. It was one of my biggest highlights of our time together playing cricket.'

Mark reached his ton in 146 balls and Steve his in 183. He'd given only one chance, at 42, to the debuting West Indian keeper Courtney Browne, an outside edge hitting him in the wrist and bouncing harmlessly away.

The Australians were to amass 531, Waugh last out for 200,

Australia's No. 11 Glenn McGrath seeing him to his double century, his first in Test cricket. In his autobiography, Steve said that he was so focused he felt like he could have batted for a week.

### THE WAUGH TWINS' CENTURY STAND IN TESTS AND ODIs

| | |
|---|---|
| **Tests** | |
| 153 | Australia v England, Edgbaston, 1993<br>M Waugh 137, S Waugh 59 |
| 231 | v West Indies, Kingston, Jamaica, 1994–95<br>M Waugh 126, S Waugh 200 |
| 153 | v New Zealand, WACA Ground, Perth, 1997–98<br>M Waugh 86, S Waugh 96 |
| 116 | v South Africa, Sydney, 1997–98<br>M Waugh 100, S Waugh 85 |
| 190 | v England, Sydney, 1998–99<br>M Waugh 121, S Waugh 96 |
| 112 | v West Indies, Kingston, Jamaica, 1998–99<br>M Waugh 67, S Waugh 100 |
| 133 | v England, Edgbaston, 2001<br>M Waugh 49, S Waugh 105 |
| 107 | v England, Lord's, 2001<br>M Waugh 108, S Waugh 45 |
| 197 | v England, The Oval, 2001<br>M Waugh 120, S Waugh 157* |
| **One-Day Internationals** | |
| 113 | Australia v Zimbabwe, Bellerive Oval, Hobart, 1991–92<br>M Waugh 66*, S Waugh 55 |
| 207 | v Kenya, Visakhapatnam, 1995–96<br>M Waugh 130, S Waugh 82 |
| 107* | v South Africa, Port Elizabeth, 1996–97<br>M Waugh 115*, S Waugh 50 |
| 129 | v Zimbabwe, Lord's, 1999<br>M Waugh 108, S Waugh 45 |
| 120 | v Zimbabwe, Bellerive Oval, Hobart, 2000–01<br>M Waugh 102*, S Waugh 79 |
| **And their highest in first-class cricket:** | |
| 464* | New South Wales v Western Australia, WACA Ground, Perth, 1990–91<br>M Waugh 229*, S Waugh 216* |

* Unbeaten

**Cricket's New World Champions:** The 1995 Australian team which re-won the Frank Worrell Trophy and the world championship. Back row, left to right: Errol Alcott (physiotherapist), Shane Warne, Justin Langer, Ricky Ponting, Glenn McGrath, Brendon Julian, Carl Rackemann, Paul Reiffel, Michael Slater, Greg Blewett, Mike Walsh (scorer). Front: Bob Simpson (coach), Tim May, Steve Waugh, Ian Healy, Mark Taylor (captain), David Boon, Mark Waugh, Jack Edwards (manager).

It was a triumph for Steve and for Australia's coach Bobby Simpson, who had worked for hours in the nets improving his technique against short-pitched bowling.

Facing a deficit of 266, the Windies lost all chance they had of saving the game on the third night when medium pacer Paul Reiffel took the first three wickets in an inspired 45-minute burst. Included was the dynamic Brian Lara lbw for a duck to one which scuttled through low – having pitched outside his leg stump.

By early on the fourth day, the Windies succumbed for 213 to lose by an innings, Reiffel's four for 47 and seven wickets for the game the pivotal bowling contribution.

The twins had broadsided the best the Windies had to offer and the Australian team, revelling in their new world-champion status, celebrated into the wee hours. When Waugh finally found his room at the Pegasus, he was still in his full cricket gear, his baggy green welded to his head. Jamaica 1995 was to be the defining moment in a career as fabled as almost any Australian, bar the Don and Golden Age hero Victor Trumper.

**Recalled:** Just a few weeks before his forty-ninth birthday, Wilfred Rhodes (sitting, second from right) was recalled to England's team for the deciding Ashes Test of 1926 and, with six wickets and 42 runs, made a massive all-round contribution in a famous victory. England's winning team, back row, left to right: Harold Larwood, Maurice Tate, Greville Stevens, George Geary, Herbert Sutcliffe, EA 'Patsy' Hendren. Front: Herbert Strudwick, Jack Hobbs, Percy Chapman (captain), Rhodes, Frank Woolley.

# K

**'He schemed and plotted his dismissals like a chess master. Even as a 48-year-old he was a force. . .'**

## KINGS OF KIRKHEATON

Imagine it. . . Australia's elite XI featuring Victor Trumper, Clem Hill, Joe Darling and a then-willowy Warwick Armstrong bowled out for just 36! And in a Test match! Never before had a team from the colonies containing so many of the game's crème de la crème been so humbled. More than 100 years on, it's still an unrivalled low.

The two fabled Yorkshiremen who orchestrated the greatest crash of all at Edgbaston in 1902 were both from Kirkheaton. George Hirst, then 31, claimed three for 15 from 11 overs of high quality seam and swerve. Fellow left-armer Wilfred Rhodes, 25, took seven for 17, also from 11 overs. The all-star Australians were bowled out in 80 minutes, Hirst and Rhodes responsible for all but one over, Hirst dipping the ball back late into the right-handers and across the left-handers and Rhodes changing paces, landing the ball on a sixpence and making it spit and veer wickedly towards slip.

Rain thwarted England on that occasion but come the last Test of the summer at The Oval, the pair combined again, this time as batsmen, helping to score the final 15 runs to lift England to a gripping one-wicket victory. Legend has it that on meeting last man Rhodes at the wicket, Hirst said in his ever-so-broad Yorkshire brogue: 'We'll get 'em in singles, Wilfred.' It's a story which has passed on through the generations but is totally false. But the pair did lift England to a magnificent win, beating Australia for only the second time all tour.

In a match of mainly modest scores, Hirst made 43 and 58 not out and took six wickets in a pivotal all-round contribution, yet was overshadowed by the astonishing hitting of 'The Croucher', Gilbert Jessop, who on the final epic afternoon accelerated to one of the great 100s in a hurry as England's scoreline improved from a down-and-out 5–48 to its ultimate match-winning 9–263.

In four wonderful Tests that summer, Hirst averaged almost 40 with the bat and 23 with the ball. Rhodes played all five Tests, scoring 67 runs for once out and taking 22 wickets at 15.

No Golden Age cricketing pair were as valuable or as revered. Hirst and Rhodes dominated Yorkshire and English cricket for a generation, Rhodes playing in 12 championship-winning teams in 29 summers and achieving the double of 1000 runs and 100 wickets a record 16 times. Hirst played in 10 championship teams and did the double on 14 occasions, including the first 'double-double' in 1906, when he amassed 2385 runs to go with his 208 wickets. In Yorkshire's final county game that year, against Somerset at Bath, Hirst made 111 and 117 not out and took six for 70 and five for 45!

The pair tended to bowl in tandem more often than not, and nine times each took 100 wickets in the same season.

Yorkshire won four championships out of five upon Rhodes' arrival from farming community Hopton, just outside Kirkheaton, in 1898. He took more than 1000 wickets in those five years. One in three of his overs were maidens. No-one was more observant or could more quickly assess a batsman's weakness. He schemed and plotted his dismissals like a chess master. Even as a 48-year-old he was a force, being recalled into England's XI for the deciding Ashes Test of 1926 and playing a central role in one of the great English wins. His Test exploits included a triple-century opening partnership with Jack Hobbs. He was seriously good.

Don Bradman claimed Rhodes to be the greatest and most durable of all-round cricketers alongside WG Grace. The young Don was amazed by Rhodes' ease of action when he opposed him in his last major game at Scarborough in 1930. By then, Wilfred was almost 53 and still tricking the batsmen into believing the ball was pitching further up than was the case.

**Yorkshire Evergreens:** Left-arm slow bowlers George Hirst (*page 103*) and Wilfred Rhodes were champions of cricket's Golden Age.

**GEORGE HIRST AND WILFRED RHODES: THEIR 100 WICKET SEASONS**

| | George Hirst Debut 1891 | Wilfred Rhodes Debut 1898 |
|---|---|---|
| 1895 | 150 | DNP |
| 1896 | 104 | DNP |
| 1897 | 101 | DNP |
| 1898 | x | 154 |
| 1899 | x | 179 |
| 1900 | x | 261 |
| 1901 | 183 | 251 |
| 1902 | 128 | 213 |
| 1903 | x | 193 |
| 1904 | 132 | 131 |
| 1905 | 110 | 182 |
| 1906 | 208 | 128 |
| 1907 | 188 | 177 |
| 1908 | 174 | 115 |
| 1909 | 115 | 141 |
| 1910 | 164 | x |
| 1911 | 137 | 117 |
| 1912 | 118 | x |
| 1913 | 101 | x |
| 1914 | x | 118 |
| 1919 | x | 164 |
| 1920 | x | 161 |
| 1921 | x | 141 |
| 1922 | DNP | 119 |
| 1923 | DNP | 134 |
| 1924 | DNP | 109 |
| 1926 | DNP | 115 |
| 1928 | DNP | 115 |
| 1929 | DNP | 100 |
| Career wickets | 2742 | 4204 |
| 100-wicket seasons | 15 | 23 |
| Most wickets in a season | 208 | 261 |

'x' denotes played but did not take 100 wickets. DNP denotes Did Not Play

Hirst's beginnings weren't as spectacular, but he was just as deadly, especially when he perfected his swerve style. Yorkshire icon Lord Hawke considered Hirst the greatest county performer of all, and if he or Rhodes needed a momentary rest, his Lordship would call upon the medium-paced Schofield Haigh, the third diamond in the deadliest of trinities.

Thickset, bouncy and bubbly, the ultimate Yorkshire hero, Hirst had a slingy action above medium pace and competed like few others. Of his ability to swing the ball late, noted author AA Thomson said Hirst's victims felt as if the ball had come at them like a fast throw-in from cover point. Hirst also had a well-disguised slower ball which embarrassed many, especially tailenders who sometimes had finished a swipe at the ball well before it had arrived and could only watch on helplessly as they were castled.

As a pair Hirst and Rhodes complemented each other perfectly, and made a habit of mowing through opposing teams on wickets which helped and wickets which didn't. Hirst was always accorded the choice of ends and invariably he'd take the end where the wind was blowing from third man, to assist his late-swerving in-swinger. Rhodes would have liked that end too as his ability to bowl a late-dipping arm ball was one of his signatures. But rarely was he accorded the luxury when Hirst was around.

The pair were glittering stars of cricket's Golden Age and were to be feared as much as famed predecessors Bobby Peel and Johnny Briggs and the great early Australian pairs Charlie Turner and Jack Ferris, and Jack Gregory and Ted McDonald.

**Tearaway:** The fastest bowler in history, Jeff Thomson. He didn't know where they were going. . . neither did the batsmen. In back-to-back summers in the 1970s, 'Thommo' and fellow express Dennis Lillee ruled like no Australian pair before or since.

# L

**‘The rebuff left old Bert broken-hearted. He may have lacked the social graces of some and his action may not have been as pure as Blackie’s, but he’d never been no-balled for throwing. . .’**

## LAST CHANCE HERO

Danny Morrison held the world record of 24 ducks in 47 Tests coming into the opening Test of the 1996–97 New Zealand summer against England at Eden Park. The Kiwis were facing certain outright defeat at 9–142 – an overall lead of just 11 – early in the final afternoon. Back in the rooms, New Zealand captain Lee Germon was rehearsing his loser’s speech.

Nathan Astle was still not out, but one of England’s pacemen, Dom Cork, Alan Mullally or Darren Gough, only had to bowl wicket to wicket to dislodge Morrison. . . or so everyone thought.

One hundred and sixty-six minutes later, Morrison was still there, unconquered, having helped Astle to one of the great fighting centuries and New Zealand to the unlikeliest of draws.

‘Let’s just enjoy it,’ Astle had said to Morrison when they came together shortly after 2 pm.

Morrison’s sole initial aim was to stay long enough to see Astle to 50. ‘I never dreamed I’d be there when he got his century,’ he said. His 14 not out, following his unbeaten 6 in the first innings, lifted his Test career average to 8. And that’s where it stayed. He never played another Test.

## LIFE BEGINS AT 40

If it wasn't for the generosity and contacts of the St Kilda Cricket Club's livewire president RL 'Doc' Morton, Melbourne club cricket's most famous bowling duo would never have been.

Don Blackie was working in the country for the local postal service and doing little more physical than tending his rose garden at weekends when Morton, his family's doctor, arrived unannounced and invited him to once again play District cricket alongside one of his old Prahran teammates, Bert Cohen.

Fifteen years earlier, Blackie had played his one and only game for Victoria against a visiting team from Fiji. A tall off-spinner with a run-in from mid-off, a ramrod straight arm and ever-so-long fingers which encouraged spin on the flattest of surfaces, he'd rarely again challenged for higher honours despite being a four-time bowling average winner at Toorak Park.

Another mature-age recruit about to join the Seasiders was Bert Ironmonger, a left-arm finger spinner noted for his ability to consistently land a ball on a sixpence – despite having sliced off the top of his index finger in a farming accident as a child. He'd flick the ball off a corn on his shortened finger, imparting swing, seam and spin at close to medium pace. In the era of covered run-ups and uncovered wickets, he could be unplayable, especially when there was any extra juice in the wickets. He'd been the bowler of the Australian 'B' team tour to New Zealand just 18 months earlier, taking 10 wickets against Canterbury and 13 in the two representative matches against NZ.

Known as 'Dainty' because of his soft, economical run to the wicket, he'd been lured back to Melbourne after the failure of the latest of his business ventures, a hotel in inner Sydney. Within weeks of setting up a tobacconist's shop just around the corner from St Kilda's Junction Oval, he was mortified to arrive at work one morning to find it had been burgled. Little more than the shelving remained. Morton arranged an immediate cash hand-out for his family and organised Ironmonger a job mowing lawns with the local St Kilda council. Ironmonger thrived in his new Monday to Friday role, the extra fitness built from pushing hand mowers around the St Kilda parklands helping him to regularly bowl for marathon periods on the hottest of days and triggering his rise into Australia's elite XI, including his final four Tests at the grand old age of 50. No Australian Test representative has been older.

**Influential:** St Kilda Cricket Club president Dr. R. L. Morton lured Don Blackie out of retirement and found a new job for Bert Ironmonger which triggered his Test promotion.

The two 40-year-olds were pivotal in St Kilda's rise from the time they took 70 wickets in their first season together in 1922–23, Blackie playing from the opening game in October and Ironmonger, who'd begun the club season in Sydney, from November. The club's first XI narrowly missed the finals before winning an unprecedented four flags on end. In all, Blackie and Ironmonger were together in six premierships in the 1920s and early 1930s, the pair regularly bowling through an innings, making a third and fourth bowler almost unnecessary.

In the club's run of four premierships in a row in 1923–24, 1924–25, 1925–26 and 1926–27, they claimed 110 of the 138 wickets to fall to the bowlers. In six winning Grand Finals, Blackie took 38 wickets and Ironmonger 35. Seven other bowlers used in the play-offs took just 10 wickets between them, one of the little-used back-ups being a young 'Chuck' Fleetwood-Smith.

With record-breaking Bill Ponsford and Cohen dominating the batting, St Kilda could lay claim to being the champion club team in all Australasia.

It was extraordinary how often Blackie would find himself bowling against the opposition's left-handers and Ironmonger the right-handers. They'd sit in the rooms, analysing the opposition's best players, planning fielding positions and fine-tuning tactics.

## THE OLD FIRM: SEASON BY SEASON AT ST KILDA
## DON BLACKIE

| Season | Balls | Runs | Wickets | Average | BB | 5wI |
|---|---|---|---|---|---|---|
| 1922–23 | 1424 | 711 | 41 | 17.34 | 6–49 | 4 |
| 1923–24* | 1886 | 629 | 51 | 12.33 | 7–38 | 4 |
| 1924–25* | 1809 | 532 | 58 | 9.17 | 7–71 | 7 |
| 1925–26* | 2004 | 649 | 59 | 11.00 | 7–39 | 6 |
| 1926–27* | 2268 | 825 | 64 | 12.89 | 10–64 | 8 |
| 1927–28 | 1021 | 284 | 14 | 20.26 | 7–113 | 1 |
| 1928 Tas tour | 192 | 122 | 9 | 13.55 | 3–24 | – |
| 1928–29 | 1553 | 491 | 29 | 16.93 | 5–30 | 3 |
| 1929–30 | 2228 | 738 | 42 | 17.61 | 5–35 | 4 |
| 1930–31 | 1331 | 520 | 30 | 17.33 | 6–26 | 2 |
| 1931–32* | 1075 | 453 | 29 | 15.62 | 7–34 | 1 |
| 1932–33 | 886 | 340 | 24 | 14.16 | 6–56 | 1 |
| 1933–34* | 2016 | 656 | 47 | 13.95 | 6–64 | 4 |
| 1934–35 | 668 | 219 | 7 | 31.28 | 2–14 | – |
| **Total** | **20,381** | **7169** | **504** | **14.22** | **10–64** | **45** |

## BERT IRONMONGER

| Season | Balls | Runs | Wickets | Average | BB | 5wI |
|---|---|---|---|---|---|---|
| 1922–23 | 1030 | 490 | 29 | 16.89 | 8–65 | 3 |
| 1923–24* | 1852 | 654 | 59 | 11.08 | 6–37 | 4 |
| 1924–25* | 1513 | 446 | 39 | 11.43 | 6–41 | 2 |
| 1925–26* | 2126 | 719 | 60 | 11.98 | 8–47 | 4 |
| 1926–27* | 2691 | 999 | 50 | 19.98 | 6–28 | 3 |
| 1927–28 | 1064 | 340 | 19 | 17.89 | 8–39 | 3 |
| 1928 Tas tour | 272 | 131 | 17 | 7.70 | 7–31 | 1 |
| 1928–29 | 1425 | 482 | 30 | 16.06 | 5–26 | 2 |
| 1929–30 | 2743 | 893 | 57 | 15.66 | 7–48 | 6 |
| 1930–31 | 1610 | 539 | 41 | 13.14 | 6–19 | 4 |
| 1931–32* | 1208 | 385 | 39 | 9.87 | 6–50 | 5 |
| 1932–33 | 1081 | 331 | 29 | 11.41 | 6–42 | 3 |
| 1933–34* | 1150 | 361 | 27 | 13.37 | 7–53 | 2 |
| 1934–35 | 930 | 245 | 23 | 10.65 | 5–25 | 1 |
| **Total** | **20,695** | **7015** | **519** | **13.52** | **8–37** | **43** |

*premiership years
Table: Ron Harbourd

Blackie took 4 10wM and Ironmonger 5 10wM

**Bodyline Test:** Fifty-year-old Bert Ironmonger attempts a run out during the Melbourne Test of 1932–33, the only one in the controversial series which Australia won.

Both were to bowl more than 20,000 balls and take 500-plus wickets for St Kilda, Ironmonger's costing 13 runs apiece and Blackie 14. Between them they took five wickets or more in an innings 88 times, Ironmonger's best eight for 37 in his first season and Blackie's ten for 64 – eight of the 10 bowled or lbw! They took all 10 wickets to fall on 13 occasions.

Their success at St Kilda was rewarded at both Victorian and Australian level, Ironmonger playing 14 home Tests and Blackie three, including his first alongside Ironmonger in Sydney in 1928–29, the match in which a young Don Bradman served as twelfth man for the one and only time in his career.

The first time they'd teamed together at interstate level was in 1925–26 when they claimed all 10 first-innings wickets opening the bowling for Victoria against the visiting West Australians at Fitzroy, Ironmonger taking seven for 30, six bowled or lbw and Blackie three for 57. Their game haul was 13.

Ironmonger reaped damage at every level and was even called for as a substitute to bolster Australia's 1934 Ashes party, only for the austere Australian Board of Control to overrule captain Bill Woodfull, saying Woodfull could pick anyone *but* the St Kilda veteran. Woodfull said if he couldn't choose Ironmonger he didn't want anyone else. The rebuff left old Bert broken-hearted. He may have lacked the social graces of some and his action may not have been as pure as Blackie's, but he'd never been no-balled for throwing. At the time authorities were trying to rebuild calmer relations, the Australians not wanting to spark a throwing controversy so soon after the acrimonious Bodyline summer. It was known to them that PF 'Plum' Warner, England's most powerful and most profiled ex-cricketer, had questioned Ironmonger's action.

Ironmonger averaged more than five wickets per Test, 70 per cent of his 74 Test wickets coming in the top-order. Don Bradman regarded him as the best bowler never to be chosen for an Ashes campaign.

Within months Ironmonger had announced his intention to retire, playing a farewell club season at the Junction alongside Blackie in 1934–35 before being called into the unofficial Australian team which toured India and Ceylon under the captaincy of Frank Tarrant in 1935–36.

Blackie's 14 Test wickets included a six-for at the MCG in the 1928–29 Christmas Test, his victims including double-centurion Walter Hammond. He retired in 1935, his hair silver but his action still bouncy. St Kilda named its pride and joy new grandstand, which still stands, in the pair's honour.

They had one last game together in a patriotic fixture at the MCG in 1939 to aid the War Veterans Homes Trust fund.

Woodfull called them 'The Old Firm' and said they would always be one of the greatest bowling batteries in the history of the game. 'They are masters of their art,' he said.

**THE OLD FIRM: THEIR FINEST GRAND FINAL PERFORMANCES**

|  |  |
|---|---|
| 1924–25 | All 20 wickets<br>Blackie 5–34 and 6–48, Ironmonger 5–27 and 4–30 |
| 1925–26 | 18 wickets<br>Blackie 5–21 and 4–24, Ironmonger 4–45 and 5–27 |
| 1931–32 | 17 wickets<br>Blackie 4–52 and 4–61, Ironmonger 5–24 and 4–49 |

## LILLI'AN THOMSON... THE DEMOLITION MEN

It's one of Australian cricket's most immortal catch-cries: 'Ashes to Ashes, Dust to Dust, if Lillee Don't Get Ya, Thomson Must.'

Dennis Lillee and Jeff Thomson were the most menacing set of speedsters since Bodyliners Harold Larwood and Bill Voce. Furiously fast and volatile, they triggered an extraordinary Australian domination not seen since the days of Richie Benaud. In back-to-back Test summers in the mid-1970s, Australia won nine of 11 Tests against England and the West Indies, the two next-best teams in the world. England's solitary success came when Thomson was absent and Lillee injured in the first hour in the final match in Melbourne.

As a Thomson thunderbolt thudded into the gloves of wicketkeeper Rod Marsh in his unforgettable Ashes debut in Brisbane in 1974–75, Marsh winced in pain and said to first-slipsman Ian Chappell, 'Hell that hurt... but I love it.'

There was nowhere to run and nowhere to hide when Lillee and Thomson were threatening. Neither cared if they struck a batsman. If a tailender looked to outstay his welcome, he knew that he would soon be subjected to some 'chin music'. Thomson was famously quoted as saying there was nothing better than seeing blood on the pitch. Lillee wanted to hit the batsmen under the rib cage so that 'they were so hurt they didn't want to face me any more'.

In those two extraordinary summers, the most sensational since Bodyline, Lillee and Thomson changed the face of cricket forever. Having torn through the Englishmen 4–1, they humbled the West Indians 5–1. Windies' captain Clive Lloyd vowed that no team in his charge from the Caribbean would ever again be so humiliated and immediately started stacking his teams with four fast bowlers. Spin was forever after an afterthought – and helmets a necessity in even the tailender's kitbags.

In those two much-remembered Australian series of the mid-1970s, Lillee took 52 wickets and Thomson 62. They were positively lethal, Lillee downwind and 'Thommo' into it.

In Brisbane, captain Ian Chappell initially had intended to open the bowling with Lillee and the medium-paced Max Walker, thinking Thomson would be better suited following Lillee with the wind at his back. But after Lillee's opening over, on the spur of the moment, he threw the ball to Thomson.

'In the few overs that followed, I watched in awe,' Chappell said. 'Thommo was the fastest into-the-wind bowler I'd seen. I don't think the Englishmen knew what had hit them. . . there was great joy amongst us all to see the fearful pace they generated.'

England had held the Ashes since 1970–71 but were literally blown away by the two frontline pacemen – plus seam specialist Walker who netted 23 wickets.

Lillee had been riled on the second morning in Brisbane when he was dismissed by a Tony Greig bouncer which saw him finish inelegantly on his backside, with keeper Alan Knott gloving a simple catch. He was spoiling for a fight and from his first over was furiously fast.

'He also managed to make the ball leave the bat and bounce a lot,' said opener Dennis Amiss. 'Clearly I'd underestimated him.'

Amiss had averaged 75 in six home Tests in 1974 on his way to more than 1300 runs for the calendar year, yet was challenged like never before. His partner Brian Luckhurst, 36, was clearly intimidated and admitted it was one tour too many for him. Within weeks of the Tests starting he knew he shouldn't have been there.

'The Lillee-Thomson phenomenon was not pleasant,' Luckhurst said. 'It gave me an insight into how Test cricket was changing. To look at us walking out in those pre-helmet days to face two of the fastest and most dangerous bowlers the world has seen – on lightning-quick and bouncy surfaces – provides an almost ghoulish fascination.'

England's opening stands that summer averaged just a shade above 30. Amiss had his thumb broken in England's second innings in Brisbane, having been struck by both expressmen.

'We were left with an awkward last hour [on the penultimate night] in which I faced the most frightening fast bowling I have ever seen,' Amiss said.

'Thomson and Lillee ran [in] like madmen. They were not bowling bouncers but deliveries which lifted unpredictably from just short of a length. Three of them whistled by my chin and because the [Brisbane] light was poor, one of the umpires warned Thomson to pitch the ball up. Thomson was clearly not having any. The next four balls whistled past my face and off we went [for bad light].'

Only two of England's top-order, the warrior-like John Edrich and Greig, averaged 40 or more for the summer. David Lloyd, Amiss, veteran reinforcement Colin Cowdrey and Luckhurst were all sub-25.

'It was better to be watching rather than batting that summer,' said Lloyd. 'When Lillee and Thomson got it right and the pitches gave them some help, as most did, they were an awesome pairing. Get through an over from one of them and there was not a moment of respite with the other one pawing the ground. We were still playing by the old Australian regulation of eight-ball overs and there were times when five of the eight were flying past nose or chest. We weren't good enough to stem the onrushing tide.'

In Sydney on a greentop, the juiced-up crowd on the Hill began to chant 'Kill. . . KILL. . . KILLLLL' as Lillee and Thomson tore into the tourists. One Thomson bouncer sconed Keith Fletcher, whose head protection consisted of his MCC cap complete with its emblem of St George on his horse. As Fletcher collapsed, teammate Geoff Arnold jumped to his feet in the rooms and exclaimed: 'Blimey, ee's just knocked St George off 'is 'orse!'

Earlier in the game, Greig had struck Lillee on the point of the elbow, causing him to drop his bat in pain. He was unimpressed when Fletcher, fielding in the gully, asked: 'Did it hurt?' Fletcher had picked up Lillee's bat but after Lillee's stream of invective, tossed it back on the ground, leaving Lillee to retrieve it himself.

Having already forced Edrich to retire hurt with broken ribs, Lillee found an extra gear when he sighted the next-man-in, Fletcher, and began to pitch relentlessly short.

'At least half a dozen times I flicked my head out of the way through sheer instinct as balls I had not seen at all whipped past the end of my nose,' said Fletcher. 'Some missed me by only a fraction of an inch.' Of the searing Thomson lifter, which he failed to evade, Fletcher said he'd simply frozen, despite having 'a reasonable sight of it'.

'For some inexplicable reason, my reactions just didn't work in time,' he said. As he ducked, he got only the lightest of gloves onto the ball before it struck him directly on the skull.

Fletcher said he tired that summer of using his bat purely as a shield. One delivery from Thomson in Perth spat back at him late with such venom that he could only just cover his face with his gloves, the ball deflecting through to Marsh who took a juggling catch.

'That ball was the quickest of my career,' said Fletcher. 'It convinced me that Thomson must rank alongside the quickest of all Test bowlers. I only just had time to get my gloves in front of my face. The deflection was travelling so fast it actually thumped the chest of Marsh standing more than 20 metres back before he got his gloves to it.'

In Perth, Lloyd had his box inverted by a Thomson screamer. After his dismissal he lay on the rubdown table, shaking involuntarily.

Forty-two-year-old Cowdrey said the sheer pace and unpredictability of the Lillee-Thomson combination made them the most difficult pair he'd ever opposed in his prime, including Lindwall and Miller, the West Indians Hall and Griffith, and the South African expresses Heine and Adcock.

Greg Chappell said Thomson often bowled at speeds in excess of 160 km/h (100 mph). 'You can name anyone you like: Roberts, Holding, Marshall. . . Thommo was two yards quicker than them all. Before he did his shoulder he was frighteningly quick.'

Nineteen of their 26 Tests together were in Australia where they were at their most effective and lethal. Surprisingly, Lillee's home ground of Perth was his weakest ground, where his wickets came at an average of 27.2. Perth was Thommo's second weakest, his wickets also coming at 27.2.

Leading into his demolition of the English, Thomson had played only one Test, against Pakistan in Melbourne several years earlier, when he carried an injury into the game and failed to take a wicket.

'We'd never even heard of him,' said Lloyd. 'He'd played one Test, a couple of years earlier, and taken nought for a hundred and plenty. Why would we waste time worrying about him?'

From mid-tour, at the suggestion of the team's physiotherapist Bernard Thomas, most of the Englishmen strapped on made-to-measure foam rubber chest guards.

'Never in my career have I witnessed so much protective gear applied to individuals before they went out to bat,' said captain Mike Denness, who stood down for a Test in mid-series. 'On the plane flying from Australia to New Zealand, the players were clearly relieved that they had left Australia intact and without fatal injury.'

Thomson's Brisbane blitz inspired Lillee, who had played only grade cricket in Perth the previous summer as a specialist batsman while recuperating from a back breakdown.

Lillee had been genuinely surprised to make it past the first Test and in his early comeback Sheffield Shield matches with Western Australia, had despaired of ever bowling truly fast again, despite his exhaustive winter fitness campaign.

Buoyed by Thomson's outstanding performances, the further the Test series went, the more confident and aggressive Lillee became. He stared, gesticulated and pointed at the English batsmen, going out of his way to be cranky and outrageous. He *wanted* a mid-pitch war.

In Sydney on the fastest wicket in the east, his first ball to Amiss soared over both the batsman and keeper Marsh and thudded one bounce into the sightscreen. 'We were always ducking and weaving and not always successfully,' said Amiss.

The English could use their own expressman Bob Willis sparingly in only very short spells because of his battle-scarred knees, and possessed no-one else who could engender the same heat as Lillee and Thomson.

'It was no use thinking of taking a single off Thomson to get to the other end,' said Denness. 'You then had Lillee thundering in at you.'

The West Indies were similarly intimidated the following summer, with only a young Viv Richards, on his first tour, enhancing his reputation, though fellow rookie Michael Holding showed great promise.

Only two batsmen, Keith Boyce and captain Clive Lloyd, averaged in excess of 40. The worldbeating Lawrence Rowe averaged just 24 and champion-in-the-making Gordon Greenidge, 2.

The Windies won only three of their 13 first-class matches, their solitary Test win coming in Perth when Roy Fredericks teed off and Andy Roberts bowled seriously fast, taking nine wickets for the match including seven for 54 as the Australians were beaten by an innings. Lillee went for six an over, Thomson, seven, left-armer Gary Gilmour almost eight, and Walker, five.

It was an aberration in a series otherwise dominated again by the Aussie speedsters. In Melbourne, Lillee and Thomson took 13 wickets between them to restore the balance. Almost 86,000 attended the opening day, Thomson taking the first five wickets and Lillee four of the last five. Only the in-form Fredericks made 50, though Lloyd's 102 in the second innings was a brave effort against the odds.

Along with Brisbane, 1974, it was the pair's most successful Test match together.

'In Thomson and Lillee they possessed the best combination of fast bowlers any captain could wish for,' Lloyd said, 'and our batsmen, especially early in an innings, were constantly under pressure. None of them had ever encountered bowling of such speed before.'

In Perth, Lloyd was struck in the jaw and Alvin Kallicharran's nose was cracked by Lillee. In Sydney, stand-in opener Brendon Julien had his thumb broken by Thomson.

'If no-one else received any actual broken bones, everyone at some stage did feel the pain of a cricket ball thudding into their bodies at 90 miles an hour,' said Lloyd.

**DENNIS LILLEE'S TEST OPENING PARTNERS**

| Matches | |
|---|---|
| 17 | Jeff Thomson |
| 13 | Terry Alderman |
| 11 | Max Walker |
| 9 | Rodney Hogg |
| 8 | Geoff Dymock |
| 6 | Gary Gilmour, Bob Massie, Len Pascoe |
| 3 | Geoff Lawson |
| 1 | David Colley, Tony Dell, Ashley Mallett, Carl Rackemann, Alan Thomson |

Injuries and Kerry Packer's rebel World Series Cricket movement were to restrict their future influence as a pair. Lillee was one of the headline early WSC signings, but Thomson remained in traditional ranks, being rewarded with his country's vice-captaincy for the 1978 tour of the West Indies under Bobby Simpson. He even led in an island game and ambled out with 11 others and calmly said, 'I'm bowlin'. The rest of yez spread out.' On being told that Australia had 12 players on the field, he said, 'One of youse nick off.'

It wasn't until Mr Packer funded a WSC tour of the Caribbean in 1979 that the Lillee-Thomson partnership resumed. In five Supertests they amassed 39 wickets between them, Lillee 23 and Thomson 16, including 11 in the first Supertest at Sabina Park, Jamaica. They were still fast and threatening, but by then Thomson had had his shoulder reconstructed after a collision with teammate Alan Turner and had lost just a little of his zip.

The following 'compromise' summer, they played the first two of the summer's six Tests together, without sharing the new ball. Their last appearance side-by-side was against the West Indies in Adelaide in 1981–82, Lillee breaking down with a groin injury in his fifth over. In the second innings, acting captain Marsh opened with Thomson and Len Pascoe. Even off-spinner Bruce Yardley was preferred to Lillee. A pulsating, ever-so-pacy era was over.

**Supremos:** Melburnians Bill Ponsford (left) with Bill Woodfull. Together they shared 23 century stands, three in Tests.

# M

**'No, Ken,' he told me, his eyes twinkling. 'I couldn't tell you that. The income tax people might be after me...'**

## MUTT AND JEFF

Few pairings have ever been as celebrated as Bill Ponsford and Bill Woodfull, Australia's prolific openers who flattened bowlers' spirits and the seams of cricket balls with ruthless efficiency. The Melbourne Cricket Ground was their stage. Only Dolly the Clydesdale spent more time in centre pitch, daily hauling the roller up and down the famed wicket square prompting a stream of extraordinary run feasts.

Twice in the timeless 1920s, Victorian XIs amassed 1000 runs-plus. Ponsford scored 429 in the first match and 352 in the second. When the ball rolled off his boot onto the stumps, robbing him of another quadruple, he muttered: 'By cripes, I'm unlucky!'

Eight of his 23 century stands with Woodfull came in Melbourne, including their biggest three: 375, 236 and 227, all at interstate level just months after they'd opened for Australia for the first time. On witnessing the toss and seeing the broad frame of Woodfull preparing to take the first ball as was his habit, the team's wicketkeeper Jack Ellis, a building inspector, would take himself off to a site or two and on the way back to the ground leisurely lay some bets with a local bookmaker, so sure was he that he wouldn't be required to bat until late in the day, if at all.

Sydney pressmen had initially been aghast when two Southerners were promoted to Test openers. One dubbed them 'Mutt and Jeff' after the comic strip characters. A stream of elite New South Welshmen, from Warren Bardsley and Herbie 'Horseshoe' Collins to Charlie Macartney and Tommy Andrews, had been at the head of Australia's order for years. But so dependable were they that by the end of their reign, even the most caustic Sydney scribes were calling Ponsford and Woodfull 'The Twins'.

On wide, ever-so-white wickets, which should have carried a health warning to bowlers, 'The Two Bills' would bat for hours. Woodfull, seemingly ungainly, hands apart on the handle, all concentration; and Ponny, cap on its familiar tilt, dancing at the spinners and toying with the mediums, always showing the full face. Ponny treated net practice like it was a Test match. Bert Ironmonger once said he'd bowled at Ponny for years at St Kilda, yet rarely induced even a play and miss! The record breaker was almost always controlled and inscrutable.

As a 15-year-old in short pants on his first XI debut at the St Kilda Cricket Ground, Ponsford batted for more than an hour against the men from Fitzroy. The opposing attack included EA 'Ted' McDonald, soon to be one of the premier pacemen in the world, yet Ponny made 12, all in singles.

'I couldn't hit the ball past the bowler then,' he told me years later. 'But it wasn't bad going. I was pretty small.'

Before his massive new world record 429, Ponny hadn't made a century at club level. The closest was a 99 earlier that summer for St Kilda against South Melbourne when he was run out by a direct hit. The fielder? Woodfull!

The Ponsford-Woodfull combine became the most famous in Australian Test annals, the pair recording century stands in Australia, England and New Zealand. Few before or since could so occupy the crease or be so consistently relied upon to take the shine off the ball for the players who followed. Their signature English summer of 1930 saw them amass three centuries in four Tests; shades of Hobbs and Sutcliffe. A young Don Bradman, in at No. 3, was a beneficiary and sparkled like no-one before or since. At a send-off gala function for the team at the tour end, Sir James Barrie of *Peter Pan* fame read a specially composed poem, 'How to Get Woodfull Out'.

A fourth 100-run partnership between the two Bills came the following Australian season in Sydney, when the pair ushered in the

New Year with a fifth-wicket stand of 183 in just two hours and 20 minutes. Woodfull, captaining for the first time, batted at No. 6. It was the highest of their Australian Test stands.

Woodfull was the ultimate team man and with his no-fuss ways and caring approach was always very popular amongst his peers. He wouldn't have a drink himself, but he'd buy beers for his team. The son of a minister, he was a Methodist and worked hard for his success. As Australia's bravest captain, he'd refused to be bowed by Bodyline, and led by his own no-nonsense example. In the rooms before a game he wouldn't say much, but for a, 'Come on fellers. Remember it's straight up the centre with no short passes.'

Woodfull wasn't the fastest runner between wickets and once, sometimes twice a season, was run out. But such misfortunes were rare in combination with Ponsford, only a handful of run-outs occurring in almost 100 stands together. They trusted each other's judgment and took genuine pride in their achievements. Their stellar 375 against New South Wales during Christmas Week, 1926, remained a record for Sheffield Shield cricket for 65 years. It stamped their authority as a world-renowned opening pair. . . and it came at a rare old clip:

1–50: in 28 minutes
51–100: 47
101–150: 40
151–200: 17
201–250: 24
251–300: 34
301–350: 25
381–375: 8

When Woodfull was dismissed for 133, Ponsford was 232 and scoring at a run a minute. He was 170 when Woodfull reached 85. No mega-score had ever been amassed so quickly in the Sheffield Shield. Of 190 eight-ball overs bowled by New South Wales, just five were maidens. The Victorians batted six sessions for 1107, a new world-record score, before keeper Ellis was run out. The New South Wales attack included the whimsical leg-spinner Arthur Mailey who said his

**WOODFULL AND PONSFORD IN TESTS**

| Opponent | Tests | Innings | Not Out | Best | Runs | Average | 100s |
|---|---|---|---|---|---|---|---|
| England | 8 | 13 | 0 | 162 | 569 | 43 | 3 |
| South Africa | 4 | 6 | 1 | 185 | 738 | 37 | 0 |
| West Indies | 2 | 3 | 0 | 50 | 106 | 35 | 0 |
| **Total** | **14** | **22** | **1** | **162** | **860** | **41** | **3** |

figures of four for 362 would have been far superior, 'Had a chap in a tweed coat 20 rows back near the shilling stand not kept dropping Jack Ryder!' He was sorry Ellis had succumbed at the end as he was 'just striking a length!'

Late on the first day of Victoria's epic, Victoria's No. 3 HSTL 'Stork' Hendry suggested to Ponsford that they hit out, only to be told that he could do so if he wanted, 'But I might just try and hang around a bit longer, Stork!'

It wasn't until the first hour the following day that Ponsford mis-hit a delivery from New South Wales change bowler Gordon Morgan onto his foot, the ball trickling back onto his stumps. As he whacked his leg in annoyance, New South Wales captain Alan Kippax said: 'What are you crook about? You've been there long enough.' Years later Ponsford told me he could still remember the moment. 'I was just starting to see them too!' His 352 came in just six hours and three minutes and included thirty-six 4s. He did not give a chance until he was 265. He'd wanted to better Clem Hill's Shield record of 365 as several of his teammates had laid some bets. He felt he'd let them down.

Ponsford and Woodfull remained Australia's first-choice openers until the conclusion of the 1934 Ashes tour, when both retired, Woodfull at 37 and Ponsford 34. Woodfull had a teaching career to follow and played little cricket afterwards. Ponsford, a clerk and for a time a journalist, continued at club level at Melbourne. The Bodyline summer of 1932–33 soured the international game for them both, Woodfull's widow years later saying the terrific hit under the heart her husband had taken in Adelaide had shortened his life.

In an interview that the normally publicity-shy Ponny agreed to only after daily phone promptings from his old teammate Leo

O'Brien, Ponny told me that Bodyline 'wasn't the game'. He'd loved each of his three trips to England but felt 1938 and the next scheduled Ashes tour was too far away, so he retired too.

Ponsford's ultimate first-class batting average was 65.18, Woodfull's average just a boundary short of 65. Of those to make 10,000-plus first-class runs only two, India's Vijay Merchant with 71.22 and Bradman with 99.94, have superior averages.

As Victoria's long-time Sheffield Shield openers Woodfull and Ponsford averaged 70 together, including 120 in 1926–27 and 104 in 1927–28. While Ponny was the more fluent and generally reached the major milestones quicker, Woodfull had his moments, most notably on the 1934 Ashes tour in a county game in Bristol when the pair started with 183, Woodfull reaching his 100 in three hours, half an hour before Ponsford was out for 54. With the arrival of Bill Brown, who opened in the final four Tests, Woodfull dropped himself down the list but remained a force.

Their final match together was a testimonial in their honour in Melbourne, in November 1934, shortly after the return of the Ashes touring team. Appropriately they shared in their twenty-third and final century stand, 132 for the fourth wicket, Ponny in at No. 5 making 83 and Woodfull, No. 6, 111, having been cheered all the way to the wicket after lunch to the Northcote Boys' Band's rendition of 'For They're Jolly Good Fellows'. Early rain on the Saturday seemed likely to affect the crowd, but more than 22,000 still came to celebrate with two of Australia's finest.

'We were a little unlucky though,' said Ponsford. 'It was wet. In those days people worked on a Saturday morning. When it rained people would go home instead of going to the cricket. Our fund diminished somewhat.' They each received more than 1000 pounds, but Ponny was uncomfortable divulging the exact figures. 'No, Ken,' he told me, his eyes twinkling. 'I couldn't tell you that. The income tax people might be after me if I start making statements!' One thousand pounds then was the 2000s equivalent of $65,000. A fair return indeed for two of Australia's finest.

## CENTURY STANDS BETWEEN 'THE TWO BILLS'

**First wicket (18)**

| | |
|---|---|
| 375 | Victoria v New South Wales, Melbourne Cricket Ground, 1926–27<br>Ponsford 352, Woodfull 133 |
| 236 | Victoria v South Australia, MCG, 1927–28<br>Ponsford 336, Woodfull 106 |
| 227 | Victoria v New South Wales, MCG, 1927–28<br>Ponsford 202, Woodfull 99 |
| 223 | Australians v The Rest, Sydney Cricket Ground, 1926–27<br>Ponsford 131, Woodfull 140 |
| 214 | Australians v Otago, Dunedin, 1927–28<br>Ponsford 148, Woodfull 107 |
| 184 | Australian XI v New Zealand, Auckland, 1927–28<br>Ponsford 86, Woodfull 284 |
| 183 | Australians v Gloucestershire, Bristol, 1934<br>Ponsford 54, Woodfull 131 |
| 162 | Australia v England, Lord's, second Test, 1930<br>Ponsford 81, Woodfull 155 |
| 159 | Australia v England, The Oval, fifth Test, 1930<br>Ponsford 110, Woodfull 54 |
| 158+ | Victoria v South African XI, MCG, 1931–32<br>Ponsford 84 not out, Woodfull 73 not out |
| 138 | Victoria v New South Wales, SCG, 1932–33<br>Ponsford 200, Woodfull 78 |
| 122 | Australians v Wellington, Wellington, 1927–28<br>Ponsford 58, Woodfull 165 |
| 118 | Australians v An England XI, Folkestone, 1930<br>Ponsford 76, Woodfull 34 |
| 117 | Australians v Warwickshire, Birmingham, 1926<br>Ponsford 144, Woodfull 51 |
| 115 | Victoria v Queensland, MCG, 1926–27<br>Ponsford 151, Woodfull 56 |
| 106 | Australia v England, Manchester, fourth Test, 1930<br>Ponsford 83, Woodfull 54 |
| 104+ | Victoria v South Australia, MCG, 1926–27<br>Ponsford 84, Woodfull 34 |
| 104 | Woodfull's XI v Richardson's XI, MCG, 1933–34<br>Ponsford 42, Woodfull 118 |

+ unfinished

| | |
|---|---|
| **Second wicket (1)** | |
| 109+ | Victoria v South Australia, Adelaide Oval, 1924–25<br>Ponsford 77, Woodfull 67 |
| **Fourth wicket (3)** | |
| 178+ | Victoria v New South Wales, SCG, 1925–26<br>Ponsford 138, Woodfull 126 |
| 133 | Victoria v South Australia, Adelaide Oval, 1922–23<br>Ponsford 108, Woodfull 123 |
| 132 | Woodfull's XI v Richardson's XI, MCG, 1934–35<br>Ponsford 83, Woodfull 111 |
| **Fifth wicket (1)** | |
| 183 | Australia v West Indies, Sydney, second Test, 1930–31<br>Ponsford 183, Woodfull 58 |

+ unfinished

## PONSFORD AND WOODFULL AS OPENERS

| | Innings | Not Out | Runs | Best | Average |
|---|---|---|---|---|---|
| Test cricket | 22 | 1 | 860 | 162 | 40.95 |
| Australia on tour | 21 | 0 | 1024 | 184 | 48.76 |
| Australian XI games (in Australia) | 5 | 1 | 513 | 223 | 128.25 |
| Testimonial games | 3 | 0 | 142 | 104 | 47.33 |
| Victoria (Sheffield Shield) | 29 | 0 | 2046 | 375 | 70.55 |
| Victoria v overseas teams | 6 | 0 | 99 | 67 | 16.50 |
| **Total** | **86** | **2** | **4684** | **375** | **55.76** |

**Prolific:** Bill Woodfull (*left*) with the equally-remarkable Bill Ponsford in Sydney.

**Big Bertha:** Bill Ponsford with his ever-so-broad bat 'Big Bertha'. He hated getting out at any time.

**Reliable:** a badge featuring the great Bill Woodfull, 1934.

**Surrey Kings:** Jim Laker (left) and Tony Lock (far right) with another strike bowler, noted fast-medium Peter Loader. They were among those most responsible for lifting Surrey to unprecedented success at English county championship level in the 1950s.

# N

**'They were sitting ducks for Laker, who drifted and spun his off-breaks so wickedly across the batsmen that his leg trap arsenal, including the eagle-eyed Lock, thought Christmas had come early. . .'**

## A NEAR MIRACLE

Putting aside, for now, the Edgbaston epic of 2005, it was as gripping a finish to a cricket match as any I have witnessed in 50 years. To be one of the 18,000 filing into the Melbourne Cricket Ground on the fifth day of the heart-stopping 1982 Christmas Test was a privilege and a pleasure.

Set 292 runs to win and reclaim the Ashes, Australia was cruising at 3–171 before England's Jamaican-born speedster Norman Cowans engineered a middle-order collapse. The Australians lost six wickets for 47, including top-scorer David Hookes for 68, as England revived. Only one wicket separated England from a convincing win and a 2–1 mid-series scoreline with the deciding Test to come in Sydney.

Enter Australia's No. 11, Jeff Thomson, an express bowler of still intimidating pace, but without the accompanying batting credentials.

Meeting him in centre wicket was 27-year-old Allan Border, highest score 32 all summer, fighting for the right to remain in Australia's top six. Having been out for 2 in the first innings in Melbourne, Border knew he was on the brink. He either had to make runs in the second innings or be replaced for the final Test in his home town of Sydney the following week.

'I hadn't been playing particularly well and my position in the side was in question,' he said. 'I started that [second] innings under a lot of pressure. There was a two-fold situation at the beginning of the innings. One was to get Australia over the line and [two to] make sure I scored enough runs to keep my Test career going. It was touch and go for a while. I had nothing much to lose. I went out there and played my own game.'

Demoted one slot to No. 6, he was in at 4–171 and watched on as Cowans tore through the middle and late order on a relaid wicket starting to keep menacingly low. Rod Marsh and Rodney Hogg were lbw and Bruce Yardley bowled, giving Cowans three more wickets for just five runs from 20 balls. It had been a sensational return given that he'd failed to take a wicket in the first two Tests and been dropped from the third. At 9–218, Australia still needed an additional 74.

'Given Jeff's previous batting history, it was unlikely we were going to win the game,' said Border. 'As we lost wickets it became more important for me to hang in there and dig a little bit deeper.'

The umpires Tony Crafter and Rex Whitehead extended play by half an hour, thinking the game would finish in four days. But rather than capitulate meekly, Thomson played some solid defensive shots, backing his partner, who began to play with his old authority, using a bat, minus its stickers, borrowed from Ian Botham.

Border expertly manipulated as much of the strike as possible, Thomson having to face only one or two deliveries most overs. Slowly but surely, the Australians whittled down the required runs to 60, 50 and then 40.

The crowd willed the Australians on. By stumps, the scoreline had improved to 9–255. Just 37 more were needed. It shaped to be a magnificent finish. . . or so the public thought.

Walking down from the Hilton Hotel the next morning, the Australians were amazed to see Yarra Park alive with so many streaming in. Greg Chappell thought they were all mad. He'd written the game off.

The gates had been thrown open on the fifth morning, the Australians dispensing with their normal team warm-up, only Border and Thomson having a brief hit-up.

They couldn't help but sense the expectation. Even before 11 am, the crowd had swelled to almost 10,000 and was to double during one of the best-remembered hours at cricket's colosseum.

As they walked out to roars of approval, Thomson said if it was good enough for all the fans to come, they should give it their absolute best. In the dressing rooms the Australians resumed the exact seats they'd been in the night before. Those like Geoff Lawson, who'd been downstairs, remained in the dungeon, relying on updates from the room attendant.

'We were something like 200/1 to win,' said Border. 'Eighteen thousand people get lost a little at the MCG but they were making enough noise for 40,000 or 50,000. Their support made us all the more determined to win or, at worst, lose gloriously.'

Tracking a seven-for, Cowans bowled the first over from the members' end and Thomson either let the ball go or defended like he was an accomplished top-order player. There was widespread cheering and applause as each ball was successfully negotiated. Cowans' second over, too, was a maiden, Thomson in little discomfort against the old ball.

Border, meantime, was scoring ones and twos. England captain Bob Willis had spread the field wide, allowing Border easy runs to help get Thomson back on strike.

Play had re-commenced at a somewhat leisurely pace, but as the partnership grew so did the noise in the crowd, the confidence of the two batsmen and the anxiety of the Englishmen.

When Cowans took the second new ball at 11.29 am, there were cheers as, after a prolonged delay with the field being re-set, Thomson confidently square-cut his first delivery to third man for a single.

Only five runs came in the first half an hour – a hush proceeding every delivery before excited chatter and applause as deliveries were either defended or allowed to fly harmlessly through to wicketkeeper Bob Taylor.

The 50 stand came in 92 minutes, when Thomson played another cut shot, this time squarer through point, and the batsmen scampered three.

There was a further roar when Allan Lamb and substitute fieldsman Ian Gould collided as Border stole a daredevil single to again keep the strike. When the replay of the collision was shown on the big board – in use for the first time – the crowd erupted again. The Englishmen were now the hunted. Willis was fast running out of options. By not pressuring the Aussies early, he'd allowed both to settle and they were playing beautifully, the crowd an increasing factor.

'Every time a single was scored or Jeff played out an over, the crowd went berserk,' said Border. 'The pressure built up. You could see the Englishmen succumbing. It was a couple of great hours of Test cricket. Extraordinarily 18,000 people turned up to see what possibly could have been one ball. They were the smart people that morning.'

Less than 20 were needed for a famous win and there were gasps when Border nicked Bob Willis through where second slip would have been, only for Willis' insistence at spreading the field. He was playing Border back into form.

Minutes before, Thomson had played an ungainly cut shot which ballooned towards point and landed safely. It could so easily have been caught, only for him to take a single and escape to the safety at the non-striker's end. Looking up at the replay screen he quipped to umpire Crafter: 'Arrrr, that didn't look too good, did it!'

Crafter said the tension was almost unbearable. Having given Thomson not out to an ever-so-close run-out call the night before – and seen a replay vindicating his decision later that night – Crafter prayed that no-one would be hit on the pads.

Having bowled five overs for eight runs, Willis introduced Ian Botham, but even the champion all-rounder couldn't induce a false stroke and, to screams of delight, Border and Thomson further reduced the target. Less than a dozen were needed and there were often two and three minute delays between overs for consultations between a clearly worried Willis and his deputies.

'It was an incredible situation,' said Border. 'Here was the No. 11 bloke trying very hard and [together] we were pulling something special out.'

Thomson was on strike and just four were needed as Botham was again entrusted with the ball. In between overs there had been

**Epic Partners:** Yorkshiremen Herbert Sutcliffe (*left*) and Percy Holmes shared 69 century stands, the highest a monumental 555 against Essex at Leyton in 1932. *Stephen Chalke*

**He Refused a Knighthood:** Australia's between-the-wars cricketing statesman Bill Woodfull, who formed one of Australia's most revered opening partnerships with the recordbreaking Bill Ponsford. Woodfull was offered a knighthood for his services to sport – and refused it.

**Australia's Hobbs and Sutcliffe**: The two Bills, Ponsford and Woodfull, as featured on the cover of the English *Cricketer*'s *Winter Annual* for 1928–29.

**Jewels in the Crown:** Jack Hobbs (left) with his illustrious partner Herbert Sutcliffe. Together they amassed 15 century stands and averaged 87 per innings.

**They Batted all Christmas Day:** Alan Kippax and Hal Hooker scored 254 runs on Christmas Day on their way to a world record 307 run tenth wicket stand, against Victoria in late December 1928–29. NSW's team, back row, left to right: Archie Jackson, Sam Everett, Frank Jordan, CDB Wright (manager), Hooker, Charlie Nicholls, Tommy Andrews. Front: Dudley Seddon, 'Hammy' Love, Charlie Kelleway, Kippax (captain), Don Bradman, Alan Fairfax. *Colin Clowes/NSW Cricket*

| | | | | | |
|---|---|---|---|---|---|
| 5-24 | 59 | 3 | Andrews T J | 3133111212322 1142 | Bow |
| | 387 | 4 | Kippax A | [illegible] | not |
| 5-41 | 3 | 5 | Bradman D G | 1 | Bow |
| 5-44 | 1 | 6 | Kelleway C E | | Bow |
| 5-55 | 8 | 7 | Seddon D | | LB |
| 5-59 | 2 | 8 | Love H.D. | | LB |
| 11-44 | 9 | 9 | Nicholls C | 3412 | Bow |
| 12-23 | 36 | 10 | Everett S | 211411411 | LB |
| 12-19 | 304 | 11 | Hooker A | 113111211111131111111122413141131421 | Caught |

Byes
Leg B
Wides
No Bal

of Innings
minutes

| | 1 | 2 | 3 | 4 | 5 | 6 | 7 | 8 |
|---|---|---|---|---|---|---|---|---|
| Fall of Wickets ... | 2 | 46 | 54 | 55 | 55 | 57 | 58 | 74 |
| Batsman Out ... | Fairfax 2 | Andrews 33 | Jackson 19 | Bradman 1 | Kelleway 0 | Seddon 0 | Love 0 | Nicholls 1[illegible] |
| " Not Out ... | Jackson 0 | Jackson 11 | Kippax 0 | Kippax 0 | Kippax 0 | Kippax 1 | Kippax 2 | Kippax 7 |

**Rejuvenation:** NSW rallied in its first innings from 9–113 to 420 all out to force a draw in the game played over five days in Melbourne. *Colin Clowes/NSW Cricket*

**'We'd Better Get You to Your 100, Bill,'** said Don Bradman to fellow New South Welshman Bill Brown with the second new ball due in the opening Sheffield Shield game of the 1933–34 season in Brisbane. Once Brown reached three figures, Bradman once again cornered the strike, making 120 between lunch and tea on his way to 200 in three and a half exhilarating hours.

**Caught Marsh, Bowled Lillee:** Rod Marsh's birds-eye view from behind the wicket as Dennis Lillee prepares to bowl to England's Tony Greig, WACA, Perth, 1974–75.

*Cricketer magazine*

**Escape Artists:** Allan Border and Australia's No. 11 Terry Alderman batted 95 minutes to ensure a draw against the rampaging West Indies at Port-of-Spain, Trinidad in 1983–84. Back row, left to right: Steve Smith, Tom Hogan, Carl Rackemann, Dean Jones, Kepler Wessels, David Hookes, Wayne Phillips, Greg Ritchie, Geoff Dymock, John Maguire, Geoff Lawson. Front: Rodney Hogg, Alderman, Border, Kim Hughes (captain).

**How Sweet It Is:** Courtney Walsh takes the final match-winning wicket of the thrilling 1992–93 Adelaide Test to the jubilation of West Indian teammates Phil Simmons (left) and Keith Arthurton. Walsh's new-ball partnership with Curtly Ambrose was pivotal as the West Indies dominated world cricket into a second decade in the early '90s.

*Left:* **Trent Bridge Titans:** Geoff Marsh (left) and Mark Taylor celebrate Australia's four-day Ashes win at Nottingham in 1989. They batted through the entire first day, amassing 301 runs on their way to a first wicket stand of 329, a record for all Tests in England. *Patrick Eagar*
*Right:* **Sub-Continental Masters:** Wasim Akram (left) with fellow express Waqar Younis. Their command of swing and seam was extraordinary. In tandem they took almost 500 Test wickets together.

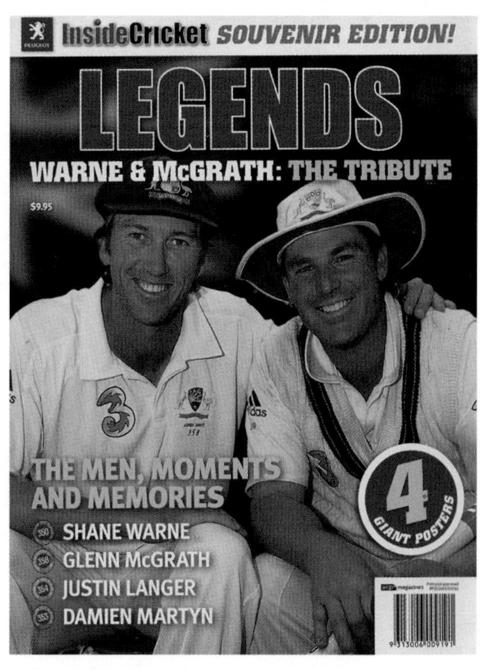


*Left:* **Champion Twins:** Gifted brothers Steve and Mark Waugh shared 15 century stands in international cricket, including nine in Tests, the standout their double-century stand in the deciding Test in the Caribbean in 1995. *Cricketer* magazine
*Right:* **1001 Wickets Between Them:** World cricket's finest ever bowling pair Glenn McGrath and Shane Warne, as featured on the cover of *Inside Edge* magazine. Together they averaged more than 70 wickets a calendar year for 14 consecutive years.

**Pride of Tasmania:** Jamie Cox (left) and Dene Hills from the tiny coastal town of Wynyard built a remarkable first-class record without ever being called up by Australia.

**Premature Congratulations**: Chaminda Vaas, Sri Lanka's most successful new ball bowler was set to play his 100th Test in Hobart during the 2007–08 Australian tour only to be controversially dropped from the side, and the trophy was never bestowed. Vaas had to wait a fortnight for a home Test against England before he played his 100th. *David and Cathy Cruse*

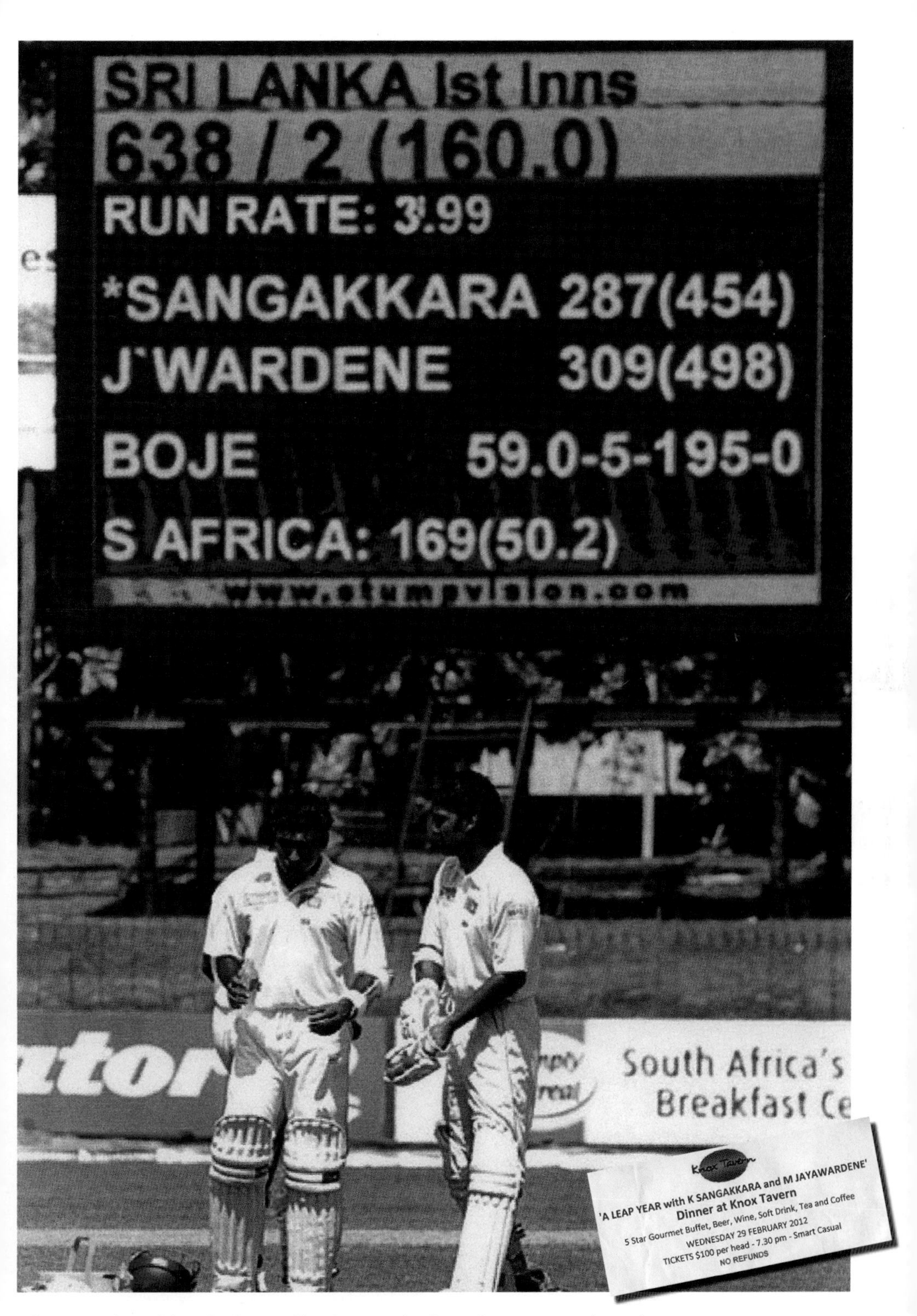


**The Grand-Daddy of Them All:** The stand of 624 from Sri Lankan champions Kumar Sangakkara (*right*) and Mahela Jayawardene against the South Africans at the Sinhalese Sports Club in July 2006, remains the world record for any wicket in any match. Inset: the pair met many of their Melbourne admirers at a sell-out function at Wantirna's Knox Tavern in 2012.

**Teeing off, Again:** Michael Clarke (*left*) and his captaincy predecessor Ricky Ponting during their epic stand of 386 in better than even time against the 2011–12 Indians in Adelaide. Earlier in the month they'd added 288 in Sydney. *Peter Argent*

screams of support. Many stood as Botham ran in to deliver the first ball of his twenty-sixth over. It was a little wide and Thomson fanned at it only to get a big edge. At the non-striker's end Border initially thought it was sailing over the slips to the boundary, only to see it loop virtually straight into the hands of second slipsman Chris Tavare. He grabbed at it, the ball ballooning over his shoulder, only for some quick-thinking by Geoff Miller at first slip to turn and take the ball on the rebound.

England had won by three runs in the closest Ashes Test since 1902. Miller and Botham embraced and sprinted for the pavilion and an afternoon of celebration.

Thomson was close to tears as he entered the Australian rooms.

'He took the defeat badly, having fought so hard for so long, only to be pipped by three lousy runs,' said Hookes. 'The atmosphere in our room was suitably sombre. Then Marshy sang out: "Don't worry, we'll get 'em in Sydney." For once [captain] Greg Chappell was not impressed with Marsh's timing and snapped: "Rodney, just shut up and let the batsmen sit down and console themselves."'

With 68 not out, Border had been incredibly stoic. Never again was his place to be in jeopardy.

'We'd gone within a whisker of pinching it,' he said. 'It was another defeat, unfortunately. But it captured people's imagination and bought that Test series to life. We had been 2–0 up coming to Melbourne. Now the Poms were back in the series.'

The fifth and deciding Test in Sydney was to be drawn, the revitalised Border scoring 89 and 83. Promoted to No. 10, in his final Test on Australian soil Thomson made 0 and 12.

For all of his sheer pace, frightening spells and 200 Test wickets, the big Queenslander is remembered just as much for that one last famous stand with Border. It had been a near miracle.

SCORES: England 284 and 294 defeated Australia 287 and 288.

## NEW ZEALAND'S FINEST

Ian Smith can still remember the battering his hands took standing back to master paceman Richard Hadlee on the 1984 tour of Sri Lanka. New Zealand's long-time stumper says he nursed ice-packs courtesy of Hadlee every night and sometimes during the day as well.

Despite all the bruises, they had a great relationship, and at Lancaster Park in 1988, on the morning that Hadlee was due to become Test cricket's new wickets record-holder, Smith approached and wished him good fortune.

'Get it quickly so we can all relax a bit.'

'If it wasn't for you, pal, I would already have the record by now!'

'Caught Smith, bowled Hadlee' appeared in New Zealand Test scorebooks on 43 occasions. There were another 19 catches in one-dayers. They were a great combo, New Zealand's finest of all.

## NINE DEFINING DAYS

For all of their hundreds of wickets together, and their pivotal roles in Surrey's remarkable run of championships in the 1950s, the careers of spin-twins Jim Laker and Tony Lock were defined in nine early summer days when England stormed from one Test down to retain the Ashes in the final riveting fortnight of July 1956.

In taking 18 Australian wickets at Leeds and all 20 at Manchester, the pair bowled Australia out four times in nine days, England winning back-to-back Tests by an innings.

'Laker was an ogre,' said Australia's captain Ian Johnson. 'That we succumbed so repeatedly to him is a credit to his bowling rather than an indictment of our batting.'

At Headingley, the Australians were bowled out for 143 and 140, and at Old Trafford for 84 and 205, Laker taking 11 wickets and Lock seven at Leeds, and Laker an incredible 19 and Lock one at Old Trafford.

Having won the second Test on a grassy green wicket at Lord's, the Australians were told by opposing captain Peter May, 'That's the last one of those you'll see.'

**Lethal:** At his very best, Tony Lock was almost as destructive as Jim Laker. Neil Harvey fell to him in both innings at Trent Bridge in the opening Test of the 1956 Ashes tour.

Leeds was a dustbowl and Manchester even worse. Old Trafford's curator Bert Flack had been ordered on the eve of the match to cut and re-cut the remaining grass by England's selection chairman GOB 'Gubby' Allen. Initially he'd complained, saying the pitch couldn't possibly hold together. When rain came in mid-match, it made the wicket as treacherous as any Melbourne sticky-dog. Laker launched through the star-studded Australian batting line-up from the Stretford end, taking nine for 37 in the first innings – including a run of seven for 8 in 22 balls – and all ten for 69 in the second.

In wreaking unparalleled havoc on the Australians, who boasted first-class centurions in every position from No. 1 to No. 11, Laker became an instant celebrity and the bowler who beat the might of Australia with just one hand. It had been 55 years since England had twice defeated Australia in a home series. Without the combative Lock building pressure like few left-arm spinners before or since,

Laker admitted his fairytale figures wouldn't have been achievable.

So often did the Australians play and miss at the vicious turn of Lock, that he became totally exasperated. Often he would pitch outside leg and it would still miss off. Several deviated almost at right-angles to slip and were simply too good for the batsmen. There were only two left-handers in Australia's side, Neil Harvey and Ken Mackay. The rest were right-handers and they were sitting ducks for Laker, who drifted and spun his off-breaks so wickedly across the batsmen that his leg trap arsenal, including the eagle-eyed Lock, thought Christmas had come early. In his only two Ashes Tests, Alan Oakman took two catches at Headingley and five at Old Trafford.

Ex-England wicketkeeper Les Ames said: 'The Australians were not good players of off-spin. They gave up the ghost. Jim, with his marvellous control, turned the ball at right-angles.'

As the players were walking off, Laker in front having taken his nineteenth and final wicket, England captain May approached Lock and said: 'Well bowled, Tony. Forget the scorebook. You played your part too.'

Writing a generation later, English cricketer and cricket journalist Robin Marlar said it still amazed his contemporaries that Laker had so dominated the match, given the quality within the Australian team and the presence not only of Lock, 'the most avaricious of bowlers', but of Brian Statham and Trevor Bailey, 'who bowled 46 overs without even one strike'.

'Even if you accept that the 1956 Australians were not one of the best teams from that country, there were still great cricketers in the team: Harvey, Miller, Lindwall and Benaud,' he wrote. 'In truth, even though it happened, we can describe Laker's feat only as incredible.'

Oakman had stood so close at leg slip that Miller came in and said: 'That's a dangerous position, Oakie. If I middle one, they'll have to carry you off.' Three balls later he was out: c Oakman, b Laker!

Despite bowling as well as he had at any time in his career, especially early in the match, Lock's 'share' in 69 overs was just one wicket: opener Jim Burke, who was the third to fall in Australia's first innings.

'If my performance was unbelievable, then so was his,' Laker was to say later. 'If the game had been replayed a million times it surely would not have happened again. Early on he bowled quite beautifully without any luck at all and beat the bat and stumps time after time.'

Richie Benaud, who was out for 0 and 18, said the Australian right-handers 'couldn't lay a bat on Lock', so far was he spinning the ball.

As Laker added scalp after scalp, Lock became increasingly frustrated at his failure to gain his share of the spoils. According to teammate Peter Richardson, also part of the leg trap, Lock began to bowl faster and faster and the right-handers were able to let many of his deliveries pass, whereas with Laker they were forced to defend, not being able to distinguish his top-spinner, which hurried straight on, from his signature off-break.

'If Lockie had pitched the ball up more,' said Richardson, 'and bowled at a sensible pace, he must have got 10 out of 20.'

Lock left Old Trafford 'in high dudgeon', according to biographer Alan Hill. 'The rift between them simmered for years,' he said.

Laker may have been his bowling buddy but he was also his arch rival. Lock treated every innings of every game as a personal competition.

Laker was everything Lock wasn't: right-arm, rhythmic, pure of action, more stable and gifted. Lock was left-arm, crustier, colourful, aggressive and very mercurial. He was also more controversial, being 'called' six times for throwing, including in a Test at Sabina Park.

'Lockie was the greatest competitor I ever saw,' said Laker, who years before had helped a teenage Lock with his grip and talked of the need to have a change-up ball, all the time learning to land it on a sixpence. The nets at the local Indoor School were low and Lock changed from having a high, pure action to a more jerky, flatter delivery which enabled him to bowl without hitting the top of the net. His faster ball was a good 25 per cent quicker than his orthodox finger spinner and his immediate returns for Surrey were astonishing.

Looking back on Old Trafford, 1956, Laker years later admitted that he should have shown more empathy with his long-time Surrey teammate.

**JIM LAKER AND TONY LOCK FOR SURREY, 1949–59**

| Season | Laker wickets | 5wI | Lock wickets | 5wI |
|---|---|---|---|---|
| 1949 | 97 | 7 | 37 | – |
| 1950 | 111 | 9 | 53 | 1 |
| 1951 | 101 | 9 | 65 | 3 |
| 1952 | 86 | 7 | 85 | 3 |
| 1953 | 43 | 2 | 62 | 6 |
| 1954 | 96 | 10 | 94 | 6 |
| 1955 | 82 | 2 | 130 | 13 |
| 1956 | 45 | 2 | 57 | 5 |
| 1957 | 80 | 4 | 113 | 11 |
| 1958 | 83 | 6 | 95 | 6 |
| 1959 | 46 | 4 | 65 | 6 |
| **Total** | **870** | **62** | **856** | **60** |

'On reflection over many years – and remembering that Tony has had to live with his "1–106" – I think I should probably have shown a bit more sympathy towards him than I did at the time,' Laker said. 'I have often tried to imagine how I would have felt if the boot had been on the other foot – as it could so easily have been.'

Australia was bowled out in 40.4 overs in its first innings and 150.2 in its second.

Coming into his game of games, Laker, then 34 and seven and a half years Lock's senior, had taken just eight wickets in six Tests at Old Trafford, but from the first delivery of the game from Ray Lindwall, which barely bounced stump high, the Australians knew that it was an uneven playing field and that the grassless crew-cut wicket had been deliberately 'doctored' to suit the two Surrey champions.

Laker had taken 10 wickets in an innings against the tourists earlier in the summer when Surrey became the first county in 44 years to defeat an Australian touring team.

In the first Test he'd taken six wickets and in the second, three, before launching into the fortnight of his life. Umpire Frank Lee had the best seat in the house at Old Trafford and said many of the

Australians pre-empted their shots, either going forward or back as Laker bowled, 'without treating every delivery on its merits'.

'Apart from Richie Benaud,' he said, 'no-one really tried to attack the bowling of Laker, which was very strange when one recalls how harshly he was treated by the Australian batsmen of 1948 at Lord's, in numbering nine 6s hit during one morning session.'

The Laker-Lock mastery that memorable summer was to continue into the fifth Test at their home ground The Oval, where the pair took 10 wickets, Laker seven and Lock three, increasing their summer aggregate to 61 (Laker a record 46 and Lock 15).

In 10 more Tests together, they collected 14 or more wickets in a game three times:

- 19 v New Zealand, Leeds, 1958
- 16 v West Indies, The Oval, 1957
- 14 v New Zealand, Lord's, 1958

Their performances with Surrey were remarkable, the club winning eight championships in their time, including an unprecedented seven in a row from 1952 to 1958. Not once were they placed outside the top six counties during their incomparable golden era.

Laker was to achieve an ambition and finally tour Australia in 1958–59 – alongside Lock. In a strange twist, despite his pre-eminence as England's finest post-war spin bowler, between his first and last Test matches he played just 46 of England's 99 Tests and was not selected for back-to-back Ashes tours in 1950–51 and 1954–55.

Stunned to have missed the Ashes tour down under in 1962–63, Lock became one of the people most responsible in the rise of Western Australia as a Sheffield Shield power.

# O

**'Gees I am tired,' said Ollie, 'I can't lift my friggin bag. . .'**

## 'OHHH, THAT NO-BALL!'

Kumar Sangakkara was walking off the Sinhalese Sports Club's ground, having been bowled by emerging South African paceman Dale Steyn, when he was stopped by the umpires. It had been a no-ball. At the time, Sangakkara was 7. Two days later he and his captain, Mahela Jayawardene, were still batting, having broken every Test and first-class record in establishing a 624-run stand for the third wicket.

'It was surreal to still be batting late on the third day,' said Sangakkara. 'Instead of being three for not many, we were two for 600 and plenty! Dale and I linked up later at Warwickshire and every time we ran into each other he'd say: "Ohhh, that no-ball!" It meant three days out in the field for South Africa, and in Sri Lanka that's tough.'

Both amassed personal bests, Sangakkara 287 and Jayawardene 374, their partnership extending to 624, the grand-daddy stand of them all.

'We thought one of them might get a bit bored once they'd gone past 150,' said South Africa's wicketkeeper, Mark Boucher. 'That's what normally happens in a big stand – someone will try and hit the ball out of the park. But they were phenomenal.'

---

**Charismatic:** Yorkshireman 'Fiery Fred' Trueman (pictured), the senior partner in England's most prolific new ball combine with the great Lancastrian Brian Statham.

Having offered some initial life, the wide, white wicket at the Sinhalese Sports Club flattened out to its most benign and batting-friendly and the two Sri Lankans prospered like no pair before or since.

'We never planned it,' said Jayawardene. 'You can't plan a partnership like that. It was a wonderful moment for us but it was also very nerve-wracking. Come tea on the third day we were told that we were just 16 behind the all-time record by Sanath [Jayasuriya] and Roshan [Mahanama at the Premadasa Stadium almost a decade earlier]. Never have I been more nervous over the scoring of 16 runs. We crawled our way there. I didn't want to let my partner down. In the end we got there with four byes. It was a wonderful moment for us. Very enjoyable. We had so wanted to get over that hurdle. All these fire crackers went off as part of the celebrations. It was really something to be out there. Hopefully there'll be another two Sri Lankans who will break our record.'

On both nights they were not out, the pair went out to dinner together with their families.

'We certainly saw a lot of each other that week,' said Sangakkara. 'Mahela and I have always been close. I love batting with him. It's so insightful to the way you should be batting. He sets a magnificent example.'

Six of the pair's 14 century stands at Test level have come at the SSC. In 2004 against the South Africans they'd added 192.

The Proteas' attack was world-rated. Ntini was ranked the No. 2 bowler in the world at the time. Steyn, then 23, was averaging almost four wickets a Test at home, while Andre Nel and finger spinner Nicky Boje were consistent.

Chancy early, Sangakkara had been dropped in the gully as well as being castled by an over-stepping Steyn before settling down and playing gloriously, the pair going virtually run for run, hardly offering even another half-chance.

At stumps on Day 1, Sangakkara was 59 and Jayawardene 55. On the second day they added 357, Sangakkara's share 170 and Jayawardene 169, Sangakkara's footwork sparkling as he took on Boje, often meeting him on the full toss and half volley and caressing

## THE SCOREBOARD: SRI LANKA v SOUTH AFRICA

**First Test**

Sinhalese Sports Club, Colombo, 27–31 July, 2006

**Toss:** South Africa

South Africa 169 (de Villiers 65, Fernando 4–41, Muralidaran 4–41) and 434 (Rudolph 90, Hall 64, Prince 61, Boucher 85, Muralidaran 6–131)

**SOUTH AFRICA**

HH Gibbs, AJ Hall, JA Rudolph, HM Amla, AG Prince (c), AB De Villiers, MV Boucher+, M Boje, A Nel, DW Steyn, M Ntini

**SRI LANKA**

| | | |
|---|---|---|
| WU Tharanga | c Boucher, b Steyn | 7 |
| ST Jayasuriya | lbw Steyn | 4 |
| KC Sangakkara | c Boucher, b Hall | 287 |
| DPMD Jayawardene (c) | b Nel | 374 |
| TM Dilshan | lbw Steyn | 45 |
| CK Kapugedera | not out | 1 |
| Extras | | 38 |
| **Total** | | **5–756 declared** |

**Fall:** 6, 14, 638, 751, 756

**Did not bat:** HAPW Jayawardene+, MF Maharoof, SL Malinga, CRD Fernando, M Muralidaran

**Bowling:** Ntini 31–3–97–0, Steyn 26–1–129–3, Nel 25.1–2–114–1, Hall 25–2–99–1, Boje 65–5–221–0, Rudolph 7–0–45–0, Prince 2–0–7–0, de Villiers 4–0–22–0

**Umpires:** MR Benson and BF Bowden

**Third umpire:** EAT de Silva

**Referee:** J Srinath

**Close of play scores:**

**First day:** Sri Lanka 2–128 (Sangakkara 59, Jayawardene 55)

**Second day:** Sri Lanka 2–485 (Sangakkara 229, Jayawardene 224)

**Third day:** South Africa 0–43 (Rudolph 24, Hall 13)

**Fourth day:** South Africa 4–311 (Prince 60, Boucher 38)

**Man of the match:** Mahela Jayawardene

**Sri Lanka won by an innings and 153 runs**

**Second Test (P. Saravanamuttu Stadium):** Sri Lanka won by 1 wicket

**Sri Lanka won series 2–0**

+ denotes wicketkeeper

## CENTURY PARTNERSHIPS IN INTERNATIONAL CRICKET BETWEEN KUMAR SANGAKKARA AND MAHELA JAYAWARDENE

| Test Cricket (14)* | |
|---|---|
| 624 | v South Africa, Sinhalese Sports Club, Colombo, 2006 |
| 311 | v Bangladesh, Asgiriya Stadium, Kandy, 2007 |
| 193 | v India, Sinhalese Sports Club, Colombo, 2010 |
| 192 | v South Africa, Sinhalese Sports Club, Colombo, 2004 |
| 173 | v Pakistan, Gaddafi Stadium, Lahore, 2001–02 |
| 173 | v New Zealand, Sinhalese Sports Club, Colombo, 2009 |
| 168 | v South Africa, Durban, Kingsmead, 2000–01 |
| 162 | v West Indies, Galle, 2001 |
| 158 | v Pakistan, Sinhalese Sports Club, Colombo, 2005–06 |
| 135 | v Bangladesh, Shere Bangla National Stadium, Mirpur, 2008–09 |
| 122 | v England, Kandy, 2007–08 |
| 119 | v South Africa, Pretoria, 2002–03 |
| 101 | v Australia, Pallekelle, 2011 |
| 101 | v Australia, Sinhalese Sports Club, Colombo, 2011 |
| **One-Day Internationals (13)** | |
| 200 | v India, Bellerive Oval, Hobart, 2011–12 |
| 179 | v Canada, Hambantota Cricket Stadium, 2010–11 |
| 159 | v England, Headingley, Leeds, 2011 |
| 153 | v India, Adelaide, 2007–08 |
| 151 | v India, Jaipur, 2005–06 |
| 150 | v Bermuda, Port-of-Spain, Trinidad, 2006–07 |
| 145 | v New Zealand, Wankhede Stadium, Mumbai, 2010–11 |
| 140* | v England, Chester-le-Street, 2006 |
| 121 | v Australia, Dambulla, 2003–04 |
| 116 | v India, Dambulla, 2004 |
| 104 | v India, Dambulla, 2010 |
| 102 | v Pakistan, Sharjah Cricket Association Stadium, 2011–12 |
| 100 | v Australia, Brisbane, 2005–06 |
| **Twenty20 Internationals (1)** | |
| 166 | v West Indies, Bridgetown, Barbados, 2010 |

* all third-wicket stands

**TEST CRICKET'S TOP FIVE BATTING PARNERSHIPS**

| Runs | Wicket | Batsmen |
|---|---|---|
| 624 | Third | Kumar Sangakkara (287) and Mahela Jayawardene (374)<br>Sri Lanka v South Africa, Colombo (SSC), 2006–07 |
| 576 | Second | Sanath Jayasuriya (340) and Roshan Mahanama (225)<br>Sri Lanka v India, Colombo (RPS), 1997–98 |
| 467 | Third | Andrew Jones (186) and Martin Crowe (299)<br>New Zealand v Sri Lanka, Wellington, 1990–91 |
| 451 | Second | Bill Ponsford (266) and Don Bradman (244)<br>Australia v England, The Oval, 1934 |
| 451 | Third | Mudassar Nazar (231) and Javed Miandad (280*)<br>Pakistan v India, Hyderabad, 1982–83 |
| **And also:** | | |
| 446 | Second | Conrad Hunte (260) and Garry Sobers (365*)<br>West Indies v Pakistan, Kingston, 1957–58 |
| 438 | Second | Marvan Atapattu (249) and Kumar Sangakkara (270)<br>Sri Lanka v Zimbabwe, Bulawayo, 2003–04 |
| 437 | Fourth | Mahela Jayawardene (240) and Thilan Samaraweera (231)<br>Sri Lanka v Pakistan, Karachi, 2008–09 |

*denotes not out

the ball delicately through the offside. Jayawardene was just as technically correct and at 340 passed Jayasuriya's Sri Lankan national record. He was zeroing in on Brian Lara'a Test high of 400 before missing a low one from Nel which cut back wickedly and scuttled his middle and off stumps. He'd batted for 14 hours and 32 minutes. Sangakkarra had earlier succumbed, flashing at a wide one. He'd batted for 11 hours and 15 minutes.

Not only did the pair break the all-time Test partnership record of 576, they went past the previous highest first-class partnership record of 577 held by Vijay Hazare and Gul Mohamed in India's Ranji Trophy in 1947.

Along with the World Cup triumph in 1996 and Muthiah Muralidaran's 800 wickets, it remains the proudest moment of all in the annals of Sri Lankan cricket.

## THE OLD FIRM

There has been no more celebrated English new-ball pairing than Brian Statham and Freddie Trueman. While not as physically threatening as Bodyliners Harold Larwood and Bill Voce, or as enduring as Yorkshire's Golden Age combo George Hirst and Wilfred Rhodes, they were mighty warriors: the larger-than-life Trueman downwind, froth, bubble and swing; Statham into it, patient, probing and pacy, the true master of economy.

As new-ball partners, they would occasionally gift singles to turn around batsmen, allowing Trueman open season on the right-handers with his natural, often-late outswing, and Statham, the lefties with his signature nip-backers.

Side-by-side they took 284 wickets in 35 Tests together at eight a match: Trueman 143 at 25.76 and Statham 141 at 25.71. It's one of cricket's quirks that only once did they each take four or more wickets in the same innings, against the star-studded West Indies on the final day of the Trent Bridge Test in 1957.

The Statham-Trueman pairing was responsible for 52 of the 79 South African wickets taken by English bowlers in their golden summer of 1960. England dominated from the opening Test at Edgbaston, winning 3–0.

Possessing the purest of side-on actions with the shoulder strength of a prize fighter, the ego-driven, limelight-seeking Trueman was essentially all attack. He'd bowl his bouncer often and at the throat, even if only to wake up the crowd. Occasionally he overstepped the mark, but a smile and an appeasing one-liner would invariably follow, like in the opening over of the Melbourne Test of 1962–63 when he struck local hero Bill Lawry clearly outside the line of the leg stump, yet appealed vociferously for leg before. Walking back past first-time umpire Bill Smyth, he joked in that broad Yorkshire accent of his: 'Just wanting to see if thee were awake!' Later that tour, a young Greg Chappell was among the crowd in Adelaide when there was a 21-gun salute to mark Australia Day. On hearing the first shots, Trueman, at the head of his run-up, immediately tumbled over as if he'd been shot.

'It was great theatre,' said Chappell. 'That was Fred for you. He always liked the limelight.'

Trueman's smile and earthly manner opened doors wherever he went. In 1956 when the Australians were Lakered on a monstrous wicket, they initially baulked at signing a bat for the curator Bert Flack, who they felt had bowed to pressure from the top and provided unfair conditions. Trueman, who was twelfth man, marched into the visitors' rooms with the bat and obtained the signatures himself, one-by-one.

As a bowler, Trueman offered more width and scope for batsmen than Statham, but his best balls could be unplayable, as he regularly reminded tailenders: 'Wasted on thee,' was a favourite one-liner.

He'd cornered the headlines from the time he smashed and grabbed 29 wickets in four maiden Tests against a terrified India in 1952, and survived just as many downs as ups, becoming the first, in 1964, to 300 Test wickets. Along the way, in 1963, he passed Statham as the world's new No. 1 wickets record holder, a milestone Statham enjoyed for just six weeks.

The sheer quality of his bowling enabled him to survive and keep his many detractors at bay. On the 1958–59 trip, Marylebone manager and ex-captain Freddie Brown twice threatened to send Trueman home, once when they were boarding the SS *Iberia* when Trueman spoke sharply to him in front of the squad, and again after the first Test, which Trueman missed with lumbago. Only the timely intervention by captain Peter May, who told Brown to give Trueman space, stopped what was building towards a career-ending Full Monty of altercations.

The ever-smiling, highly durable Statham was England's premier bowler in the 1950s, despite Frank Tyson's speed blitzes of 1954–55 and Jim Laker's heroics of 1956. Had he not made himself unavailable, 'George', as he was affectionately known, could easily have found himself on a fifth Ashes tour in 1965–66. A captain's dream, he could bowl a maiden over with his eyes closed. And they were eight-ball overs on tour back then. No international-class bowler could build pressure as effectively. So rarely did the double-jointed Lancastrian ever bowl a bad one that master cricket writer Neville Cardus once asked, semi-seriously, whether Statham had ever bowled a wide! Consistently faster than Trueman, his off-cutter could be lethal, and in 1958–59 in Adelaide, he almost bent Australia's opening batsman Colin McDonald in two with the opening delivery of the match.

'I still don't know how it missed the off bail,' said McDonald, who went on to make 170. 'It was just about as good a delivery as I ever received. . . certainly the best not to get me out.'

Statham's motto was, 'If they miss, I hit.' He loved bowling extended spells *à la* Alec Bedser, and at breaks would often talk to his feet: 'Come on lads,' he'd say. 'Just another two hours and I can put you up for the night.' Tyson said he never saw Statham have breakfast. Instead, he'd content himself with a cigarette, a cough and a cup of coffee.

On four tours to Australia, the first as a reinforcement, Statham took more than 100 wickets, including 43 in the Tests. In 1954–55, when Trueman controversially missed selection for reasons other than cricket, Statham shared the new ball with the cyclonic Tyson, and was integral to England's remarkable revival.

While Tyson built ferocious, near-100-mph pace from a shorter run-up he'd first trialled at Alf Gover's cricket school, the almost-as-quick Statham maintained high pressure, shutting down the Australian players and taking 18 wickets himself. On the New Zealand leg of the tour, without even a warm-up, Tyson was timed at 99 mph and Statham at 97 mph.

In England's famous 38-run win in Sydney, Tyson said his fast bowling mate 'burst his lungs bowling into the breeze for 85 minutes, while I surfed downwind to take 10 wickets. It was the same in Melbourne where he breasted the breeze for 90 minutes to take two for 19 as the Aussies collapsed. [Tyson taking seven for 27 as Australia was bowled out for 111, the two walking off with their arms around each other's shoulders.] My 28-wicket series contribution was in no small part due to Australian batsmen's eagerness to escape from Brian.'

The MCC team's manager, Geoffrey Howard, said Statham's relentless accuracy was the perfect foil for Tyson's thunderbolts.

'Brian always got a lot of wickets for the bowler at the other end,' he said. 'He gave nothing away and the Australians like to get on with it. They don't like maiden overs.'

With his fluid approach and rhythmic, front-on action, Statham could bowl at high speed, not as rapid as Tyson at his top, but still consistently around 90 mph. Old foe McDonald felt him consistently quicker than Trueman, and second only to Tyson, as the best English fast bowlers he faced in the 1950s.

For a fast bowler, Statham was the gentlest of souls. So much effort did he put into his delivery action that the knuckles of his bowling hand all but kissed the pitch. At just 12 st 4 lb he was pencil-thin, and the rigors of bowling long spells most days would see him lose 8 or 9 lb most tours. The shock of having to bowl in 100-degree heat on his first tour in Australia taught him to conserve his energy. He streamlined his action and bowled even faster with the minimum of effort. In 1953, on his Ashes debut at Lord's, he thumped a lifter flush into the chest of Australia's centurion Keith Miller, who was visibly discomforted. Rather than intimidate opponents with bouncers, he'd much rather hit their stumps. In the 1953–54 Test at Port-of-Spain, West Indian Frank King felled England tailender Jim Laker with a bouncer, breaking the code that tailend batsmen should not be subjected to bouncers. Come the next match in Jamaica, Trueman was all about retribution and readily involved himself in 'chin music' to the retreating King. Urging Statham to do the same, he was told, 'Nay Fred, I think I'll just bowl him out.'

Trueman and Statham were paired in one Ashes Test in 1956, two in 1958–59, three in 1961 and in all five in 1962–63, when Trueman took 20 wickets and Statham 13.

Neil Harvey, Australia's finest batsman of the 1950s, considered Trueman the finer all-round bowler, yet he fell more often to Statham (10 dismissals to nine). The only other international to be dismissed more times by Statham was also left-handed: South Africa's Trevor Goddard. In 1958–59 in Melbourne, the Test in which Ian Meckiff torpedoed England, Statham's Ashes-best seven for 57 kept England in the game early. Four of his wickets were bowled or lbw and two more caught by wicketkeeper Godfrey Evans. His line was immaculate.

**FREDDIE TRUEMAN'S FAST BOWLING PARTNERS**

| Number of Tests | |
|---|---|
| 35 | Brian Statham |
| 5 | Alec Bedser, Peter Loader |
| 3 | Len Coldwell, Alan Moss, Derek Shackleton, Frank Tyson |
| 2 | Trevor Bailey, David Larter, Fred Rumsey |
| 1 | Jack Flavell, Les Jackson, John Price, Harold Rhodes |

Trueman's mega Ashes moment came at Leeds in 1961 before his adoring home crowd, when he took 11 wickets for the match to beat Australia almost single-handedly. Having lost at Lord's, England revived emphatically with an eight-wicket win, Trueman following his five for 58 with six for 30. In the second innings, he slowed his pace and at one stage had five for 0 in 27 balls, his lethal off-cutter triggering Australia's remarkable slump from 2–99 to 120 all out.

The legendary commentator John Arlott was an unabashed fan, writing: 'Statham was accurate, Tyson was fast; Fred was everything.'

## THE OLD GREY MARE

When Alan Davidson asked bosom buddy Wally Grout for a complimentary copy of his autobiography, *My Country's Keeper*, in 1965, he was immediately told that he could afford to buy his own! Within days, however, one duly arrived, signed and inscribed: 'To the man I made!'

'Davo' always reminded his long-time mate that for Grout to get his name into the scorebook, *he* had to hit the edge first! The pair shared a wonderful rapport and friendship and remain among the greatest of all Australian bowler-wicketkeeper combinations.

Grout, cricket's ultimate team-man, was a talented extrovert who had the eye of an eagle and rare anticipation. He provided another set of ever-so-expert eyes for his captains, urging, encouraging and plotting, and along the way taking some of the great catches as

Australia prospered again after the dim, dark days of the Ashes-forfeiting tour of England in 1956.

Davo was integral in Australia's rejuvenation. Thrust key responsibility with the retirements of champion new-ball duo Keith Miller and Ray Lindwall, he was a master of his craft, becoming the best performing left-arm paceman in the world with the rare ability to swing the ball around corners, from right to left and left to right. He could bend it even on the sunniest days when everyone else was bowling gun-barrel straight. His party trick was to duck one or two back into the right-handers before, with no discernible change of action, running one across them, often inducing an edge through to the willing mitts of Grout.

In 28 Tests together, 'c Grout, b Davidson' was responsible for 44 catches at a rate of 1.6 wickets per Test, a superior ratio than even the record-breaking combo of 'c Marsh, b Lillee'. Most notably there

**Old mates:** Alan Davidson (*left*) with his long-time wicketkeeping buddy Wally Grout.

was a forty-fifth wicket for the pair, a Grout-inspired stumping in Madras, 1959–60, that was one of the great post-war dismissals.

During Australia's extended tour of the sub-continent, Grout noticed an increasing number of grey hairs around the Davidson temples, ensuring lively banter between the two. Madras was the seventh of eight Tests in 10 weeks and Davidson's workload had finally caught up with him. The heat and humidity this mid-January day was stifling, and so exhausted was Davidson that he'd slowed from his normal briskish medium to slow medium. Had the speed gun been in vogue back then, he would have been lucky to have clocked a Mike Hussey-ish 115 km/h. On the first two deliveries of this particular over, Grout shuffled closer and closer to the stumps, and as Davidson wearily trudged back to the top of his mark for his third delivery, Grout cheekily took up occupation right next to the stumps, as if Davidson was bowling slow spinners like Benaud or Lindsay Kline.

Grout knew what was coming next. Davidson stopped at the top of his run and angrily eyeballed the Queenslander, and told him to resume his normal position – otherwise he'd land one straight between his eyes!

Instead of retreating, Grout stayed where he was and began singing a few bars of '*The old grey mare she ain't what she used to be. . .*' followed by another most-audible aside to slipsman Neil Harvey: 'Has anyone ever stood in front of the stumps?'

Satisfied he'd sufficiently upset his mate, he went into his normal crouch, grinning like a Cheshire cat.

Davidson's initial reaction was to bowl as fast a bouncer as he could and make Grout's hands tingle. If he happened to get his head in the way, so much the better. It would teach the so-and-so a lesson. Just as he was running in, he changed his mind, opting to sling one wide, which Grout wouldn't be able to stop. The resultant four byes would be a bigger blow to the Grout ego than any hit to the head. Down it went, way wide of off-stump with all of Davidson's remaining energy, and the Indian batsman MM Sood did his best to connect, only to over-reach and lose his balance. Just as Grout was taking the ball ever-so-nonchalantly in his outstretched right hand, he saw Sood spreadeagled in front of him, with not even a shoelace behind the crease. Cartwheeling his arm at the stumps, he broke the wicket in an instant. Sood was out – the only stumping of Davidson's illustrious career! It was an inspired take. Glancing sideways at the square leg umpire for confirmation, Grout calmly walked up the wicket and handed the ball back to Davo with a deadpan: 'And it didn't even spin, Al!'

**STATS FACT:** Grout also had a telling combination with Richie Benaud with 15 catches and 11 stumpings in 32 matches.

## OLD PALS

They opened together for just one riotous season but the fun, frivolity and happy memories remain.

Colin 'Ollie' Milburn, Western Australia's roly-poly English import, captivated crowds throughout the 1968–69 Sheffield Shield season with his daredevil strokeplay. Built like a tank, 17-stone Ollie would whack cuts, pulls and drives all off the front foot. Teammates would try to retreat to other nets for fear of being hit by one of his explosive straight hits.

His opening partner, Derek Chadwick, was a Perth sporting star good enough to represent his state at both football and cricket and also make an Australian B team to New Zealand.

On practice nights, Ollie and 'Chaddie' loved to have their net and, still with their pads on, wander back into the rooms early and devour the king's share of the large plate of quarter-cut sandwiches faithfully laid out by the West Australian roomie, Alfie Morgan. No-one could eat like Ollie. He'd grab a handful and without even bothering to see what was in them, down them in a single gulp. Then he'd go off for 'a feed'. By the time the rest of the team came in, invariably only a few offcuts would remain.

'We decided enough was enough,' said Western Australia's long-time vice-captain Ian Brayshaw, 'so we had the girls in the kitchen prepare some "special" sandwiches for Ollie and Chaddie, and Alfie duly brought them out. We sneaked in early to have a look and both

**TOP AVERAGES OF OPENING PAIRS IN SHEFFIELD SHIELD CRICKET**

| | Team | Span | Innings together | Best | Total | Average |
|---|---|---|---|---|---|---|
| Victor Trumper and Reggie Duff | New South Wales | 1902–08 | 14 | 298 | 1332 | 102 |
| Colin Milburn and Derek Chadwick | Western Australia | 1968–69 | 11 | 328 | 1007 | 100 |
| Jack Fingleton and Bill Brown | New South Wales | 1932–35 | 24 | 249 | 1719 | 78 |
| Kepler Wessels and Martin Kent | Queensland | 1980–82 | 18 | 246 | 1063 | 66 |
| Bob Simpson and Grahame Thomas | New South Wales | 1962–66 | 22 | 308 | 1244 | 62 |
| Sam Trimble and Ray Reynolds | Queensland | 1959–64 | 35 | 256 | 1928 | 56 |
| Ken Meuleman and Colin McDonald | Victoria | 1947–50 | 11 | 337 | 621 | 56 |
| Bill Lawry and Ian Redpath | Victoria | 1962–69 | 51 | 204 | 2857 | 56 |
| Bob Simpson and Ian Craig | New South Wales | 1961–62 | 15 | 161 | 772 | 55 |
| **And the most prolific:** | | | | | | |
| Matthew Elliott and Jason Arnberger | Victoria | 1996–05 | 98 | 353 | 5084 | 53 |
| Matthew Hayden and Trevor Barsby | Queensland | 1991–97 | 87 | 243 | 4423 | 52 |

**Test Cricket Resumes:** Bill Brown and Ken Meuleman open for Australia in the first post-war Test match in Wellington in 1946. While Brown topscored with 67, Meuleman was dismissed without scoring in his one and only innings for Australia.

**Interstate Champions:** Jason Arnberger (left) and Matthew Elliott built a remarkable combination at Sheffield Shield level for Victoria. Together they made more than 5000 runs with 16 century starts.
*Getty Images/Cricket Victoria*

boys were looking decidedly green, especially when we brought out the just-opened half-empty can of Pal dog food!'

The pair were great mates, Chadwick happy to have the best seat in the house as Ollie whacked them. The only time the rotund one would take a single was from the last ball of an over so he could stay on strike.

In that 1968–69 season they made century starts three times, including an extraordinary 328 in four explosive hours against Queensland at the Gabba. One hundred and forty-seven runs came in the first session and 181 in the second. The temperature hovered at around 100 degrees and Milburn was absolutely spent by tea. Within a minute or two afterwards he was out.

Chadwick had a wicked sense of humour and one day borrowed a hammer and some extra long nails from the curator's shed and hammered Ollie's kitbag to the floor.

'Gees I *am* tired,' said Ollie, 'I can't lift my friggin bag!'

The payback came within days. Chadwick arrived in the rooms to find his brand new Slazenger hanging from the rafters with a dozen holes power-driven from back to front. Advantage Milburn.

Chadwick never did admit to a follow-up episode when a live cat was found in Ollie's locker, but it made one ungodly mess!

They averaged 100 runs per partnership throughout 1968–69. The only other pair to surpass their average were Golden Age heroes Victor Trumper and Reggie Duff, who averaged 102 for New South Wales at the turn of the century.

## OUTSTAYING THEIR WELCOME

Bill Brown and Jack Fingleton were among the most successful of all between-the-wars Sheffield Shield openers, but they could outstay their welcome.

'On good days we'd bat until lunchtime,' Brown said. 'But if we happened to go along too much afterwards, the crowd would start to get restless. You see, you were batting in Bradman's time! If you happened to get hit on the pads, not only would the bowler and the field go up, but so would everyone else in at the ground. When you got out you got the most tremendous ovation, not because you'd played well, but because you were getting out of the way for Don! It was nothing for the crowd to double and even treble over lunch with the prospect of Bradman batting. If he happened to get out, there'd be this mass exodus for the turnstiles.'

Brown loved batting with the Don. He had the best seat in the house as the master went about his business.

'One day we [New South Wales] played Victoria at the [Sydney] Cricket Ground. I got going early and needed about 30 for my 100 and the second new ball was just about due. Don was batting with me and he said: "Bill, we must get your 100 before the next new ball" and proceeded to just take singles, feeding me the strike at every opportunity. I duly got my 100 and he was about 16 or 17. By the time I was into my 120s, he'd passed me! And all in about an hour's cricket.'

In addition to averaging 78 opening up for New South Wales, Brown and Fingleton averaged 103 together during their golden tour of South Africa in 1935–36. Included were three century stands and a 99 in four Tests.

## OVER TO YOU, ARTHUR

Vic Richardson and Arthur Gilligan would chat away like two old married magpies during their Ashes cricket broadcasts on the ABC. So popular were the two old Ashes captains that the Sydney *Bulletin* even devoted a page of cartoons to the pair's one-liners: 'What do you think, Vic?' and 'What do *you* think, Arthur?'

From 1936 to 1937 and again after the War, the Richardson-Gilligan combine was synonymous with cricket on the airwaves.

Their friendship stood the test of time, Gilligan even sending a special cheerio to Vic from 13,000 miles away during the fifth Test in one of his last broadcasts at The Oval in 1964.

# P

**'When he wasn't playing cricket, he'd be charming the members at Ascot in top hat and tails. He was the classiest of all wild colonial boys. . .'**

## POST-WAR DYNAMOES

For reasons other than cricket, their union was to last just 10 Tests, but in the pantheon of Australia's finest openers, Sid Barnes and Arthur Morris rate among the most dynamic.

Both were wonderfully gifted: Morris, polished and poised, as good a left-hander as Australia has produced – Neil Harvey included; and Barnes, a right-hander with flair, flamboyance and attitude. They combined in three century stands in eight Ashes Tests, including 117 at Kennington Oval in 1948 after England had been shot out for just 52.

'Sid was my all-time favourite opening partner,' said Morris. 'We were able to get our singles, especially on the on-side, and being different types of batsmen made it more difficult for bowlers. Sid was the finest opening batsman I ever saw – and the most affected by the wartime.'

As a 22-year-old, early on his first Ashes tour in 1938, Barnes broke his wrist and returned only in time for the final pre-war Ashes Test at The Oval, where he made 41 and 33. He was 30 by the time Ashes cricket resumed in 1946.

---

**Prolific:** Bill Brown (left) and Jack Fingleton enjoyed one of the great summers in South Africa in 1935–36, sharing opening stands of 12, 93 unfinished, 105, 17, 233, 99 and 162 in the five Tests.

Ambitious to make an immediate mark and wanting to be an integral part of the post-war Australian teams, which included his hero Don Bradman, he agreed to open the innings alongside Morris, who had made twin centuries on debut for New South Wales in one of the final representative games before the war.

'Much better to get in before him [the Don] than to come later,' Barnes explained, 'like flat beer after champagne.'

Morris admired his mate's skill and loved his sense of humour. After Barnes, just beginning to settle, had been athletically caught by Alec Bedser in the first innings in Brisbane, he joined a disconsolate Morris, already back in the rooms. He took one look at his mate and said: 'We'll go back to our room, lock the door and sulk!'

Morris conceded that often one would get out before the other prospered. He would have loved to have opened more often with

**Beneficiary:** Jack Moroney cashed in on Sid Barnes' self-imposed exit from Test cricket and opened with Arthur Morris regularly during the 1949–50 tour of South Africa. Together they averaged almost 40 per innings before Jack went back to his schoolteaching in Orange.

**Reliable:** Arthur Morris' most noted opening partner was Sid Barnes but the Morris-Colin McDonald combine was more consistent and prolific. They are pictured during the opening first-class game of the 1953 tour, in Worcester.

### MORRIS AND BARNES IN TESTS

| Opponent | Tests | Innings | Not Out | Best | Runs | Average | 100s |
|---|---|---|---|---|---|---|---|
| England | 8 | 12 | 0 | 126 | 661 | 55 | 3 |
| India | 2 | 3 | 0 | 29 | 68 | 23 | 0 |
| **Total** | **10** | **15** | **0** | **126** | **729** | **49** | **3** |

Figures include their partnerships down the order

### MORRIS'S OPENING PARTNERS

| Innings | Partner | Runs | Average | 100s |
|---|---|---|---|---|
| 15 | Colin McDonald | 949 | 63 | 3 |
| 13 | Sid Barnes | 706 | 54 | 3 |
| 11 | Jack Moroney | 425 | 38 | 1 |
| 11 | Lindsay Hassett | 303 | 27 | 0 |
| 9 | Ken Archer | 182 | 20 | 0 |
| 5 | Les Favell | 134 | 26 | 0 |
| 3 | Jim Burke | 32 | 10 | 0 |
| 2 | Graeme Hole | 30 | 15 | 0 |
| 2 | Ian Johnson | 13 | 6 | 0 |
| 2 | Merv Harvey | 134 | 67 | 1 |
| 2 | Bill Brown | 63 | 31 | 0 |
| 1 | Len Maddocks | 6 | 6 | 0 |

Barnes, but Sid withdrew from the 1949–50 tour of South Africa saying he couldn't afford the time away from his business interests. He never played Test cricket again.

Morris' other favourite partner was Don Bradman, the pair responsible for Australia's famous win at Leeds in 1948 when they chased 400 in less than a day and won with just three wickets down.

'No doubt that was Don and my most important partnership, because it was the most difficult and certainly the most unexpected given our expectations,' Morris said. Morris made 182 and Bradman 173 not out, the pair adding 301 for the second wicket in three hours and 35 minutes on a worn fifth-day wicket. It was the highlight win of Bradman's career.

A fortnight later Morris made another big century, this time 196, but few remembered it as Bradman, in his last major innings, was out for a second ball duck.

With Barnes retiring prematurely, Morris had eight different opening partners in the next six years.

The most successful was the Victorian Colin McDonald, who considered it one of his lifetime thrills to bat with such an acknowledged master. Together they averaged 63.

'Jimmy Burke and I often opened but I always felt most comfortable going in with Arthur,' McDonald said. 'Arthur was a magnificent player. No-one is impregnable, but you knew you were batting with a great batsman.'

## PRIDE OF THE NORTH-WEST

They were the pride of the Tasmanian north-west coast, buddies since starting school and openers of distinction for virtually a decade.

From the early 1990s and into the 2000s, Jamie Cox and Dene Hills went from being neighbours in the tiny rural town of Wynard to being Australia's outstanding domestic opening combination. No pair at state level opened more often – or were more prolific. In amassing almost 6500 runs at an average of 45-plus in a decade of domination, the pair shared 20 century stands, at an average of one three-figure score every seven first-class innings.

Cox is one of the most prolific Sheffield Shield batting 'specialists' not to gain Australian selection. A right-hander, he enjoyed a golden period in his late 20s and found a willing ally in Hills, a high-quality, very-focused leftie. They were forever coaching and encouraging each other.

'We grew up together,' said Cox. 'Dene lived literally 30 seconds away over the back fence and across the street. We played backyard Test matches growing up and they could be pretty extreme. It didn't do much for Dad's front lawn.'

Family photo albums show the pair together at birthday parties from the age of seven and eight. They were virtually inseparable and got to know each other's games backwards. As a kid, Hills wore big thick-rimmed glasses.

'Coke-bottle glasses they were,' said Cox. 'His eyes were always giving him grief. He was colour blind and half blind. It makes me wonder what a player he could have been!'

Cox said their lives followed 'ridiculously silly paths'.

'We were born a year apart. We started university a year apart. We both worked for the same bank a year apart. We got married three weeks apart. We had children six months apart. Everything followed each other.'

The pair roomed together on tour and often would run between wickets even without a call or any eye contact. They just knew that the other was coming. Cox says the intimate knowledge of each other was the core reason for their consistency and success.

'It wasn't often said in words,' he said. 'It was often a look or a raised eyebrow, a stare to say: "Mate, what the hell are you doing?" It wasn't telepathic or anything, but we didn't call a lot. We just knew if runs were on offer. When we started batting together [Cox having originally been in the Tasmanian middle order], we bloomed. It felt comfortable. . . it was instinctive.' Years after they retired from playing, Hills still regards Cox as another brother.

Highest of their stands together was a record 297 against Victoria in 1997–98, when Tasmania chased 400 in the fourth innings at Bellerive Oval and won by seven wickets, the catalyst in the team's barnstorming season finish which saw them make the Sheffield Shield final. Victoria's attack included Testmen Shane Warne and Damien Fleming, yet they took just one wicket between them. In one over from Warne, Hills hit four 4s.

The previous season Cox and Hills had five century starts, including 215 against the Victorians. No set of Tasmanian openers had enjoyed such success. Yet such was the strength of Australia's top-order, with competition from the likes of Michael Slater, Matthew Elliott, Justin Langer and Matthew Hayden, that they were never seriously considered for higher honours.

## OPENING PAIRS IN SHEFFIELD SHIELD

| | Number of innings opened |
|---|---|
| Jamie Cox and Dene Hills (Tasmania) | 144 |
| Trevor Barsby and Matthew Hayden (Queensland) | 87 |
| Geoff Marsh and Mike Veletta (Western Australia) | 81 |
| Andrew Hilditch and Glenn Bishop (South Australia) | 77 |
| Mark Taylor and Steve Small (New South Wales) | 66 |
| Robbie Kerr and Andrew Courtice (Queensland) | 64 |
| Sam Trimble and Des Bull (Queensland) | 54 |
| Rick McCosker and John Dyson (New South Wales) | 52 |
| Bill Lawry and Ian Redpath (Victoria) | 51 |

## JAMIE COX AND DENE HILLS IN SHEFFIELD SHIELD CRICKET

| Season | Innings | Not Out | Highest Score | Total | Average | 100s |
|---|---|---|---|---|---|---|
| 1993–94 | 12 | 0 | 213 | 772 | 64 | 3 |
| 1994–95 | 19 | 0 | 89 | 597 | 31 | 0 |
| 1995–96 | 17 | 1 | 125 | 751 | 46 | 3 |
| 1996–97 | 20 | 1 | 215 | 1086 | 57 | 5 |
| 1997–98 | 21 | 1 | 297 | 1199 | 59 | 3 |
| 1998–99 | 15 | 0 | 112 | 503 | 33 | 1 |
| 1999–2000 | 17 | 1 | 205 | 610 | 38 | 2 |
| 2000–01 | 16 | 0 | 106 | 445 | 27 | 1 |
| 2001–02 | 7 | 0 | 205 | 329 | 47 | 1 |
| **Innings:** 144 | | | | | | |
| **Highest stand:** 297 v Victoria, Bellerive, 1997–98 | | | | | | |
| **Runs:** 6292 | | | | | | |
| **Average:** 44 | | | | | | |
| **Century partnerships:** 19 | | | | | | |

Cox did receive an offer to cross the Strait and play with Victoria, but he remained loyal to Tasmanian cricket, not wanting to play against his closest mates.

'The ultimate would have been if we'd both got to play for Australia,' said Cox. 'We often discussed how nice it would be to play a Test match but we also conceded that it would not have been quite the same unless we were doing it together. Changing both Test openers at the time was unlikely to happen.'

Tasmania's coach Greg Shipperd said the pair were central in Tasmania gaining new respect from the mainland states.

'They were a big part of the journey and made fantastic contributions,' he said. 'It helped that they'd come from the same town, were a similar age and were left- and right-handers. They were also very hungry [to achieve] and could bat for long periods. It was tough bowling against them as they were both good drivers and cutters. At a different time, Jamie in particular would have been a fine international cricketer. He made some big scores against some excellent attacks, especially New South Wales. But he was competing with Michael Slater. "Slatts" got the nod and so he had to bide his time again. That happens in cricket. Timing is everything.'

Cox and Hills' record of opening together in 144 Shield innings, including 70 times in a row from 1995–96 to 1998–99, is unlikely to be surpassed.

The next most prolific pairing at domestic level were the Queenslanders Matthew Hayden and Trevor Barsby with 87 innings together, followed by the West Australians Geoff Marsh and Mike Veletta with 81.

They had one peculiarity as a pair: Hills always ran onto the ground first and took the first ball.

'He thought he was the tough guy for doing it,' said Cox.

# Q

'Keith Miller was one who rebuked Barnes for not going past 234. He and Bradman had never been mates. . .'

## QUADRUPLE FUN IN SYDNEY

Sid 'Bagga' Barnes worshipped Don Bradman. He regarded his 405-run stand with Bradman at the Sydney Cricket Ground in 1946–47 as a lifetime highlight and was fiercely proud that his ultimate Test average of 63 was second only to that of his all-time hero. Their quadruple century remains the highest partnership in the first 135 years of Test cricket down under.

A charismatic strokemaker of rare genius, Barnes was emerging as a world-class player before the world went to war again, forcing a cessation of international cricket.

A top-order specialist who had rarely opened before the war, Barnes was parachuted into opening regularly afterwards following a chat with Bradman. The Don felt Barnes' technique was ideally suited to going in first and he could be very successful, especially if he tempered his aggression just a little.

Barnes was at the other end, initially, for Bradman's triumphant return Test in Brisbane in 1946, falling at 31 to the bouncy Douglas Wright in his first Ashes Test on Australian soil. After a modest start, the Don went on to make 187.

Come Sydney, Bradman spent a whole day off the field with a thigh injury and a gastric complaint. He dropped himself down the list, the game being well balanced on the third day with Australia

---

**Sydney Spree:** Don Bradman and Sid Barnes during their epic Ashes partnership of 405 in Sydney in 1946–47.

4–159, chasing England's 255, when the Don came in to a tumultuous reception. This was the home-town hero's first Test at the SCG for a decade, a Monday work-day crowd of more than 51,000 thrilling to see the great man take centre stage again.

'The partnership with Bradman and I was the important one,' said Barnes in his autobiography. 'Arthur Morris, Lindsay Hassett, Keith Miller and [nightwatchman] Ian Johnson had all gone and Don impressed on me that he was not feeling well. . . I simply had to keep my wicket intact.'

Throughout Saturday's play and into Monday, Bradman reinforced the importance of Barnes remaining at the wicket if Australia was to win.

'It was as if the whole Test rested on me,' said Barnes. 'After a while, I began to feel that I was carrying the house of Bradman as well as Australia's cricket fortunes on my shoulders.'

Normally Bradman would score all around the wicket, his free-flowing drives a feature of his play, but he was so hampered by his thigh injury that he played mainly off the back foot, square and behind the wicket. His fleet-of-foot running between wickets wasn't as sharp as usual, either. Yet his focus was unerring. The pair worked hard against a keen attack headed by Alec Bedser and Wright, going to stumps at 4–252 with Barnes 109 and Bradman 52. In five hours' batting, Barnes had added 88. According to Bedser, the outstanding seam bowler in the world, his bat seemed as wide as a barn door. It was his first century in Tests.

The Sunday off allowed Bradman vital extra time in which to recuperate. Ever the entertainer, Barnes took some of his teammates out on Sydney Harbour on his boat for a little skylarking. His mates hoped he could turn one century into two. Barnes liked the prospect of being a double-centurion, especially in a game involving Bradman. But in making 16 previous first-class tons, he'd been able to convert only one into a double, the season before in an interstate game in Brisbane. He knew that a truly big score could be his, especially if he could work his way through the first half an hour the following morning. Particularly though, he was revelling in the opportunity to have such a key involvement with the Don.

**Dynamic Duo:** Don Bradman (*left*) with Sid Barnes added a record 405 for the fifth wicket against Wally Hammond's 1946–47 Englishmen in 1946–47.

'Batting with Bradman never ceased to be a tremendous thrill, no matter how often you were lucky to do so,' said Barnes. 'No cricketer ever minded handing over the strike to the little maestro. He'd keep up a running commentary in between overs. He was always full of information about what the other captain and his bowlers were thinking and trying to do.'

Having reached his maiden Test century in the slow-coach time of six hours and 23 minutes, Barnes would normally have accelerated and played in a more cavalier fashion, but with the Don's urgings in between overs, he curtailed his natural game and hardly changed pace. Opposition opener Cyril Washbrook thought Barnes' powers of patience and concentration 'astounding'.

He'd been on 48 when Bradman came in, and kept his score ahead of Bradman's until the Don took 16 from a Denis Compton over and reached a Sydney Cricket Ground record 234 before falling lbw in the final half an hour. Their stand had been worth a mammoth 405. The Don had batted for six hours and 37 minutes.

Taking a single from Norman Yardley, Barnes moved to a record-equalling 234, only to be dismissed four balls later in the following over, lofting a catch to mid-on. He claimed it was deliberate. Others said Barnes would never willingly have forfeited his wicket – even to his grandmother. He'd wanted to break Bradman's record with a six straight down the ground only to misjudge it. Keith Miller was one who rebuked Barnes for not going past 234. He and Bradman had never been mates.

'I knew another single would have given me the Australian record on my own,' said Barnes. 'But I preferred to have my name associated with Don's in holding the joint record. I worshipped him. He could do nothing wrong as far as I was concerned, so I tossed my wicket away, hitting one above my head and walking off [having been caught by Jack Ikin].'

On return to the pavilion, having batted just 11 minutes short of 11 hours, Barnes was congratulated by the Don: 'Well done Bagga,' he said. 'You have done a great job for Australia.'

'You didn't do so bad yourself.'

Years later Barnes admitted he could have gone on *à la* Len Hutton at The Oval in 1938 and made a triple-century – 'but I'd rather share an honour with Bradman than surpass it,' he said. At the time it was the slowest double century ever made in a Test. It also remained the signature moment in Barnes' colourful career of massive highs and lows, culminating in his death in 1973 from an overdose.

Australia won the match by an innings.

### BARNES AND BRADMAN: AN EPIC STAND

An Australian record 405 runs, fifth wicket, v England, Sydney Cricket Ground, December, 1946

| Sid Barnes | | Don Bradman | |
|---|---|---|---|
| **In:** 14 Dec 12.45 pm | | **In:** 16 Dec 3.51 pm | |
| **Score** | **Minutes** | **Score** | **Minutes** |
| 50 | 159 | 50 | 110 |
| 100 | 323 | 100 | 225 |
| 150 | 467 | 150 | 305 |
| 200 | 579 | 200 | 376 |
| 234 | 649 | 234 | 397 |
| **Out:** 17 Dec, 5.46 pm | | **Out:** 17 Dec, 5.43 pm | |

## QUE SERA SERA

When Allan Border met Australia's No. 11, Terry Alderman, in mid-pitch at Queen's Park Oval, Port-of-Spain, the Test virtually over, he spoke only a few words: '*Que sera sera*, mate. . . whatever will be, will be.'

It was the start of an epic tenth-wicket stand which was to deny the West Indies what seemed to be a certain first win in the autumn of 1983.

At 9–238 in their second innings, Australia had only a slender 25-run overall lead, and with 105 minutes remaining seemed certain to be beaten, the fury of the West Indian fast bowlers simply swamping the Aussies.

With a previous highest Test score of just 12, Alderman was one of the renowned No. 11s and he was mighty relieved to face four or five overs of gentle spin from Viv Richards before the second new ball was taken.

'By then I'd had the chance to get my eye in,' said Alderman. 'Viv had taken a couple of cheap wickets and in me saw a likely third. AB was doing it easy at the other end. My instructions were to simply try and block the ones on the stumps and leave the ones which weren't. We were to save that game. . . but not the series. The Windies were a pretty handy outfit.'

So successful was Alderman that he made it into the 20s for the first time in Tests, his determined defence also allowing Border to reach one of his greatest 100s late in the final session before Richards called off the game with four overs to go, Australia having extended their lead to an unreachable 86.

'Border was simply Border,' wrote leading cricket writer Peter Roebuck later. 'Predictable, secure, unemotional, a battler from birth.'

Having made 98 not out in the first innings, he'd again defied the might of the West Indians led by Joel Garner, Malcolm Marshall and Wayne Daniel to engineer one of cricket's great escapes.

# R

**'The Guyanese fans were beside themselves with joy, laughing and chanting and urging Clarke and Phillip to "Keep bumpin' 'em maarn, keep bumpin' 'em". . .'**

## RETREATING TO THE ROOMS

Bobby Simpson did not dare watch. His young Australians were clawing towards an improbable first victory in the Caribbean and the tension was unbearable.

He retreated into the Georgetown dressing rooms, relying only on updates from the players' balcony on how the Australian run chase was progressing.

Even with a remodelled team, the West Indies was surging towards a third consecutive Test win against Simpson's 1978 tourists after setting a fourth innings' target of 360. At a disastrous 3–22, with Rick Darling, David Ogilvie and Simpson the victims of a searing first five overs from debutant Sylvester Clarke, the Test was heading for an early finish. The Guyanese fans were beside themselves with excitement, laughing and chanting and urging Clarke and the almost-as-pacy Norbert Phillip to 'Keep bumpin' 'em, maarn, keep bumpin' 'em.'

Enter Craig Serjeant on a pair to join fellow Perth boy Graeme Wood. Only once all series had he made double figures. Clarke was near express and immediately bounced one straight at Serjeant. In self-preservation he could only glove the ball and it ballooned high

---

**Pivotal:** Craig Serjeant (pictured) and Graeme Wood shared a matchwinning partnership of 251 against the West Indies at Bourda in the third Test of the 1977–78 tour of the Caribbean. *Ken Kelly*

and gently into the air, towards backward square. But new captain Alvin Kallicharran had only one close-in leg-side fieldsman, Derick Parry, who was at forward short-leg and he had no time to double back and make the catch.

Soon afterwards, Wood, on 23, hooked high towards the square leg boundary only for outrider Larry Gomes to initially be unsighted by the dark background of the grandstand. Once he picked up the ball in flight, it was too late. Another opportunity squandered.

In cricket, half-chances can be pivotal to match fortunes and so it proved as both West Australians settled and began playing with reassuring comfort. By lunch the score was an improved 3–76. Importantly, the menacing Clarke had been spelled, having taken three for 19 from his searing first eight overs.

Afterwards, against the second-stringers, they unleashed some handsome shots, Australia enjoying its best session of the tour, scoring 123 at better than a run a minute.

The wicket was shiny and flat, beautifully bound and sealed with an even grass cover that had been shaved with a razor-sharp scythe on the eve of the game. The locals had then polished the wicket, giving it a rare sheen. It was a belter, as good as most of the Australians had seen. They'd always felt confident chasing a big target.

'One great partnership can win you a Test match and this one did,' said Bruce Yardley.

Wood was the first to his half-century, in 136 minutes. Serjeant reached his half-century with two consecutive cover-driven boundaries from the bowling of local lad Sew Shivnarine, a slow left-armer. His 50 had taken 137 minutes and included eight 4s. The hesitancy which had often seen him struggle in previous Tests was gone. There was more urgency in his footwork as he drove the fuller-length deliveries and cut and pulled anything short. He even crunched Parry into the mid-wicket bleachers.

Realising his mate was 'on song', Wood fed him the strike but still scored freely himself, picking up runs square of the wicket with deft cuts and flicks. The pair also ran brilliantly between wickets.

At tea, the Australians were 3–199 and victory was no longer remote. Wood was 94 and Serjeant 81. In a team talk just before the resumption, Simpson earnestly reinforced the need to start again, build slowly and make the most of anything loose.

Kallicharran was persevering with Shivnarine and Serjeant was first to three figures with a slashing on-drive and a delicate back-cut. He'd hit seven 4s and one 6 in his rapid second 50. It was his maiden Test century.

Having played two maiden overs from medium pacer Vanburn Holder, Wood reached his own milestone with a cut from Shivnarine for his seventh boundary. It had been a triumph of discipline. Since being fast-tracked into the Australian team with the defection of the best cricketers to World Series Cricket, Wood had been a revelation. This was one of his finest innings and the first of nine Test 100s.

Victory seemed assured, even after Serjeant was caught on the square leg fence against the second new ball. But next-man-in Gary Cosier (0) and Wood were also to fall in the last half an hour's play and the Australians went to stumps at 6–290, still needing 70 more runs to win and be 2–1 down heading into the deciding Tests in Port-of-Spain and Kingston.

Debutant Trevor Laughlin was known for his power hitting in Melbourne club cricket and he rallied the Australians on the fifth and final morning with a quickfire 24, peppering the leg-side boundaries as was his habit before holing out to a rank full toss from off-spinner Parry. Wicketkeeper Steve Rixon played a higher percentage game, working the ball for singles, while No. 9 Yardley, 'The Roo', was typically proactive, mixing a deft late cut to the boundary from Parry with some sound defence. Yardley may have been one of the most happy-go-lucky of the tourists, but no-one was prouder donning the baggy green. He played every match like it was his last.

The Australians edged closer and closer to one of the great on-tour wins before Yardley seized on a shorter one from Parry and struck it clean over the top of mid-wicket's head, one, two, three bounces into the crowd before being hugged mid-pitch by Rixon. Only rarely do Test teams ever chase 350-plus in a fourth innings and win.

Simpson had been so gripped that he couldn't bring himself to watch the final stages of the game. While Rixon, Laughlin and Yardley were winning the game, Simpson stayed inside the dressing room, relying on a running commentary from the players on the balcony. He emerged just in time to see Yardley's pull shot disappearing into the crowd.

'I've never known a Test to be so desperate,' Simpson said. 'It's most unusual for me to be so nervous. . . it was so utterly vital I just couldn't watch. We had to win today or the tour wasn't worthwhile any more. As far as the series was concerned it was absolutely vital, but just as importantly, it was vital for the players themselves. Some of them on the thresholds of their career were facing the possibility that they wouldn't play Test cricket any more. I've never known a situation like this. It meant everything for us to win here.

The Wood-Serjeant partnership was the highest for the fourth wicket in West Indian-Australian Tests. They were two ever-so-proud West Australians and had produced their best when it counted most for their country. 'We didn't talk much in the early stages,' said Wood, 'but as we got closer and started to realise that we could win the match, the chats became very regular.'

Back home in Perth there had been a huge storm, much of the inner suburbs losing power. With their son nearing his first Test century, Wood's parents retreated into the garage and continued to listen to the ABC's Alan McGilvray via the car radio!

The peace treaty between the warring Mr Packer and the Australian Cricket Board was to see Serjeant relinquish his international place, but Wood, all grit and determination, remained a fine player at the head of the Australian order for years, his career average of 31 not a true indication of his long-time worth to the Test team.

The Windies were to win the fourth Test in Trinidad before drawing the fifth, Simpson's last as Australian captain. He'd been preparing to go on and have one last Ashes tilt, before having a 'thanks, but no thanks' lunch with Sir Donald Bradman. Suddenly he was back in retirement again. . . with a host of fresh memories.

**Winning Hit:** After the fine work of Graeme Wood and Craig Serjeant, another West Australian Bruce Yardley made the winning hit, ensuring one of Australia's great Test tour victories, at Georgetown, Guyana in 1977–78.

CORNHILL
CORNHILL
CORNHILL

# S

**'When JB Hobbs is out in the centre, he calls the tune and we dance to it. . .'**

## SERVICE ABOVE AND BEYOND

Influential St Kilda Cricket Club president RL 'Doc' Morton and his right-hand man, the club's long-time secretary Bert Inskip, formed a wonderful off-field partnership, ushering in a halcyon period for the famous seaside club that resulted in six between-the-wars premierships, including an unprecedented four in a row from 1923–24 to 1926–27. Few matched Inskip's passion for the game. He attended every club committee and sub-committee meeting for 38 years – in one season there were 34 meetings – and during the war years worked for nothing. He was also a club delegate at Victorian Cricket Association level and served on the St Kilda Football Club committee, lifting his meetings aggregate to 1000-plus!

## SIMPLY PEERLESS

As soloists they were sublime; as a pair, scintillating. For a decade Jack Hobbs and Herbert Sutcliffe formed England's mightiest and most revered partnership of all. Even 80 years after their last appearance, their average of 87 runs per innings is unsurpassed.

Their epic liaison hastened an English cricket renaissance. In England's first 15 Tests after World War I, 10 other openers apart

---

**Tearaway:** Even Wasim Akram conceded the wind to his formidable pace partner Waqar Younis (*pictured*), one of the masters of high speed reverse swing. *Patrick Eagar*

from Hobbs had been tried, several never to be picked again. In the very first over of their first innings together against the 1924 South Africans at Edgbaston, Sutcliffe was all but run out without having even faced a ball after Hobbs called him through for a sharpish single, only to suddenly send him back. Sutcliffe was still yards short when the throw from close range at mid-on missed the stumps. The throw wasn't backed up by the bowler and the opportunity was lost. The pair added 136, the first of 15 century stands in Tests.

As they'd walked to the wicket for the first time, Hobbs, then 41, said nothing more than, 'Play your own game, Herbert.' Sutcliffe, 12 years his junior and appearing in his first Test, took one look at Hobbs with his confident, assured stance and immediately felt at ease.

'There I felt was a man in complete control of himself as well as the situation we were facing. . . he was. . . a rare source of inspiration and strength to the youngster at the other end.'

Sutcliffe, a Yorkshireman with a cool temperament and a thumping hook shot, was to amass in excess of 50,000 first-class runs. His Test average of 60 eclipsed even Hobbs, scorer of a record 197 first-class centuries. Hobbs was more stylish and adaptable on all wickets, but Sutcliffe had a 'an unruffled calm' and tenaciousness which distinguished him from every other champion of the generation. He had no problems with Hobbs cornering the strike and said he never stopped learning from 'The Master'. Once when Hobbs played and missed several times in one over – a most unusual occurrence – Sutcliffe walked down the wicket at the end of the over and said: 'Stick it, Jack. He [the bowler] can't keep that up.'

The pair would toy with opposing fielders, luring them closer as they stole short singles, to help open the boundaries for their attacking shots.

Australia's captain Herbie Collins dubbed Hobbs 'The Ringmaster'. When asked to explain, he said: 'When JB Hobbs is out in the centre, he calls the tune and we dance to it.'

HSTL 'Stork' Hendry said no pair could judge a run like Hobbs and Sutcliffe. 'You knew they were going to steal singles. It didn't matter a damn how you placed the field, they still got the singles.'

The great alliance was never more effective than on back-to-back Australian tours from the mid-1920s, where they amassed six of their 11 century stands, four in 1924–25 and two in 1928–29.

The wickets down under were like billiard tables, wide, white and flat. Games often spilt into a second week. Only the run-ups were covered, however, and if there was any rain, combined with fierce sun, as often occurred down south in Melbourne, batting conditions could be hazardous. But wet, dry, sunny or overcast, the Hobbs-Sutcliffe union prospered.

Their stands were worth 97 runs per innings in 1924–25 and 54 in 1928–29, when Hobbs turned 46. Series by series they made:

- 1924–25: 157, 110, 283, 36, 63, 126, 0 and 3
- 1928–29: 85, 25, 37, 28, 105, 143, 1, 64 and 1

From their appearance in the opening Test in Sydney in 1924–25, when the pair survived the menacing bounce of expressman Jack Gregory and the testing outswing of Charlie Kelleway, they played confident, dominating cricket. Sutcliffe felt Hobbs was initially a little unbalanced by Kelleway's away swing and, after the first over, met him in mid-pitch advising him to leave anything angling towards the slips alone, especially while the ball was new. Hobbs was the game's most celebrated player and Sutcliffe's advice could have been deemed impertinent, but Hobbs welcomed it. Later he wrote: 'I knew we'd found the right opener for England.'

Having added 157 in the first innings, they started with 110 in the second, only for the Englishmen to be easily beaten.

Coming to Melbourne for the New Year, where the Test was to last seven days, they shared their most famous stand, 283, and became the first to bat through an entire day's play, a monumental achievement given Australia had amassed an Ashes-best 600 over the first two days.

Neither gave a chance, Hobbs going to stumps on 154 and Sutcliffe 123. It was riveting, near-perfect cricket, one of the finest achievements in Ashes annals. Remarkably, Sutcliffe was also to bat through the sixth day on his way to twin hundreds.

'It was English cricket at its best,' wrote former Australian Test captain MA 'Alf' Noble. 'You only had to remember the total that glared in the face of these men as they went out to open the innings to realise the mental as well as the physical effort that was necessary to overcome the feeling of hopelessness, which certainly dominated the minds of every well-wisher in the crowd. Six hundred was the greatest total ever made in a Test! It could not be beaten! But that is not England's way; and if cricket teaches anything at all, it is that you are never beaten while a wicket remains intact.

'For a whole day they defied every change of bowling that could be brought against them. They simply played on and on, now in admirable defence, now in vigorous aggression, but always cautious, always confident. . . they seemed unconquerable.'

The heat was ferocious and the Australian attack well balanced with the speed of Gregory, Kelleway's testing mediums, and the wafty leg-breaks of Arthur Mailey, who on the previous MCC visit to Melbourne had become the first to take nine wickets in an innings.

Hobbs' plan was to 'tame Jack' and 'if we can we could be here for a considerable time'. Gregory had captured seven wickets in Sydney and like the greatest fast bowlers had a habit of taking wickets in a hurry. Yet even he could not elicit even a half-chance from either Hobbs or Sutcliffe as they scored 70 in the first session, 117 in the second and 94 in the third.

'No brilliant century or two could save her [England], nothing but dogged perseverance, chanceless play, hour after hour,' said PR Le Couteur, writing in the English *Cricketer*. 'Such play these two gave us. They were content with ones and twos, stealing with complete safety scores of runs by perfect judgment in running. They scored a four only when it was utterly safe. At one period, when Sutcliffe was about 40, he brightened, hit one or two balls with full vigour, but wisely took himself to task and returned to the routine of the job. The great crowd was quite satisfied and relished the grim fight. The cheers which greeted the two weary batsmen [at the end of the day] could not have rung louder at Lord's or The Oval.'

Hobbs' own MCG first wicket record of 323 with Wilfred Rhodes seemed likely to be surpassed, but he missed a flighted full toss in Mailey's first over on the Monday and was bowled. Sutcliffe later blamed Hobbs' refusal to have even a short hit-up that morning for missing the ball, which landed on the popping crease. Teammates blamed the harsh Australian sun, saying Hobbs hadn't been sufficiently acclimatised to play the ball correctly.

Among the MCG crowd of almost 50,000 on the Saturday had been the wife of Australia's cricket-loving Prime-Minister-to-be Robert Menzies. Unlike her husband, Pattie Menzies had little interest in cricket and she went home early as Hobbs and Sutcliffe batted on and on.

'We were in England in 1926 and Bob suggested we should go to at least one game in England,' she said, 'so down to The Oval I went, Australia playing England, and there they were again, Hobbs and Sutcliffe. They were still batting!'

The 283-run partnership was the closest the pair were to get to the triple-century milestone in Australia, but there were some stellar moments ahead, especially in 1928–29 when Percy Chapman's team successfully defended the Ashes, winning the first three Tests in a row in Brisbane, Sydney and Melbourne. The MCG win was a particularly momentous one, as England successfully chased 332 on a 'sticky dog' of a wicket on which Hobbs and Sutcliffe miraculously started with 105, after Hobbs had been missed at 3, a relatively easy chance to Stork Hendry resting at slip. He'd been struck a tremendous blow in the chest earlier in the game by Harold Larwood and wore a six-stitcher bruise for a fortnight afterwards.

The game again went seven days and it seemed the Australians must win after heavy overnight rain which softened the unprotected wicket. (By law, only the run-ups were covered.) Play was delayed until almost 1.30 pm and the wicket was like putty when play resumed under increasingly sunny skies. The ball left divots and pock marks on the drying pitch, encouraging extraordinary, steepling bounce and danger to the batsmen. Test veteran Hugh Trumble, the secretary of the Melbourne Cricket Club, felt an all-out score of 100 would be a good effort on 'such an unplayable wicket'. Even Hobbs conceded that the Englishmen were 'up against it'.

Watching on from the old open-air press box adjacent to the MCC committee room, Englishman Percy Fender felt the wicket had 'behaved as badly as it could'.

'About three balls in five hopped head- or shoulder-high, some turning as well and some stopping almost visibly as they hit the ground. The batsmen were hit all over the body from the pads to the shoulders and in two or three cases, even on the neck and head – all from good or nearly good length balls.'

Behind the stumps, Bert Oldfield was having a nightmarish time, conceding more than a dozen byes.

Sutcliffe preferred to be hit rather than offer a catch to any of the close-in fieldsmen clustered around the bat. One spitting delivery to Hobbs knocked his cap off and the cap flew just wide of the wicket. Among the few aggressive shots either allowed themselves was the cross-batted pull. They played back at every opportunity, dropping their hands expertly to allow rising balls to harmlessly pass. It was as fine a defensive display as any seen at the cricketing colosseum.

Australia's captain Jack Ryder changed his bowlers frequently, realising that the wicket must improve and that unless the Australians made more inroads into the top-order, the extra rolling of the wicket on the following morning would all but cancel any wet weather advantage the Australians had enjoyed. While Hobbs finally succumbed in the final session, Sutcliffe and Douglas Jardine carried England through to 1–171 at stumps and within sight of a famous victory. Sutcliffe registered his fourth century in five innings on the final day, England securing victory with seven wickets down. It had

**Windies greats:** Jeff Stollmeyer (left) with Allan Rae.

**English Icons:** Geoff Boycott (left) with John Edrich.

**Springboks:** Trevor Goddard (left) with Eddie 'Bunter' Barlow.

**TEST CRICKET'S ELITE OPENING PAIRS, ON AVERAGE**

| | Innings | Not Out | Runs | Best | Average | 100s |
|---|---|---|---|---|---|---|
| Jack Hobbs and Herbert Sutcliffe (England) | 38 | 1 | 3249 | 283 | 87 | 15 |
| Allan Rae and Jeff Stollmeyer (West Indies) | 21 | 2 | 1349 | 239 | 71 | 5 |
| Jack Hobbs and Wilfred Rhodes (England) | 36 | 1 | 2156 | 323 | 61 | 8 |
| Len Hutton and Cyril Washbrook (England) | 51 | 3 | 2880 | 359 | 60 | 8 |
| Bill Lawry and Bobby Simpson (Australia) | 62 | 3 | 3596 | 382 | 60 | 9 |
| Sadiq Mohammad and Majid Khan (Pakistan) | 26 | 3 | 1391 | 164 | 60 | 4 |
| Trevor Goddard and Eddie Barlow (South Africa) | 34 | 2 | 1806 | 134 | 56 | 6 |
| Roy Fredericks and Gordon Greenidge (West Indies) | 31 | 2 | 1593 | 192 | 54 | 5 |
| Sunil Gavaskar and Chetan Chauhan (India) | 59 | 3 | 3010 | 213 | 53 | 10 |
| Matthew Hayden and Justin Langer (Australia) | 113 | 4 | 5655 | 255 | 51 | 14 |
| Geoff Boycott and John Edrich (England) | 35 | 2 | 1709 | 172 | 51 | 6 |
| **And the most prolific:** | | | | | | |
| Gordon Greenidge and Desmond Haynes (West Indies) | 148 | 11 | 6483 | 298 | 47 | 16 |

been one of the great fourth-innings chases, Hobbs and Sutcliffe again playing pivotal roles on a wicket on which others would almost certainly have succumbed.

On the penultimate night, Hobbs had called for a new bat and Jardine, due to bat at No. 6, took it out ahead of the twelfth man Maurice Leyland. According to Hobbs' biographer Leo McKinstry,

**JACK HOBBS'S MOST FAMOUS PARTNERS IN FIRST-CLASS CRICKET**

| | 100 stands |
|---|---|
| Andy Sandham | 67 |
| Tom Hayward | 40 |
| Andy Ducat | 29 |
| Herbert Sutcliffe (15 in Tests) | 26 |
| Ernie Hayes | 15 |
| Wilfred Rhodes (eight in Tests) | 14 |
| Tom Shepherd | 12 |

**100-RUN OPENING STANDS IN TESTS BETWEEN HOBBS AND SUTCLIFFE**

| | |
|---|---|
| 283 | v Australia, Melbourne, 1924–25 |
| 268 | v South Africa, Lord's 1924 |
| 182 | v Australia, Lord's 1926 |
| 172 | v Australia, The Oval, 1926 |
| 157 | v Australia, Sydney, 1924–25 |
| 156 | v Australia, Headingley, 1926 |
| 155 | v West Indies, The Oval, 1928 |
| 143 | v Australia, Adelaide, 1928–29 |
| 136 | v South Africa, Edgbaston, 1924 |
| 126 | v Australia, Melbourne, 1924–25 |
| 125 | v Australia, Trent Bridge, 1930 |
| 119 | v West Indies, Old Trafford, 1928 |
| 110 | v Australia, Sydney, 1924–25 |
| 108 | v Australia, Old Trafford, 1930 |
| 105 | v Australia, Melbourne, 1928–29 |

Jardine was whispering some congratulations about Hobbs' brave stand with Sutcliffe when Hobbs cut him off in mid-sentence and said: 'I want you to come in next.'

Jardine had a rock-solid defensive game and was more suited to the situation than England's champion No. 3 Walter Hammond. While Jardine made only 33, he lasted until stumps and on the following day, on an improved wicket, England made the Ashes-securing runs despite a flurry of late wickets by the Australians, which saw four wickets go down for just 10 runs when the tourists were within 15 runs of victory.

Hobbs had been long talking of Test retirement but was so pivotal to the fortunes of English cricket that he continued to be picked, including for all five 1930 Tests against the Australians, when he and Sutcliffe averaged almost 65 with century stands at Old Trafford and Trent Bridge.

Hobbs, 47, retired with a record 3636 Ashes runs at an average of 54. Sutcliffe continued in Tests until 1935, when he was 40. His Ashes average was 66. They were remarkable players and, as a pair, cricket's incomparable supremos.

## SRI LANKA'S FINEST

No Test team has had a greater reliance on two frontline bowlers than Sri Lanka with its two 'go-to' men, Muthiah Muralidaran and Warnakulasuriya Patabendige Ushantha Joseph Chaminda Vaas – the fast bowler with the longest name in cricket.

Paired together in 95 Tests, Murali, from Kandy and Chaminda Vaas, from tiny Wattala, a fishing town just north of Colombo, captured 62.2 per cent of Sri Lanka's wickets at almost 10 wickets a Test. Even their high-profile contemporaries Shane Warne and Glenn McGrath collectively averaged just 50 per cent of Australia's wickets.

Seventy-two of their 95 Tests were on the sub-continent or in Zimbabwe, where they are particularly famed. They played together just three times in Australia and five times in England.

Their ability to bowl long spells and build pressure from each end was pivotal, both at Test and One Day International level, where they were similarly successful.

Murali, the *Wisden* Bowler of the Century and the first to 800 Test wickets, was incredibly successful, his extraordinary flexibility of shoulder and wrist allowing him to turn the ball both ways. His detractors reckoned he simply threw the ball, but from birth both he and his brother Sasi Daran had both been unable to fully straighten their arms. Murali may have bowled with a bent arm, but he also *finished* with a bent arm.

He polarised opinions from the time he opposed Allan Border's Australians in 1992–93.What was never questioned was his extraordinary ability to spin the ball *à la* Shane Warne on even the flattest, most batting-friendly wickets. His perfecting of an off-spinner's flipper to go with his ripping off-break and doosra ushered in a halcyon period of personal and team success for the Test cricketing minnow. Warne's action may have been purer, but Murali struck more often. And, as his team's only Tamil, he helped unite a nation torn for years by civil war.

In a 20-year period, Sri Lanka won only six of 39 Tests when Murali was absent.

Vaas was also a wonderful ambassador, mentor and hero for hundreds of thousands of Sri Lankans. His rare ability to curl his left-arm swingers at medium pace, no matter the state of the ball, saw him become the youngest Sri Lankan, at 21, to take 10 wickets in a Test against the 1994–95 New Zealanders in Napier, when Sri Lanka won its first-ever overseas Test.

When both Murali and Vaas played, the Sri Lankans won 43 per cent of their matches. That percentage plunged to just 23 per cent if one, or both, were absent.

With Vaas in the same team, Murali averaged 6.17 wickets per Test and 5.63 when he wasn't. Vaas averaged 3.25 wickets per Test when Murali played and 2.88 when he didn't.

'It was always reassuring to see Chaminda at the other end,' said Murali. 'He is a very proud Sri Lankan and it showed every time he went out. It didn't matter the ground, the conditions or who we were playing, he always had a wide smile and he wanted the ball in his hand. If you have that sort of attitude, appetite and passion for the game, you're a long way down the road to success.'

Murali was Sri Lanka's player of the series 11 times and man of the match 19 times, his best match analysis a staggering 16 for 220 against England at The Oval in 1998. He took 10 wickets in a match in four consecutive Tests in 2001 and repeated the feat in 2006 as part of an amazing calendar year which saw him collect a near-record 90 wickets.

Vaas was to amass more than 350 Test wickets and remained competitive even when his pace had slowed. Due to play his one hundredth Test against the Australians in Hobart in 2007, he was dismayed to be dropped and told a friend who had arranged a commemorative trophy in his honour to throw it in the bin.

## STOUSHING AT KENSINGTON OVAL

It was a stand which all but caused an almighty stoush – between Australia's captain and vice-captain!

Tempers rose at cricket-crazy Kensington Oval, Bridgetown, as the West Indians clawed their way back into the fourth Test of the 1955 series courtesy of a mammoth 348-run partnership between local heroes Denis Atkinson and Clairmonte Depeiza.

Australia had started with 668 and seemed assured of another huge win when, in reply, the Windies slumped to 6–147 late on the third day. There was just half an hour to play when wicketkeeper Depeiza joined his Barbados teammate Atkinson. Rather than defending, they played old-fashioned calypso cricket, adding 40 against the bowling of Ray Lindwall and Richie Benaud.

There was no hint of what was to come: they were about to bat through three epic sessions on the following day, mixing stern defence with some cavalier strokeplay which had the locals dancing in delight. In five hours, the pair remained unbeaten, taking the score to 6–494; Atkinson adding 196 and Depeiza, known as 'The Leaning Tower', exactly 100.

**Loggerheads:** Australian captain Ian Johnson all but came to blows with his deputy captain Keith Miller at Kensington Oval, Bridgetown in 1954–55.

**Newboy:** Collie Smith from Jamaica made a century on debut earlier in the series, but missed out at Kensington Oval.

Australia's vice-captain Keith Miller had been dealt some severe treatment by 18-year-old local phenomenon Garry Sobers, who struck seven 4s from his first three overs. Kensington locals pointed and whistled at Miller as he aimed some retaliatory bouncers at their rising young champion. In his second spell, bowling against a strong crosswind, Miller took two of the first six wickets to fall, Everton Weekes and Collie Smith in the same over, both caught at the wicket by Gil Langley from slower-than-normal curling deliveries which bent away to the slips.

Instead of allowing Miller an extended time at newcomer Depeiza, captain Ian Johnson immediately replaced him with Lindwall.

'It was the one point on which the captaincy of Johnson could be criticised,' said Percy Beames in the Melbourne *Age*. 'Miller was openly displeased at being taken off. He was anxious to atone for the loss of face suffered at the hands of the young left-hand opener Sobers.' His first seven overs had cost 43, but he had claimed two key wickets.

The Australians toiled throughout the fourth day without even one wicket. Colin McDonald at cover point grassed the only genuine chance late in the day, with Atkinson on 195, from the bowling of Lindwall.

'It was a sitter, too,' said McDonald. 'Straight in and straight out again.'

The two West Indians scored 95 in the first 90-minute session, 135 in the second two-hour session, and 77 in the last 90-minute session, Miller being given just 15 overs all day, despite the taking of the third new ball at 427.

In the morning session Johnson had preferred to use Ron Archer with the second new ball alongside Lindwall, Miller not having his first bowl until immediately after lunch.

Atkinson and Depeiza raced to their first 100 in just 84 minutes before the introduction of spin saw the skiddy wrist spinner Jack Hill. Johnson so slowed the scoring rate that six maidens were bowled in a row, Depeiza defending his wicket as if it was the last match he'd ever play. Hill tried to force him back and set him up for his 'lbw ball', the quicker top-spinner, but Depeiza kept reaching forward, his concentration unerring. At one stage he'd advanced his score by just two while Atkinson made 50.

The scoring rate lifted again with Miller's reintroduction. Atkinson greeted Miller with a four for his century immediately after lunch and Depeiza also started to play more freely. Unhappy at his team's lack of success, Johnson recalled the spinners, but Atkinson was as severe on Benaud as Sobers had been on Miller the previous afternoon.

With the third new ball due, Johnson recalled Miller and he bowled a particularly furious spell, striking Depeiza several times on the chest and arms before he was replaced again. It had been an incredibly frustrating day for the Australians.

No Australian team in 30 years had ever fielded through a single day's play without a wicket. Atkinson and Depeiza had batted 91 overs without being separated. The volatile Miller felt he'd been under-bowled and said so in the tiny visitors' rooms, openly accusing Johnson of inept captaincy and how he couldn't lead a bunch of

## MOST RUNS IN PARTNERSHIP (BATTING TOGETHER TWICE)

| Partnerships total | | | |
|---|---|---|---|
| 480 | Don Bradman and Bill Ponsford (Australia) | 451 and 29 | v England, The Oval, 1934 |
| 457 | Ricky Ponting and Michael Clarke (Australia) | 386 and 71 | v India, Adelaide, 2011–12 |
| 433 | Dilip Vengsarkar and Sunil Gavaskar (India) | 89 and 344* | v West Indies, Calcutta, 1978–79 |
| 422 | Colin Cowdrey and Peter May (England) | 11 and 411 | v West Indies, Edgbaston, 1957 |
| 402 | Inzamam-ul-Haq and Younis Khan (Pakistan) | 324 and 78* | v India, Bangalore, 2004–05 |
| 397 | Justin Langer and Ricky Ponting (Australia) | 248 and 149* | v West Indies, Georgetown, 2003 |
| 390 | Javed Miandad and Mushtaq Mohammad (Pakistan) | 252 and 138 | v New Zealand, Karachi, 1976–77 |
| 389 | Bob Simpson and Bill Lawry (Australia) | 382 and 7 | v West Indies, Bridgetown, 1965 |
| 384 | Mohammad Yousuf and Younis Khan (Pakistan) | 142 and 242 | v India, Faisalabad, 2005–06 |
| 379 | Mohammad Yousuf and Younis Khan (Pakistan) | 363 and 16 | v England, Headingley, 2006 |
| 374 | Clairmonte Depeiza and Denis Atkinson (West Indies) | 347 and 27 | v Australia, Bridgetown, Barbados 1955 |
| 372 | Don Bradman and Jack Fingleton (Australia) | 26 and 346 | v England, Melbourne, 1936–37 |

* denotes not out

schoolboys. Johnston bristled with rage and immediately invited Miller outside.

'Things got nasty and blows were threatened,' said McDonald. 'The players had the highest possible regard for Miller, but in this case, we all knew he was in the wrong. We immediately put a stop to the silly nonsense and the journalists covering the tour missed a bonanza.'

Miller and Johnson may have hailed from the same club, South Melbourne, and been in the same Victorian and Australian teams, but they were never close, Miller knowing Johnson to be a 'Bradman man'. Once the more conservative Johnson was preferred as Test captain, the rift widened even further.

'I find there are times when I like Keith immensely,' Johnson wrote soon after the tour, 'and there are times when I dislike him intensely.'

Years later when Brian Hansen and I were launching *Wild Men of Cricket*, Miller was one of the past champions happy to attend.

'You have names in the book [from Miller's childhood] that I'd forgotten about,' Miller said. Asking who else had been invited to the launch, he was told he could sit beside his old teammate Johnson.

'Why invite him?' he said. 'You don't want any wowsers there. Isn't it all meant to be a bit of fun?'

Atkinson and Depeiza's stand was to last into the fifth morning. Generations on, it remains the highest seventh-wicket stand in Test history. They paired up again late on the sixth and final day, adding 27 more without being separated as the West Indies clinched a most meritorious draw.

Their two Barbados partnerships totalled 374 runs, breaking the 20-year record held by Don Bradman and Jack Fingleton of 372 over two innings in the 1936–37 Melbourne Test.

More than 50 years and 1600 Tests later, their two innings' aggregate still remains among the top 10 match partnerships of all time.

## STRIKING EVERY 46 BALLS

'If I was able to come back as a cricketer,' Allan Border said once, 'I'd come back as Wasim Akram.' A Rolls-Royce among cricketers and, in Sir Donald Bradman's view, the most menacing and successful left-arm fast bowler in history, Wasim mowed through even the most elite batting line-ups, his late each-way swing the envy of even the legends. Tall and whippy, Wasim captured more than 900 international wickets and was Pakistan's pivotal player for almost two decades. Steve Waugh faced all the name fast bowlers from Malcolm Marshall and Curtly Ambrose to Michael Holding and Allan Donald, but one super-charged spell from Wasim at Rawalpindi in 1994 was 'quicker and meaner' than anything he'd faced before or since.

'Either Wasim didn't like me or I was in the wrong place at the wrong time,' said Waugh. 'Nothing was in my half of the wicket and it was all genuinely quick.'

When his explosive sidekick Waqar Younis arrived with his late-dipping, express yorkers, suddenly there was nowhere to run and nowhere to hide. Waqar welcomed Waugh this day with a searing, high-speed bouncer which all but cleaned him up, helmet and all. As he extended his follow-through he hissed at the Australian, 'I'm gunna kill you today!'

'Thought you were supposed to be quick,' said Waugh, as usual revelling in the fight.

It remains one of his few regrets in cricket that a lifter from Waqar cracked his ribs, landed on his toe and spun back onto his wicket, dislodging the leg bail when he'd made 98.

Despite the Wasim-Waqar onslaught, Australia scored 500-plus, one of the few times the fury of the two champion Pakistanis went unrewarded.

Throughout their outstanding reign as cricket's most successful new-ball pairing, Wasim and Waqar averaged five wickets an innings at an average of one strike every 46 balls. Even on flat wickets and in heat-wave conditions they were electric, Wasim with his reverse swing and steepling bounce from just short of a good length, and Waqar with his sheer pace and late swing. Had they had more back-up and had the Pakistanis assumed a more appealing profile as one of the game's genuine powers and been granted full-length series, instead of just two and three Tests here and there, they could have added the world Test championship to their one-day silverware.

England's Graham Gooch said batsmen never felt settled when opposed by Wasim.

His lethal second spell was pivotal in the Pakistanis winning the 1991–92 World Cup in Australasia, including the final against England at the Melbourne Cricket Ground in front of almost 88,000 fans. He was the outstanding player in the match, his withering efforts from around the wicket accounting for England's last big hope, Allan Lamb, and the dangerous Chris Lewis, both bowled just when the Englishmen were threatening.

'It was a do-or-die spell and Wasim dismissed Lamby and Chris Lewis in successive balls, each one almost unplayable,' said Gooch. 'He always had the ability to raise his game on the big occasion.'

Wasim was equally effective bowling over or around the wicket, when he could lope in behind the umpire and explode into his delivery stride at the very last moment. The Australians reckoned he was playing peekaboo, but no-one dared complain – not until he'd retired! On approach he'd cup the ball in both hands until the very last moment so the batsman on strike couldn't see the shiny side of the ball and anticipate which way it was likely to swing.

Umpire Rudi Koertzen said Wasim's momentum through the crease was 'incredible' and, with the clatter of his spikes on the wicket, he made so much noise it was sometimes impossible to hear the nicks. 'He was just so hard to umpire,' he said.

Even from his shorter than normal run-up, Wasim bowled a 'heavy' ball. Melburnians who witnessed Wasim taking his first five wickets for just 13 runs in a World Championship of Cricket match one Sunday in the mid-1980s knew that the teenager from Lahore had special talents. He beat Kepler Wessels and Kim Hughes for pace and Allan Border was so flustered by a short one that he hit his own wicket. Dean Jones was another in the Australian top-order to succumb. Teammate Javed Miandad said he'd simply 'paralysed' the Australians. It was an extraordinary burst.

**All Smiles:** Another of Dennis Lillee's famed new ball partners was the Tasmanian-born Max Walker. They took 16 wickets between them in the 1977 Centenary Test. Cricketer *magazine*

After his mentor Imran Khan was too old to bowl fast, Wasim carried Pakistan's attack for years before the arrival of Waqar, 'The Burewallah Express', who surged to the wicket with increasing momentum before an explosive delivery leap and whippy, slingy action which saw him deliver the ball at speeds upwards of 90 mph.

So fast was the teenage speedster that Wasim soon relinquished the wind and found his unique late swing was even more pronounced.

'I didn't mind,' said Wasim. 'Waqar had the longer run-up and coming into it was good for reverse swing. He was an incredible bowler. He'd run in [with purpose] every ball. He had real attitude about him. He was good on every sort of wicket and that's what a young bowler needs to aspire to.'

In 1989, the pair first shared the new ball in the opening Test against India at Pakistan's cricketing capital Karachi, both taking four wickets. Among debutant Waqar's first four was Bombay teenager Sachin Tendulkar, making his maiden appearance.

In tandem, they were to amass 476 Test wickets together, ahead even of the great West Indians Curtly Ambrose and Courtney Walsh.

**PARTNERS IN PACE**

| Innings opened | | Last Test together |
|---|---|---|
| 89 | Waqar Younis and Wasim Akram (Pakistan) | 2001–02 |
| 86 | Courtney Walsh and Curtly Ambrose (West Indies) | 2000 |
| 82 | Glenn McGrath and Jason Gillespie (Australia) | 2004–05 |
| 65 | Freddie Trueman and Brian Statham (England) | 1963 |
| 61 | Ray Lindwall and Keith Miller (Australia) | 1956–57 |
| 57 | Kapil Dev and Manoj Prabhakar (India) | 1993–94 |
| **Other Australians:** | | |
| 26 | Craig McDermott and Merv Hughes | 1993–94 |
| 22 | Dennis Lillee and Jeff Thomson | 1981–82 |

**WASIM AND WAQAR: CRICKET'S DEADLIEST COMBO**

| | Wasim Akram | | | | |
|---|---|---|---|---|---|
| | Matches | Wickets | Average | Best | Strike-rate |
| Tests | 104 | 414 | 23.62 | 7–119 | 54 |
| ODIs | 356 | 502 | 23.52 | 5–15 | 36 |
| | **Waqar Younis** | | | | |
| | **Matches** | **Wickets** | **Average** | **Best** | **Strike-rate** |
| Tests | 87 | 373 | 23.56 | 7–76 | 43 |
| ODIs | 262 | 416 | 23.84 | 7–36 | 30 |

In all they opened together a record 89 times. They were just as lethal in one-day cricket and if either sniffed a hint of fear from 22 yards away, they would accelerate up into another intimidating gear.

Waqar dismissed the star Indian Kris Srikkanth six times in consecutive innings and the New Zealander Mark Greatbatch eight times in eight matches. Imran Khan said he'd never known another cricketer to rise so quickly from such obscure beginnings to be among the best bowlers in the world. Waqar wasn't as naturally gifted as Wasim, but he was more athletic and just as hungry. As he strengthened his lean frame, he bowled as fast as anyone, even the South African express Donald, known as 'White Lightning'. And no-one, not even Wasim with his incredible late flurry at the crease, could bowl a yorker at such devastating speed. In Hobart in 1995, one of his in-swinging yorkers collected Shane Warne directly on the big toe, the resultant crack stopping him being able to bowl.

Best in short bursts, Waqar powered to his first 50 Test wickets in 10 matches and his first 100 in 20, along the way overcoming injuries, slipshod slips catching and charges of ball tampering from those unused to seeing an old ball veer in and out at speed – depending on which side was scuffed and which side wasn't.

At Lord's in 1992, there was a hue and a cry after England's captain Lamb asked for the ball the Pakistanis were using to be changed. He believed it had been deliberately damaged. The world champions won by three runs, Wasim and Waqar taking five wickets between them. Nothing was proved that the Pakistanis had acted inappropriately and on the pair careered, creating devastation virtually everywhere they played.

At The Oval Test that year, Wasim took five for 8 in 22 balls on his way to nine wickets for the game. Waqar grabbed six and Pakistan won the decider by 10 wickets.

Earlier, as batsmen, they combined in a vital 46-run stand at Lord's to allow Pakistan to narrowly win the second Test.

'Wasim was the one who calmed me down and made me believe we could win it,' said Waqar. Set 141 to win, Pakistan was 8–95 before Wasim (45) and Waqar (20) made the runs in a riveting final hour. It remains the closest ever Test at Lord's.

Their most devastating Test together came against New Zealand in Hamilton in 1992–93, when Wasim took eight wickets and Waqar nine. The Kiwis were beaten in three days. Set 127 to win, the Kiwis were bowled out a second time for just 93.

Eighteen months later in Kandy, they bowled unchanged as Sri Lanka was dismissed for 71 on the first morning. Wasim took four for 32 and Waqar six for 34. Only two other pairs in the last 50 years have bowled through an innings unchanged: West Indians Ambrose and Walsh (against England, 1993–94) and Australians Glenn McGrath and Jason Gillespie (West Indies, 1998–99), both games at Port-of-Spain.

None of the illustrious new-ball pairs have bowled a fuller length; almost 60 per cent of Waqar's wickets and more than 50 per cent of Wasim's either bowled or lbw.

Unlike some of the great pairs, they were close without being great mates. Waqar was among those within Pakistan's team unhappy with Wasim's demanding leadership style and said so.

'He was too young, too rash,' he said. It tested their friendship, but both had the utmost respect for each other's skills, Wasim backing his strike bowling with his incredible hitting.

'He smashed the bowling. It didn't matter who it was,' said teammate Mushtaq Ahmed. 'He was so incredibly talented.'

Waqar said the pressure the pair were able to build from both ends was good for both of them.

'We got wickets for each other with some batsmen desperate to get down to the other end, away from the one of us who was making life hard for him,' said Waqar. 'When we were going well as a unit it was a fantastic feeling. We felt we could bowl out any side in the world. If "Was" got four wickets, I'd want to get five. It was good for the side to have such pride in our performance.'

# T

**'It was seriously dangerous out there so I took them both off. They weren't happy with me or the limit I had imposed throughout the series. But it was cricket, not war. . .'**

## TEARAWAY TWOSOME

Clive van Ryneveld feared someone could be seriously injured. On a lively St George's wicket and in fading light, his two tearaways, Peter Heine and Neil Adcock, had been giving the 1957–58 Australians a farewell to remember, bombarding them with short balls in a lethal display of near-Bodyline bowling. Less than 40 runs were needed with lots of wickets in hand. It was the last week of the tour and, rather than let his fired-up speedsters continue their onslaught, he withdrew them from the attack.

'A barrage of short balls at this juncture just wasn't appropriate,' said van Ryneveld, one of South Africa's most popular and versatile sportsmen known for his liking for 'playing the game'.

'Their bowling this night in Port Elizabeth was the most hostile I ever saw,' he said. 'Three short balls from Adcock went perilously close to [Colin] McDonald's head and soon after he snicked another to [Hugh] Tayfield in the slips. [Wally] Grout and [Neil] Harvey were also peppered with rising balls and the umpire walked across to me [at mid-off], asking me to ensure that the bowlers pitched the ball up. After another over from each I switched to [the mediums of Trevor] Goddard and [off-spinner] Tayfield.

---

**Ashes Bound:** Bill 'Tiger' O'Reilly leaves the WACA Ground in 1938 headed for England, without – to his lifelong regret – his long-time spin partner Clarrie 'Grum' Grimmett.

**Brutal:** South Africans Neil Adcock (*left*) and Peter Heine were as frightening a set of fast bowlers as anyone in world cricket in the mid to late 1950s.

'Apart from the umpire having taken a hand, I had throughout the series asked Adcock and Heine to limit the number of bumpers they bowled to an average of one per eight-ball over. The incident [four years earlier] at Ellis Park against the New Zealanders, when [Bert] Sutcliffe was hit on the head by Adcock and taken to hospital, had made a considerable impression on me.

'Batsmen didn't have helmets. It was seriously dangerous out there so I took them both off. They weren't happy with me or the limit I had imposed throughout the series. But it was cricket, not war. In retrospect we could legitimately have used more bouncers and maybe the series may have been closer.'

Australia's opener McDonald was to face all the expresses of the 1950s and early 1960s from Tyson, Trueman and Statham to Hall and Chester Watson. All could be discomfortingly fast, but none were as lethal or as intimidating as Heine and Adcock on this night.

'It was virtual Bodyline and very nasty,' said McDonald. 'In making four runs from the four balls I faced, I never felt closer to death!'

**PETER HEINE IN TEST CRICKET**

| | |
|---|---|
| **Debut:** 1955 | |
| **Tests:** 14 | |
| **Wickets:** 58 | |
| **Average:** 25.08 | |
| **Best bowling:** 6–58 v Australia, Wanderers, Johannesburg, 1957–58 | |
| **5wI:** 4 | |

**NEIL ADCOCK IN TEST CRICKET**

| | |
|---|---|
| **Debut:** 1953–54 | |
| **Tests:** 26 | |
| **Wickets:** 104 | |
| **Average:** 21.10 | |
| **Best bowling:** 6–43 v Australia, Kingsmead, Durban, 1957–58 | |
| **5wI:** 5 | |

The Australians had wanted the local umpires to invoke the law relating to unfair play, but they refused, van Ryneveld's prompt action ensuring cooler tempers. Noted South African cricket writer and commentator Charles Fortune called it 'the most terrifying eruption of fast bowling' he'd ever seen.

'The light was drab and the evening chilly. Heine and Adcock between them sent down seven overs of electrifying pace and soaring trajectory. Adcock gave McDonald three successive bumpers all of which missed him by hairsbreadths. Then both umpire and skipper van Ryneveld called for a stop to this type of attack. Adcock promptly sent down the daddy of all bumpers. From it McDonald was caught at slip.'

In the first innings the two South Africans had struck Australian batsmen six times: Jim Burke three times, and Richie Benaud, Ken Mackay and captain Ian Craig once each. McDonald finished on his back trying to avoid one Heine bouncer.

Having played two titanic series against England home and away, the South Africans were beaten 3–0 by the Australians, despite the intimidating presence of the two expresses, who accounted for 31 wickets between them.

In his memoirs van Ryneveld says they were South Africa's all-time premier fast-bowling pair, ahead even of Mike Procter and Peter Pollock from the famous 1970 series.

'Both were tall and very fast. Adcock [191 cm] had a beautifully fluent run-up and delivery of the ball. Heine [195 cm] was less fluent but when he got to his delivery stride he gathered his considerable strength and delivered the ball with all his might. His body language was all menace and if he managed to hit the batsman it encouraged him. He did not like to be taken off. Adcock was more accepting of being asked to take a rest.'

This was the only series in which they opposed the Australians, Adcock taking 14 wickets with his normally fuller-of-length quick in-duckers and the even more aggressive Heine, 17.

Pairing together in 12 Tests they took 95 wickets at almost eight a match, their best performance coming against England at Old Trafford in 1955 when they claimed 14 wickets in a famous three-wicket win. Both possessed the fire batsmen fear. . . in spades.

## THE TERRIBLE TWINS

It was six months of extraordinary batting brilliance, a halcyon summer, 1947, in which 'The Terrible Twins', Denis Compton and Bill Edrich, excelled like no batting pair before or since.

'First one out buys the first round,' they'd joke to each other before plundering opposing attacks for Middlesex, England, and everyone else they represented.

In a searingly hot summer, they amassed 7355 county championship, Test and representative runs and took 100 wickets and 50 catches. Both surpassed the seemingly invincible 40-year calendar-year runs record of Tom Hayward. No pair had ever been as prolific.

'We learned to raise our standards to the other's needs and wishes,' said Edrich. 'If I was bogged down, Denis would take control. Nothing needed to be said. It just happened.'

In the post-war period of ration books, petrol coupons and general austerity, Compton and Edrich played with refreshing freedom and remarkable consistency, amassing almost 3000 runs in

**The Terrible Twins:** Denis Compton (*left*) with his Middlesex and England partner Bill Edrich at Lord's.

partnership together at an average of 100-plus. The Middlesex rooms were often in party mode as the pair invariably celebrated their centuries with champagne – and together they made 30 hundreds: Compton 18 and Edrich 12.

Five of their 11 century stands were doubles and one a memorable triple at Lord's against the Springboks, when the pair added 370 in better than even time: Compton 208 and Edrich 189.

Their superiority that summer seemed so effortless, Compton's zestful strokemaking including one 4 against Gloucestershire's Tom Goddard when he'd tripped and was lying on his back. Edrich wasn't as inventive, but he could be just as inspired. He crashed the ball even harder than his mate down the ground and through mid-on, while his explosive hook shot was compared favourably with Middlesex's between-the-wars great, Patsy Hendren.

On the opening day of the county game against Surrey at The Oval, Middlesex made 2–537 with Edrich making 157 and Compton 137, both unbeaten. Two Saturdays later at Lord's, they made 7–462, Compton racing to 178. So entertaining were they that on the last

**1947 ENGLISH FIRST-CLASS AVERAGES**

| Matches | Innings | Not Out | Runs | Highest Score | Average | 100s |
|---|---|---|---|---|---|---|
| Denis Compton (Middlesex and England) | | | | | | |
| 30 | 50 | 8 | 3816 | 246 | 90.85 | 18 |
| Bill Edrich (Middlesex and England) | | | | | | |
| 30 | 52 | 8 | 3539 | 267* | 80.43 | 12 |
| Ted Lester (Yorkshire) | | | | | | |
| 7 | 11 | 2 | 657 | 142 | 73.00 | 3 |
| Cyril Washbrook (Lancashire and England) | | | | | | |
| 28 | 47 | 8 | 2662 | 251* | 68.25 | 11 |
| Les Ames (Kent) | | | | | | |
| 22 | 42 | 7 | 2272 | 212* | 64.91 | 7 |

* denotes not out

**1947 ENGLISH TEST AVERAGES**

| Matches | Innings | Not Out | Runs | Highest Score | Average | 100s |
|---|---|---|---|---|---|---|
| Bill Edrich | | | | | | |
| 4 | 6 | 1 | 552 | 191 | 110.40 | 2 |
| Denis Compton | | | | | | |
| 5 | 8 | 0 | 753 | 208 | 94.12 | 4 |
| Cyril Washbrook | | | | | | |
| 5 | 10 | 2 | 396 | 75 | 49.50 | 0 |

day of the season, John Arlott said he and many of his 'county beat' colleagues were reluctant to go home.

'We didn't want it to end,' he said. Twenty years later Arlott released a book of the season, *Indian Summer.*

All season Compton and Edrich charged neck-and-neck at the run milestones, Compton reaching 1000 runs on 9 June, 2000 on 23 July, and 3000 on 27 August. Edrich's first 1000 came on 21 June, his second on 22 July and third on 28 August. The combined run spree has never been equalled, not even by the Australian record breakers Don Bradman and Bill Ponsford in the 1930s.

'We helped each other,' said Edrich, 'and in between us we didn't give the bowlers much hope. . . Denis was simply untouchable.'

## DENIS COMPTON'S 100S IN 1947

| | |
|---|---|
| 246 | Champion County v The Rest, The Oval |
| 208 | England v South Africa, Lord's |
| 178 | Middlesex v Surrey, Lord's |
| 168 | Middlesex v Kent, Lord's |
| 163 | England v South Africa, Nottingham |
| 154 | Middlesex v South Africa, Lord's |
| 151 | Middlesex v Leicestershire, Leicester |
| 139 | Middlesex v Lancashire, Lord's |
| 137* | Middlesex v Surrey, Lord's |
| 129 | Middlesex v Essex, Lord's |
| 115 | England v South Africa, Manchester |
| 113 | England v South Africa, The Oval |
| 112 | Middlesex v Worcestershire, Lord's |
| 110 | Middlesex v Northants, Northampton |
| 110 | Middlesex v Sussex, Lord's |
| 106 | Middlesex v Kent, Canterbury |
| 101 | South of England v South Africa, Hastings |
| 100* | Middlesex v Sussex, Hove |

* denotes not out

## BILL EDRICH'S 100S IN 1947

| | |
|---|---|
| 267* | Middlesex v Northants, Northamptonshire |
| 257 | Middlesex v Leicestershire, Leicester |
| 225 | Middlesex v Warwickshire, Birmingham |
| 191 | England v South Africa, Manchester |
| 189 | England v South Africa, Lord's |
| 180 | Champion County v The Rest, The Oval |
| 157* | Middlesex v Surrey, The Oval |
| 133* | Middlesex v South Africa, Lord's |
| 130 | Middlesex v Kent, Canterbury |
| 106 | Middlesex v Sussex, Lord's |
| 102 | Middlesex v Somerset, Lord's |
| 102 | Middlesex v Yorkshire, Leeds |

* denotes not out

The visiting South Africans didn't know where to bowl to the pair. Compton helped himself to 1187 runs with six centuries and Edrich 870, with three. England won 3–0, two of the victories coming by 10 wickets.

Touring captain Alan Melville said the brilliance of 'the twins' had helped to make it 'a summer to remember always . . . You may think we are sick and tired of Denis and his flashing bat,' he said afterwards, 'but he has scored with such style and good spirit that it has been almost enjoyable watching him accumulate his runs against us.'

Jack Hobbs' proud record of 16 centuries in a summer was beaten, as was Hayward's monumental mark of 3518, set in 1906. The crowds were huge, an average of 10,000 at every day of every game. After years of death and deprivation, the arrival of the new season had been greeted joyously and Compton and Edrich provided rare pleasure in the opening springtime days at Lord's.

Middlesex freewheeled to its first county championship since 1921, Compton scoring eleven 100s in 17 county matches and Edrich eight in 20. Compton averaged 96 and Edrich 77. One of their most astonishing feats came in the final half an hour at Leicestershire. Set 66 to win in 25 minutes after Compton had taken a five-for with his left-arm spinners, Walter Robins sent the twins in first and they took just seven overs to lift Middlesex to an astonishing win, with four minutes to spare. It was a massive effort, Edrich smashing 29 and Compton 33.

One of the few times Compton didn't dominate was at Headingley in the championship game against Yorkshire, when he made just 4 and 15, much to the delight of the staunch locals who reminded him that he wasn't a patch on local hero Len Hutton. While the golden boy missed out, Edrich scored 70 and 102 and in one new ball over from Frank Smailes started with 46440 (22).

Compton's month of August was simply stunning: 1195 runs with seven 100s. Late that month he wrenched his knee while hitting another boundary. He was never to be the same player again.

## THE TERROR AND THE FIEND

They were Australia's first truly great opening attack: CTB 'Charlie' Turner and JJ 'Jack' Ferris. Known as 'The Terror' and 'The Fiend', the New South Wales–born pair exploited uncovered wickets expertly in the late 1880s and early 1890s, taking hundreds of wickets and on consecutive tours decimating the might of England's finest professionals and amateurs.

Turner, right-arm, and Ferris, left, seamed and swung the ball both ways, even on the deadest of wickets in Australia. In 1888, during a particularly wet summer in England, they shared an extraordinary 534 wickets – Turner 314 at an average of 11 runs apiece, and Ferris 220 at 14. Their teammates accounted for just 129. Their amazing dominance continued on the 1890 tour with both bowlers taking 215 wickets and the rest only 164 between them.

Twice they bowled unchanged through an innings: in Sydney against England in 1886–87 – Ferris' debut Test – and again at Lord's in 1888.

'CTB Turner is entitled to all the credit of a favourable comparison with the greatest bowler of this or any age,' said cricket authority Charles Alcock after Turner's remarkable triple-century of wickets. 'He's one of the keenest cricketers we've ever seen and the mainstay of the team from first to last. Always confident, never tiring and full of pluck; he showed himself to be a true sportsman in every way.'

In Test matches between 1886–87 in Australia and 1890 in England, Turner and Ferris gathered 105 wickets while the other Australians took only 21. Remarkably, during the zenith of Turner and Ferris' dominance in the late 1880s, Australia won only once and lost seven times to the powerful English team. In their first Test together as a pair in Sydney in 1886–87, England was bowled out for 45 and 184 with Turner and Ferris taking 17 for 171 – yet the Australians still lost.

Ferris played eight Tests for Australia, taking 48 wickets at 14.25. He claimed five wickets in an innings on four occasions. Turner, four years his senior, was the first to 100 Test wickets, taking just 17 Tests to achieve the milestone at six a match. He took five wickets or more in an innings on 11 occasions and 10 wickets in a match twice. In 1887–88, he captured 106 wickets at 13 in just 12 first-class matches.

He remains the only Australian to take 100 wickets in a home season, a record which surely cannot be beaten given the modern emphasis on three versions of the game rather than just one.

Turner attained an even greater reputation in Australia after Ferris moved to England at the height of the pair's bowling triumphs in 1891. Unusually front-on at the point of delivery, Turner had a habit of making the ball jump sharply from a springy, graceful approach. His break-back was deadly and he also had one which seamed away from the right-handers, all at a healthy clip. The great WG Grace said Turner's deliveries skidded off the pitch quicker than any bowler he faced, except for one man, the Yorkshireman George Freeman, reputed to be the finest bowler never to play Tests.

Turner was medium-sized at 174 cm (5 ft 8 in) and 76 kg (12 st) and for a decade, without doubt, he was the world's most outstanding bowler, having first been discovered as a 16-year-old playing for Eighteen of Bathurst against Lord Harris' team in 1878–79.

Three years later, in December 1881, representing Twenty-two of Bathurst against the visiting Englishmen, he accomplished the first of many great feats – seven for 33 in the first innings and ten for 36 in the second. He soon advanced into city ranks, first with Carlton and then East Sydney, where he was an immediate handful. In just seven matches in 1886–87, he captured 70 wickets, including 14–59 for New South Wales against England in Sydney. He also took a hat-trick against Victoria in Melbourne, his victims being high-profile trio GE 'Joey' Palmer, Tom Horan and John Trumble. For this he received a small silver memento in the shape of a stove-pipe hat, with the names of his Victorian victims suitably inscribed.

Turner's greatest season in 1887–88, when he took more than 100 wickets, was remarkable for the fact that two teams of English cricketers toured Australia simultaneously and on behalf of different interests – one promoted by the Melbourne Cricket Club under the captaincy of Lord Hawke and later all-sportsman George Vernon, and the other under the management of regular down under visitors Alfred Shaw, Arthur Shrewsbury and James Lillywhite.

Then 25, Turner averaged almost nine wickets a match in an unprecedented run of success:

**CTB TURNER'S INCREDIBLE 1887–88 SEASON**

| Match | Opponent | Figures |
|---|---|---|
| 1. | Shaw and Shrewsbury | 7–107 and 0–21 |
| 2. | Shaw and Shrewsbury | 4–22 and 6–13 |
| 3. | Vernon | 7–106 and 2–40 |
| 4. | Victoria | 5–17 and 4–97 |
| 5. | Shaw and Shrewsbury | 8–39 and 8–40 |
| 6. | Victoria | 1–79 and 5–102 |
| 7. | Shaw and Shrewsbury | 1–80 and 3–19 |
| 8. | Test match v combined England | 5–44 and 7–43 |
| 9. | Vernon | 5–128 and 1–34 |
| 10. | Shaw and Shrewsbury | 5–64 |
| 11. | Vernon | 4–71 and 7–48 |
| 12. | Shaw and Shrewsbury | 7–72 and 4–135 |
| **Total: 106 wickets at 13.59** | | |

- He played twice against Victoria (for 15 wickets).
- Thrice against Vernon's team (26).
- Six times against Shaw and Shrewsbury's team (53).
- And once for Australia in the only Test of the summer (12).

In 1888 he became the first bowler to send down more than 10,000 deliveries on tour and remains among the true early icons of Australian cricket.

Ferris, from Sydney's Belvedere club, had a lovely high action and great stamina for one so young. At 21, he was the youngest player in the Australian party of 1888. He bowled an admirable length and, according to Alcock, 'with just enough break to deceive the batsman, he showed himself to be a bowler of unusual merit'.

Their stellar summer together on tour in 1888 saw them sweep through county and Test line-ups alike, as if they were opposing unfledged schoolboys. They bowled unchanged in matches against Middlesex at Lord's, Derbyshire at Derby and an England XI at Stoke.

According to another noted cricket writer, Arthur Haygarth, 'the pair created a sensation – and almost a panic – with their successes',

**AUSTRALIANS TO BOWL UNCHANGED IN A COMPLETED TEST INNINGS**

| Four-ball Overs | |
|---|---|
| Joey Palmer – Edwin Evans | v England (133), Sydney, 1881–82 (Palmer 58–36–68–7 and Evans 57–32–64–3) |
| Fred Spofforth – Joey Palmer | v England (77), Sydney, 1884–85 (Spofforth 19,1–7–32–4 and Palmer 20–8–30–5) |
| Charlie Turner – Jack Ferris | v England (45), Sydney, 1886–87 (Turner 18–11–15–6 and Ferris 17,3–7–27–4) |
| Charlie Turner – Jack Ferris | v England (62), Lord's, 1888 (Turner 24–8–36–5 and Ferris 23–11–26–5) |
| **Six-ball Overs** | |
| George Giffen – Charlie Turner | v England (9–72), Sydney, 1894–95 (Giffen 15–7–26–5 and Turner 14,1–6–33–4) |
| Hugh Trumble – Monty Noble | v England (61), Melbourne, 1901–02 (Trumble 8–1–38–3 and Noble 7,4–2–17–7) |
| Monty Noble – Jack Saunders | v England (99), Sydney, 1901–02 (Noble 24–7–54–5 and Saunders 24,1–8–43–8) |

England losing at Lord's before winning the remaining two Tests at The Oval and Old Trafford.

During the 1890 tour, Ferris signed an agreement for the tenancy of a house near the Bristol County Cricket Ground and he returned to England in March 1891, having settled his business affairs in Sydney. Before leaving Australia he received a silver cigar case and match box from the Melbourne Cricket Club, which was an active promoter of tours to and from the UK late in the nineteenth century. In Sydney, Ferris was presented with a 60-guinea gold chronometer bearing his monogram on the back and an inscription on the inside: 'Mr John J Ferris from his great admirers, 10th January 1891'.

Before his qualification with his new club Gloucestershire was completed, he visited South Africa as a member of WW Read's 1891 English team, claiming 235 wickets. Ferris joined the elite band of cricketers to represent two countries, being selected for the only Test of the tour at Cape Town. He opened the bowling and took six for 54 and seven for 37 to spearhead his adopted country to an easy win. During this tour his figures included nine for 83 in a single innings against Eighteen of Transvaal at Johannesburg; twenty-five for 70 against Twenty-two of Border at Grahamstown; twenty-one for 62 against Eighteen of Eastern Province at Port Elizabeth, and sixteen for 70 against Twenty-two of Orange Free State at Bloemfontein.

His batting also improved immeasurably and in 1893 he scored 1056 runs with a highest score of 106 against Sussex at Hove. He began opening the batting with Dr WG Grace for both Gloucestershire and the Gentleman against the Players with success. In a club match in Bath, again with WG as his partner, Ferris made 135 not out and shared in a 352-run second-wicket stand, the Doctor making 204 not out. Ferris also represented Gloucester against the 1893 Australians.

Ferris returned to Australia in 1895 but played only three further first-class matches. He was killed in the Boer War whilst serving with the Imperial Light Horse in Durban in November 1900. He was 33.

Turner continued to be a menace to the best bats in Australia until the late 1890s. During the 1893 tour of the UK he topped the bowling averages with 160 wickets at 13.76 despite a bout of influenza which sidelined him for a stretch.

After playing two Tests in Sydney and one in Melbourne during the first great Test series in 1894–95, he was dropped from the deciding match in Melbourne, despite his status as a co-selector. He'd taken seven wickets in the previous Test, yet was replaced by an unknown named Tom McKibbin. His demotion created a sensation and was akin to Keith Miller's Bradman-inspired initial omission from Australia's tour of South Africa in 1949–50 and Shane Warne being dropped mid-career from the Caribbean tour in 1999. England won the Test and Turner was embittered.

But the following summer he produced one more astonishing bowling feat which he considered to be his finest. On a perfect wicket in Sydney, he took six for 35 for New South Wales against South Australia from 43.3 six-ball overs. Twenty-five were maidens.

'Turner was on his mettle and managed to thoroughly astonish those who had relegated him to the populous realm of the has-been,' said JC Davis, one of the leading cricket writers at the turn of the century. One of his victims was 18-year-old Adelaide prodigy Clem Hill who, in the first innings, had become the youngest cricketer to make a double century. New South Wales won the game and the Sheffield Shield.

'The Terror' was to claim 992 wickets at under 15 in first-class cricket to be among the top four all-time Australian wicket-takers behind Clarrie Grimmett, 1424; Ted McDonald, 1395; and George Giffen, 1022. Ferris is in the top 10 with 813 wickets at 17.52.

In 1909–10, cricket lovers in Sydney initiated a benefit match in the Terror's honour between New South Wales and the Rest of Australia. Playing his first match in 12 years, the 47-year-old cricket coach opened the bowling and took one for 21 and made 8 and 19. The game to assist 'the best bowler who ever lived' raised 331 pounds.

## TURNER AND FERRIS REINCARNATED

One was tall, bouncy and belligerent, the other tiny, cunning and crafty. Bill O'Reilly was the confrontationist, Clarrie Grimmett the conjurer.

Had O'Reilly been a fast bowler rather than a fast-ish leggie, his idea of the perfect wicket would have been to have hit the batsmen on the chin and watch him collapse onto his stumps. His Irish temper was forever bubbling, and batsmen were his everyday prey.

Grimmett was all about the game's subtleties, delighting in deceiving with his round-arm leg-spinners, googlies and sliding top spinners. He shared a testimonial with his great friend Vic Richardson in Adelaide in the mid-1930s, the game set up around Don Bradman batting on Saturday afternoon in front of the biggest possible crowd. Richardson was beside himself when Grimmett dismissed the Don in the last over before lunch with a perfectly pitched leg-break which bit and spun sharply across the Don, taking his off bail.

'That'll teach him I can still bowl a leg-break!' Grimmett said.

'I suppose you know you've bowled us out of a thousand pounds [of gate money],' said Richardson, shaking his head.

The New Zealand–born round-armer lived in Sydney and Melbourne before settling in Adelaide where he found an ally in Richardson, who loved his hunger for cricket and his passion to practise and improve.

**Menacing:** Clarrie 'Grum' Grimmett (left) formed a magnificent combination with Bill 'Tiger' O'Reilly.

'Before he joined us [South Australia], we thought nothing of spending two days in the field dismissing New South Wales and Victoria. Clarrie reduced that time by about half,' said Richardson. 'As his captain I never once had to tell him to give of his best. He gave it all the time.'

Grimmett was the first to take 200 Test wickets and in the competitive, focused, feisty O'Reilly he found the ideal partner. 'Tiger Bill' would bound in downwind, spinning and bouncing his leg-breaks, often at impossible-to-drive speed. His wrong-'un would often stand up, catching batsmen high on the gloves, leading to catches in the leg trap.

Together they were to mow through even the elite batting line-ups like they were Turner and Ferris reincarnated.

Grimmett's biographer, former Australian spinner Ashley Mallett, regarded Grimmett and O'Reilly 'as good as any pair in history'.

'It was an odd liaison for they were direct opposites,' said Mallett. 'Grimmett quiet in the extreme, wheeling away diligently, almost blending with the scenery, and O'Reilly burly, robust and bellowing like a bull. He snorted and ranted. What hair he had was red and it often stood out like an Irish revolt. Together they formed the perfect spin bowling partnership.'

**CLARRIE GRIMMETT AND BILL O'REILLY IN SOUTH AFRICA, 1935–36**

| Tests | Test wickets | Average | Best | 5wI | Tour wickets | Average | Best |
|---|---|---|---|---|---|---|---|
| **Clarrie Grimmett** | | | | | | | |
| 5 | 44 | 14.59 | 7–40 | 5 | 92 | 14.80 | 7–40 |
| **Bill O'Reilly** | | | | | | | |
| 5 | 27 | 17.03 | 5–20 | 2 | 95 | 13.56 | 8–73 |

The tandem talents of O'Reilly and Grimmett saw Australia beaten in only three of 14 Tests they played together, spread over four series. They averaged 15 wickets in each of the eight Tests Australia won. In three drawn matches they averaged 10 a Test and in the three losses five a Test – two of these being in the extraordinary summer of Bodyline. Few pairs could so expertly build and maintain pressure at both ends. There was none of the wafty extravagances of Arthur Mailey. Both hated conceding runs, the Tiger particularly.

Their signature summer was on the Veld in 1935–36, when they were responsible for almost 75 per cent of the South African wickets. Grimmett, then 44, claimed 44 wickets (at 14 runs apiece) and O'Reilly 27 (at 17). Australia won four Tests and drew the other at high-altitude Johannesburg, where both struggled to adapt to the conditions, Grimmett taking just six wickets and O'Reilly five. At Durban they shared 17 wickets and at Cape Town and Johannesburg, 15.

In the final Test in South Africa at Kingsmead, Richardson at short leg took five of the last six wickets, three catches from the bowling of Grimmett and two from O'Reilly.

So lethal were the pair that Richardson included just one specialist new-ball bowler in Ernie McCormick in the Tests, allowing Stan McCabe to bowl his mediums for a few overs at the other end before enlisting his in-form spinners. The team's other new-ball specialist, Victorian Maurice Sievers, wasn't included in even one of the Tests.

For the tour, the pair aggregated almost 200 wickets and delivered more than 1300 overs. No-one else took even 50 wickets.

Their most successful Ashes Test together came at Trent Bridge in

1934 when they claimed 19 of the 20 English wickets to fall: O'Reilly 11 and Grimmett eight. The Australians won with just 10 minutes to spare.

Remarkably, Grimmett never played another Test after his record series haul in South Africa, despite his average of 40 wickets a year at domestic level with South Australia. Had Grimmett, rather than Frank Ward, toured England in 1938, O'Reilly always contended that the Ashes would have been comfortably retained rather than just squared. A fall-out with the all-powerful Bradman was almost certainly the key element in his puzzling non-selection. Years later I wrote to Bradman, querying in particular Grimmett's non-selection for the 1938 Ashes tour. Bradman replied that Grimmett, then 46, was 'finished'.

He didn't elaborate, but O'Reilly did, saying Grimmett had upset Bradman during a Sheffield Shield game in Melbourne when Bradman had been dismissed late in the day, just before Australia's fastest bowler, McCormick, was about to take the second new ball. In front of his teammates, Grimmett queried the timing of Bradman's dismissal – 'You didn't want to face the music, did you?' – the clear inference that the Don was intimidated by the likely onslaught of bouncers from McCormick. Bradman was said to be angered and Grimmett, O'Reilly always believed, was the victim of one throwaway line.

'Young Ken,' he told me, 'you don't piss on statues.'

Grimmett never forgave Bradman for not including him for the tour. Instead Bradman went with Frank Ward, from his old Sydney club St George, Ward playing just one unsuccessful Test. O'Reilly termed Grimmett's exclusion as 'shameful' and said his old mate carried the scars to his grave.

O'Reilly said bowling in tandem with Grimmett was always a joy and, especially early, he was pivotal in O'Reilly's bowling success as he taught him the need for patience, accuracy, change-ups and variety.

'We bowled together in perfect harmony,' O'Reilly said, 'each with a careful eye on the other. With him at the other end I knew full well that no batsman would be allowed the slightest respite. "Grum" loved to bowl into the wind which gave him the opportunity to use wind resistance as an important adjunct to his schemes.'

The pair remained the closest of friends for years and when the Test cricket came to town, they would meet up in the old open-air press box in the Mostyn-Evans Stand and saunter downstairs for a cool one or two. Until he met O'Reilly, Grimmett never touched a drink. Tiger changed all that.

## TWO OLD PROS

They first opened during the 'Victory' tests of 1945, one a Yorkie and the other a Lancastrian. Together they became England's finest opening pair since Hobbs and Sutcliffe.

Len Hutton and Cyril Washbrook combined in eight century partnerships in Tests, featured in three 100-plus stands in a row on tour against the powerful Australians in 1946–47, and a high of 359 against the South Africans in high-altitude Johannesburg in 1948–49. Another of their most satisfying matches came at Leeds against the mighty 1948 Australians, when they started with 168 and 129 in one of the great Ashes Tests of all.

Hutton would always take the first ball and was always so correct and assured that most others around him automatically gained in confidence. In Washbrook, Hutton saw a determined, resolute fellow Northerner, unperturbed by pace, who could bat for time as well as play shots, accelerating the run-rate as in Johannesburg when they

### FIFTY-THREE OF THE BEST: HUTTON AND WASHBROOK IN TESTS

| Opponent | Innings | Not Outs | Runs | Best | Average | 100s |
|---|---|---|---|---|---|---|
| Australia | 21 | 0 | 1042 | 168 | 49.61 | 5 |
| India | 5 | 1 | 200 | 81 | 50.00 | – |
| New Zealand | 4 | 0 | 177 | 103 | 44.25 | 1 |
| South Africa | 19 | 2 | 1371 | 359 | 80.64 | 2 |
| West Indies | 2 | 0 | 90 | 62 | 45.00 | – |
| **Total** | **51** | **3** | **2860** | **359** | **59.55** | **8** |

* The figures do not include two stands between the pair batting lower-down the list.

averaged 74 runs an hour in a rare assault on the South Africans.

'Without question, Cyril was the best Test opening partner I had,' said Hutton. 'We had much in common. We had learned our cricket in similar northern surroundings. We gave each other confidence. No matter how experienced a batsman might be, he likes to have some assurance from his partner and there were times when my partners were so overcome by the occasion that they were half out before they took guard.'

Above all, Hutton liked Washbrook's composure, even under direct fire as against the two Australian expresses Ray Lindwall and Keith Miller in back-to-back post-war Ashes campaigns, and against the slippery South African Cuan McCarthy in 1948–49. The artillery of short balls saw Washbrook regularly employ his favourite hooks and cuts. While others later in the order were daunted by the pace, he always portrayed a comforting calmness and assurance. In Brisbane, a nasty delivery from Miller reared and took his cap off, yet he was right in behind the next, competing, always the old pro.

In the second Test, in Sydney, their lightning stand of 49 was also memorable with Hutton making a quickfire 37 against a 20-minute bouncer blitz from Keith Miller, the one bowler Hutton admitted he never felt physically safe against. Washbrook had the best seat in the house that early afternoon as Hutton blazed away against Miller and Fred Freer.

'Len dealt with them in a manner I have never seen equalled,' said Washbrook. 'I'm quite sure the bowlers did not know where to put the ball to him. I enjoyed myself at the other end giving him all the bowling he wanted. It was a classic knock from one of the great players of them all.'

The pair shared five century stands at first-class level that memorable summer and a sixth in a second-class fixture in Canberra when they made an Australian-high 254.

Their complemented each other beautifully, Washbrook indulging himself against short bowling and Hutton, the technician, stroking the fuller-length balls through the covers. He was a master through the offside, his 364 against the 1938 Australians still the highest score by an Englishman in Tests.

**Spin Brotherhood:** West Indian spinners Alf Valentine (left) and Sonny Ramadhin on their first Australian tour in 1951–52.

# U

**'Val was asking "when does so-and-so come in?" – only to be told that he'd just got him out!'**

## ULTIMATE WILDCARDS

Until 1950 they were absolute unknowns. By the end of their remarkable first international tour together, West Indian cricket fans were singing tribute calypsos to 'Those two little pals of mine, Ramadhin and Valentine. . .'

Sonny Ramadhin from Trinidad and Alf Valentine from Jamaica together accounted for almost 60 wickets in the Tests and 258 wickets for the tour as the West Indies stunned England, winning three Tests of four in the never-to-be-forgotten summer of 1950.

The two 20-year-old spinners, Ramadhin, right-arm, and Valentine, left, perplexed and paralysed like they were O'Reilly and Grimmett.

At just 163 cm (5 ft 4 in) and barely 58 kg (9 st), Ramadhin was the size of a jockey and flicked off- and leg-breaks with the inside of his index and middle fingers with a totally stiff wrist. He insisted on keeping his cap on while he bowled. With his shirt sleeves buttoned to the wrist and each-way spin, he was very much a mystery man. He'd shuffle to the wicket from four or five paces back and propel the ball with a windmill action, hardly stopping to pivot.

The bespectacled Valentine, taller and just as slim, had also played just two games with modest returns, but like Ramadhin impressed the West Indies captain John Goddard, who believed his brand of finger spin could be ideally suited to English wickets. Like Ramadhin, whose only two previous major matches had been on matting, Valentine was largely uncoached. He looked to spin the ball as hard

**Giantkillers:** John Goddard's 1950 West Indians who stunned the might of England. Back row, left to right: Bill 'Fergie' Ferguson (scorer), Alf Valentine, Clyde Walcott, Hines Johnson, Lance Pierre, Allan Rae, Roy Marshall, Cecil Williams. Seated: Everton Weekes, Robert Christiani, Jeff Stollmeyer, Goddard (captain), J. M. Kidney (manager), Gerry Gomez, Prior Jones, Frank Worrell. Seated: Sonny Ramadhin, Ken Trestrail.

as he could each and every time, had genuine 'loop' and a big heart. Around his bowling wrist bounced a gold chain for good luck.

The pair dominated from their first Test together at Old Trafford, where they claimed 15 of the 19 English wickets which fell to the bowlers. At Lord's their share was 18, at Trent Bridge 12 and at Kennington Oval 14. So rattled were the English selectors that they played 25 in the series, including eight first-gamers. During the Notts Test, England's captain Norman Yardley suggested to his No. 1 spinner Eric Hollies that he should go and take a closer look at Ramadhin as he practised in the nets. As soon as Ramadhin saw Hollies, he put the ball in his pocket and refused to bowl any more.

Wicketkeeper Clyde Walcott said the Englishmen plunged into a complicated abyss as they sought theories on how to 'pick' Ramadhin's unique finger spins.

'Some said there were differences in his run-up for the off-break and leg-breaks. Some thought the leg-break was a slower ball, tossed further up. Some liked to play him off the back foot – but as soon

**Calypso Time:** Alf Valentine (*right*) enjoying some down time during the 1960–61 tour, Sydney.

## VICTORY AT LORD'S

A calypso* by Lord Beginner of Jamaica

*Cricket lovely cricket*
*At Lord's where I saw it*
*Cricket lovely cricket*
*At Lord's where I saw it*
*Yardley tried his best*
*Goddard won the Test*
*They gave the crowd plenty of fun*
*The Second Test that West Indies won.*

Chorus: *With those little pals of mine Ramadhin and Valentine*

*The King was there well attire*
*So they started with Rae and Stollymeyer*
*Stolly was hitting balls around the boundary*
*But Wardle stopped him at twenty*
*Rae had confidence*
*So he put up a strong defence*
*He saw the King was waiting to see*
*So he gave him a century*

Chorus: *With those little pals of mine Ramadhin and Valentine*

*West Indies first innings total*
*Was three-twenty-six just as usual*
*When Bedser bowled Christiani*
*The whole team collapse quite easy*
*England then went on*
*And made one hundred and fifty one*
*West Indies then had two-twenty lead*
*Goddard said, 'That is nice indeed.'*

Chorus: *With those little pals of mine Ramadhin and Valentine*

*Yardley wasn't broken-hearted*
*When the second innings started*
*Jenkins was right on target*
*Taking the first five into his basket*
*But Gomez broke him down*
*While Walcott licked them around*
*He was not out for one-sixty-eight*
*Leaving Yardley to contemplate*

Chorus: *The bowling was superfine Ramadhin and Valentine*

*West Indies was feeling homely*
*The audience had them happy*
*When Washbrook's century had ended*
*West Indies' voices were blended*
*Hats went in the air*
*People jump and shout without fear*
*Oh, at Lord's was the scenery*
*It bound to go down in history.*

Chorus: *After all is said and done*
*The Second Test that West Indies won*

* By September 1950, the calypso had sold 8000 discs.

**SUMMER OF SPIN: SONNY RAMADHIN AND ALF VALENTINE IN ENGLAND IN 1950**

| Tests | Matches | Overs | Maidens | Wickets | Average | Best | 5wI |
|---|---|---|---|---|---|---|---|
| | | | **Ramadhin** | | | | |
| 4 | | 377.5 | 170 | 26 | 23.23 | 6–86 | 3 |
| | | | **Valentine** | | | | |
| 4 | | 422.3 | 197 | 33 | 20.42 | 8–104 | 2 |
| | | | *Next best:* | | | | |
| | | | **John Goddard** | | | | |
| 4 | | 74.4 | 29 | 6 | 20.33 | 4–25 | – |
| **First class** | **Matches** | **Overs** | **Maidens** | **Wickets** | **Average** | **Best** | **5wI** |
| | | | **Ramadhin** | | | | |
| | 21 | 1043.4 | 398 | 135 | 14.88 | 8–15 | 15 |
| | | | **Valentine** | | | | |
| | 4 | 1185.2 | 475 | 123 | 17.94 | 8–26 | 10 |
| | | | *Next best:* | | | | |
| | | | **Gerry Gomez** | | | | |
| | 27 | 680.3 | 221 | 55 | 25.58 | 5–34 | 2 |

## OPENERS TO AVERAGE 100-PLUS IN A SERIES

| Average | Runs | Openers |
|---|---|---|
| 138.8 | 694 | Graeme Smith and Herschelle Gibbs (South Africa) v West Indies (home), 2003–04 |
| 136.8 | 684 | Desmond Haynes and Gordon Greenidge (West Indies) v Australia (home), 1983 |
| 130.3 | 521 | Terry Jarvis and Glenn Turner (New Zealand) v West Indies (home), 1971–72 |
| 118.7 | 712 | Jack Hobbs and Herbert Sutcliffe (England) v Australia (home), 1926 |
| 118 | 472 | Bill Lawry and Bobby Simpson (Australia) v England (home), 1965–66 |
| 114.5 | 458 | Michael Slater and Greg Blewett (Australia) v Pakistan (home), 1999–2000 |
| **Other Australians:** | | |
| 114 | 570 | Matthew Hayden and Justin Langer v South Africa (home), 2001–02 |
| 112.8 | 451 | Matthew Hayden and Justin Langer v New Zealand (home), 2001–02 |
| 108.5 | 434 | Arthur Morris and Colin McDonald v West Indies (away), 1955 |
| 107.7 | 323 | David Boon and Geoff Marsh v India (home), 1985–86 |
| 103 | 721 | Bill Brown and Jack Fingleton v South Africa (away), 1935–36 |
| **Most runs in a series by an Australian opening pair:** | | |
| 74 | 823 | Mark Taylor and Geoff Marsh v England (away), 1989 |

(Minimum innings 4)

as they started doing that, we knew their days were numbered,' he said.

One of the BBC commentators was so taken by the accuracy of Ramadhin and Valentine and their sequence of maidens that he quipped: 'There were more maidens than ladies at Lord's today!'

Valentine hadn't even bothered to mark out his run-up at Old Trafford, yet took the first eight English wickets to fall in a colossal start. According to historian David Frith, 'Val was asking "when does so-and-so come in?" – only to be told that he'd just got him out!'

In all he helped himself to 33 wickets at more than eight a Test. Ramadhin took 26, including 11 at Lord's, where the West Indians won for the first time. West Indian ex-pats invaded the famous field dancing and singing calypsos.

'Ram' and Val were never to be quite as startlingly effective again as a pair, but they had their moments and as wildcard selections they remain the finest of all.

## UNEXPECTED

It remains one of the few times Bangladeshi cricketers have appeared in the record books besides the highest profiled cricketers of them all. In the two-Test series in England in 2010, openers Tamim Iqbal and Imrul Kayes joined an elite group of just 14 opening pairs to average 100 over the series.

Batting four times, they shared two century stands, the most notable 185 at Lord's, just 24 hours after Test great Geoff Boycott had declared that the Bangladeshi attack was unfit for Test cricket. Taking it as a slight on the entire XI, Tamim struck England's champion slow bowler Graeme Swann for six, four, six, in three balls on his way to a 94-ball century. Asked about the quality of England's attack, Tamim declared later he'd formed no opinion as he'd been too busy putting the bad balls away!

Other opening pairs to also average 100-plus included Australians Bill Brown and Jack Fingleton (1935), Colin McDonald and Arthur Morris (1955), David Boon and Geoff Marsh (1985–86) and Matthew Hayden and Justin Langer twice (both times in 2001–02).

NatWest
NatWest
NatWest

# V

**'For hour after hour, under the pressure of knowing that if he got out, the series was lost, he produced batsmanship that was beyond the imagination. . .'**

## VERY VERY SPECIAL

Michael Slater pulled a box of cigars from his kitbag and theatrically started smelling one: 'Oh yeah baby,' he said. 'Tonight. . . here we go tonight.' Captain Steve Waugh had his customary celebratory bottle of Southern Comfort at the ready. His 2000–01 Australians, on their 'Final Frontier' tour, were poised to inflict the knockout blow at Eden Gardens, Kolkata and win a series in India for the first time in more than 30 years.

Having forfeited the first Test in under three days and been asked to follow on 274 runs behind in the second, the Indians had already lost two of their main men, Sachin Tendulkar and captain Sourav Ganguly. At 4–254, it seemed inevitable that the confident, all-conquering Australians would extend their unbeaten streak to 17 wins in a row, especially with champion pair Glenn McGrath and Shane Warne in the XI.

Most in the rooms, even wicketkeeper Adam Gilchrist, giggled as Slater clowned around. Gilchrist had played 15 Tests and not lost even one. Normally, though, he was the last to show any sign of complacency. But he, like everyone else, honestly thought the Australians were 'home'.

---

**'The Wall':** Rahul Dravid shared the epic partnership with VVS Laxman which stopped Australia's record run of 16 consecutive Test wins at Eden Gardens. *Australian Cricket Summer Guide*

**Matchwinner:** Cricket's iconic wrist spinner Shane Warne delivering one of his signature leg-breaks. He amassed more than 700 Test wickets having been fast-tracked into the Test team before he'd truly deserved selection.

India's two not-out batsmen overnight were VVS Laxman and Rahul Dravid, one an exhilarating shotmaker and the other a master of organisation with such a tight defence that he was known as 'The Wall'.

Laxman had been last man out in the first innings for 59 and was told by coach John Wright to keep his pads on after the Australians enforced the follow-on. Waugh had sought the opinion of his players on whether they should bat again – or bowl again. Only one, opener

Michael Slater, reckoned they should set a huge target and bowl when the wicket was at its most weathered. The rest wanted to go straight back out again. As Waugh was walking across to the Indian rooms to inform Ganguly, Wright was in a confab with Laxman. He wanted a strokemaker at No. 3 – someone to come in and dominate. Dravid, who normally batted three, was classy and focused, but he could be slow.

'We need to take the Australians on,' Wright said to 'VVS'. Having been so easily beaten in Mumbai and again been comprehensively outplayed in the first two days in Kolkata, he wanted India to be proactive and take risks. Wright particularly remembered Laxman's inspired 167 against the Australians in the New Year Test 15 months earlier, an innings of carefree genius which saw him dubbed 'Very Very Special' by the Australian cricket media.

Despite going into the second Test with a troublesome back injury, which made it impossible for him to stand upright, the clean-hitting Laxman was clearly his team's in-form player. Having top-scored in the first innings, he duly went in at No. 3 and rocketed to three figures, striking seventeen 4s in his second century in three Tests against the Australians. Wright's hunch had paid off beautifully, with Laxman 109 and Dravid 7 overnight.

Despite Laxman's brilliance, the Australians were still virtually unbackable favourites, especially with the second new ball due almost immediately on the fourth morning. Many were in party mood as they trailed onto India's most famous ground, smiling and cracking jokes. None had any idea that they were about to field through an entire day without even a half-chance.

Laxman set the tone early by taking four boundaries from one over from Jason Gillespie. The first was an inside edge but the others were right out of the screws, two through the covers and the third to the square boundary, backward of point.

Having caressed Michael Kasprowicz through mid-on, he danced at Warne bowling around the wicket and hit him 'inside out' over the top of extra cover. It was exhilarating batting.

'For hour after hour,' said Wright, 'under the pressure of knowing that if he got out, the series was lost, he produced batsmanship that was beyond the imagination, let alone the capability of most batsmen. It was the greatest innings I've ever seen.'

The only genuine appeal from the Australians all day came when Ricky Ponting, bowling slow mediums, struck Dravid's front pad just before lunch.

'It was our nearest thing all day,' said Gilchrist. 'They just didn't give us a sniff.'

The Indians advanced their score from 4–254 to a massive 4–589, Laxman adding 166 and Dravid 148. Warne kept aiming for the rough outside Laxman's leg stump and he kept running at him and hitting him over the infield. When he wasn't slapping him to the extra cover boundary, he was going high over mid-wicket. It was electrifying batting. At intervals, India's physiotherapist Andrew Leipus worked feverishly on Laxman's back, trying to 're-align' him. When Dravid seemed out on his feet from dehydration and was cramping, Wright yelled at Leipus to 'Get him fit!' Wright gave him a red tablet, said it was for anti-cramping, and Dravid carried on. As the pair turned one century into two and two into three, they constantly urged each other to maintain focus and not play a poor shot.

'There were times when I was tiring and not timing the ball well,' said Laxman, 'and Rahul would exhort me to keep going. I did the same when he started tiring. Our teammates, the crowd, everyone was involved.'

Both were clearly discomforted after tea but refused to relent, Laxman continuing to throw haymakers at the Australian bowlers. When Waugh stacked his offside with a seventh fieldsman, Laxman power drove a ball with such speed that even the boundary rider at point had no chance. Waugh used nine bowlers, Justin Langer, in his only over in Test cricket, being the last before stumps.

Back in the rooms Laxman and Dravid were placed on saline drips. It had been a titanic fightback and against one of the greatest teams in Test history. Australia's remarkable winning streak was all but over. With a lead of 315, India was now the hunter.

Over dinner at Ganguly's Kolkata mansion that night, Ganguly and Wright agreed India should continue batting for another hour, totally taking the game away from the Australians and yet still having five hours in which to bowl them out.

After Dravid was run out for a brave 180, ending their epic 104-over stand, Laxman was last out at 281 before the declaration at 7–657. Together they'd added 376, the second-highest stand by any set of Indian batsmen in Tests. Four of the Australians had conceded 100 runs and more, Warne the most expensive at one for 152.

Australia's target was an unassailable 384. Many thought Ganguly had unnecessarily delayed the declaration, especially when the Australians were none down at lunch. By tea, it was three down and the Indian spinners were starting to press. Steve Waugh was out almost immediately afterwards, triggering a collapse. 'The Turbanator' Harbhajan Singh took six wickets and Tendulkar three, including Gilchrist for a king pair. The crowd had swelled to close to 100,000 and the noise level was amazing as the Australian big names departed. When Waugh was the first out after the interval at 4–166, the Australian room went deathly quiet and the last six wickets fell for just 48, India winning with half an hour to spare, dozens of celebratory fires being lit all around the ground. Only two other Test teams had won following on.

Before boarding the team bus, Gilchrist saw one of Slater's celebratory cigars and snapped it in half. It had been the one that got away.

# W

**‘Australia did not lose even one home Test for 10 years while *both* McGrath and Warne were present. . .’**

## ‘WHAT ARE YOU DOING OUT HERE?’

It was cricket’s most moving and dramatic moment, an indelible chapter in the annals of New Zealand.

Emerging from the dark tunnel at Ellis Park was Wellington apprentice printer and part-time fast bowler Bob Blair, tears rolling down his cheeks, fumbling with his gloves. No-one knew he was going to bat. Earlier that day he’d learnt his fiancée Nerissa Love had been among the 151 killed back home in the Tangiwai train disaster in the centre of the North Island on Christmas Eve 1953.

Grief-stricken, he’d remained at the team’s hotel in Johannesburg, listening to the description of the match on the radio.

On a brutal green-top, the Kiwi top-order was being bruised and battered. Lawrie Miller was coughing up blood having been struck a tremendous blow on the chest. Master batsman Bert Sutcliffe was ‘pinged’ – on the left ear – by a vicious Neil Adcock bumper, splitting his ear lobe. He fell like a stone. Next-man-in John Reid took guard in a pool of blood and was hit five times in as many minutes. Matt Poore played a couple of tennis shots over the slips, before being struck by Adcock and watching helplessly as the ball trickled onto his wicket.

---

**Courage Above and Beyond:** Bert Sutcliffe’s bravery was central in one of New Zealand cricket’s never-to-be-forgotten moments at Ellis Park in 1953–54.

Meanwhile Sutcliffe, ferried straight to hospital, twice fainted during treatment. Despite complaining of double vision, he insisted on returning to the ground, his skull swathed in bandages. It was announced that he would not bat again, but the Kiwis were in dire straits with half the team out for 57, still more than 200 behind South Africa's first innings score of 271. The follow-on beckoned.

Sutcliffe called for a bottle of whisky, downed a glass and started re-buckling his pads.

'What are you doing?' asked captain Geoff Rabone.

'I'm going to bat.'

'No you're not.'

'Yes I am, Skip. Look at the scoreboard. We're in the shit.'

At the fall of the next wicket, New Zealand was 6–81, or effectively 7–81 with Blair absent.

Sutcliffe entered to an excited round of chatter, his black cap perched precariously on his head, only partially hiding the bandages. He looked dazed and was unsteady on his feet. Author Norman Harris says even the South Africans applauded his bravery in returning so soon after such a sickening blow.

Having quietly played two balls from the medium-paced Dave Ironside, Sutcliffe swung the third over the square leg fence. One of the most memorable and electrifying Test innings in history had begun.

'The pitch was still unpredictable and the score unprepossessing. Attack was the only answer,' Sutcliffe said later.

First series terror Adcock, who had repeatedly hit New Zealand's top-order batsmen on the bouncy, two-paced wicket, was brought back and Sutcliffe, with regal disdain, struck him to the point boundary. South Africa's ace slow bowler Hugh Tayfield had his first off-break lifted over the long-on fence for six. Tayfield dropped his length and Sutcliffe moved back and pulled him through mid-wicket. Another boundary.

Fifty against-the-odds runs were added in the most thrilling of half an hours before New Zealand's wicketkeeper Frank Mooney was bowled. Tailenders Tony MacGibbon and Guy Overton quickly followed and with the scoreline at 9–154 and believing Blair to be back at his hotel, the Springboks began to leave the field. Suddenly they all stopped. There was a huge roar around the ground. Blair was standing all alone in the tunnel. He was coming out after all. Inspired by Sutcliffe's heroic return, he'd taken a taxi to the ground, quickly changed and put on his pads.

An eerie silence fell across the ground. Blair walked ever-so-slowly, trying to accustom his eyes from the darkness of the tunnel to the searing sunshine. To a man the spectators around the ground rose, standing in complete and poignant silence. Looking down at the scene from the glass windows of the pavilion, Blair's teammates wept openly. The South Africans on the field were in little better state.

Blair stumbled to the wicket still struggling with his gloves to be met by Sutcliffe, head swathed in bandages. Draping his arm around his mate, Sutcliffe asked, 'What are you doing out here?'

'I want to bat.'

'Are you sure?'

'We're in trouble, so I'm out here.'

The South African fieldsmen had formed a channel and clapped as Sutcliffe walked back to the wicket with Blair. Their applause echoed around the ground, before falling silent again. Everyone was still standing. Blair had to be told which end to walk to and that he was on strike. Hardly bothering to take guard, he faced up only after wiping more tears from his eyes. Somehow he survived the final two balls of the over, which were both wide of the wickets.

One eye-witness said: 'Before he faced his first ball, Blair passed his glove across his eyes in a heart-wringing gesture of any small boy anywhere, in trouble, defiant. His was a courage unexcelled in a match which made heavy demands on the New Zealanders. To take physical knocks and come back for more is admirable, but to carry on after one's world has fallen about one's ears surely requires an effort quite out of the ordinary.'

Sutcliffe's way was to attack even more ferociously than before. With the field spread far and wide, he lifted Tayfield for three 6s for the over before taking a single from the seventh ball. To frenzied applause, Blair hit the eighth clean out of the ground. Twenty-five runs in an over! 'Toey' Tayfield, the most renowned off-spinner in the world, was on the wrong end of a new world record.

In 10 incredible minutes, 33 additional runs were added, before Blair was stumped. Sutcliffe, 80 not out, in just over even time, had lifted seven marvellous 6s. Only the South African Jimmy Sinclair and the Englishmen Walter Hammond had hit more in a Test innings.

The two gallant New Zealanders walked off together, arm in arm, back through the tunnel and into the visitors' rooms, the tremendous applause lasting long after they'd disappeared.

'They say a man should be made of sterner stuff,' said Sutcliffe, 'but without sentiment, there is nothing. This was Bob Blair's day; and it was a wonder how he stayed those 10 minutes, for he could not see properly to the other end of the pitch.'

Noted New Zealand cricket writer Dick Brittenden said: 'This was indeed triumph from tragedy, a great and glorious victory. . . a story every New Zealand boy should learn at his mother's knee.'

The Kiwis had avoided the follow-on, but were to lose the match in four days, the pace of 20-year-old Springbok express Adcock simply too much for them. He took eight wickets for the game as New Zealand, needing 233 runs for victory in the second innings, collapsed for 100.

The result was insignificant. The gallantry of Blair and Sutcliffe is forever etched in New Zealand cricket history.

'It was also the most emotional moment of all,' said Rabone. 'Blair was a character who took a bit of getting through to and the girl he had met was one who had a big influence on him. He was deeply in love with her and was totally knocked over when news of her death came through.'

## 'WHAT DID YOU DECLARE FOR?'

Steve Waugh reckoned he and twin brother Mark could have gone on and made 1000.

'What did you declare for?' he demanded of New South Wales captain Geoff Lawson as he re-entered the WACA dressing rooms.

**RECORD AUSTRALIAN FIRST-CLASS PARTNERSHIPS**

| Wicket | Runs | Batsmen |
|---|---|---|
| First | 456 | Bill Ponsford (248) and Edgar Mayne (209)<br>Victoria v Queensland, Melbourne, 1923–24 |
| Second | 451 | Bill Ponsford and Don Bradman<br>Australia v England, The Oval, 1934 |
| Third | 290* | Julien Wiener and Jeff Moss<br>Victoria v Western Australia, St Kilda Cricket Ground, 1981–82 |
| Fourth | 462* | David Hookes and Wayne Phillips<br>South Australia v Tasmania, Adelaide 1986–87 |
| Fifth | 464* | Mark Waugh and Steve Waugh<br>New South Wales v Western Australia, Perth, 1990–91 |
| Sixth | 428 | Warwick Armstrong and MA 'Monty' Noble<br>Australia v Sussex, Hove, 1902 |
| Seventh | 335 | Charlie Andrews and Eric Bensted<br>Queensland v New South Wales, Sydney, 1934–35 |
| Eighth | 433 | Arthur Sims and Victor Trumper<br>Australians v Canterbury, Christchurch, 1913–14 |
| Ninth | | Clem Hill and Edgar Walkley<br>South Australia v New South Wales, Adelaide, 1900–01 |
| Tenth | 307 | Alan Kippax and JEH Hooker<br>New South Wales v Victoria, Sydney, 1911–12 |

* denotes not out

The brothers had just created a new Australian high of 464 for any partnership at first-class level.

While Steve had been a Test regular, Mark was still a month away from making his Test debut. Neither had previously passed 50 in Perth and Steve, after a mixed season, was keen to make up for lost ground. Their partnership was cricket at its most majestic. Rod Marsh felt the entertainment surpassed even Barry Richards' 325 in a day at the WACA 20 years earlier.

Their 464 surpassed the previous record of 462 by David Hookes and Wayne Phillips for South Australia four years earlier. It was also the first time any New South Wales pair had scored so many in a single stand, surpassing the 397 by Warren Bardsley and Charlie Kelleway in 1920.

The pair scored at better than a run a minute throughout, Steve making 216 and Mark 229. Lawson's answer to Waugh was to get ready.

'You're opening [the bowling]!'

Western Australia followed on but saved the game in the final session in one of the most remembered draws of them all.

## WHERE DID THEY CELEBRATE? MACCAS OF COURSE!

Pakistan was charging towards a famous victory down under. Saqlain Mushtaq had decimated the Australians in the first innings with his combination of off-breaks, top-spinners and mysterious doosras. Speedsters Wasim Akram, Waqar Younis and Shoaib Akhtar went headhunting in the second, threatening to end the game as early as the fourth night.

Adam Gilchrist, in his second Test, joined Justin Langer in the middle at Bellerive with Australia a precarious 5–126. They'd been set 369. The Waugh twins were out. Local hero Ricky Ponting had made a pair. The light was fading. And the ball was reversing.

'You never, never know,' said Langer, who was in his mid-30s. 'If we can hang in here until stumps we might be half a chance tomorrow. Mate, we could just make Test history here.'

Gilchrist didn't take him seriously but returned his grin and started to play his shots. He knew no other way. It had taken a near-eternity for Ian Healy to be retired and 'Gilly' had moved from one side of Australia to the other to be recognised. Having made a quickfire 80 on debut in Healy-loving Brisbane and turned the hoots into cheers, he was in a hurry to show that he truly belonged and was worthy of taking the Queensland champion's place. By stumps he was 45. When it was up, he drove. When it was short, he hooked or cut. It was the type of exhilarating counter-attacking which was to become his signature. At 5–188 at stumps, the Australians were at least hanging in against the odds.

Among the guests at the game were four of Don Bradman's Invincibles, including 87-year-old Bill Brown, who had presented Gilchrist with his baggy green cap just weeks earlier at the Gabba. At breakfast the following morning, Brown said to Gilchrist: 'We'll need a century out of you today!' Overnight Gilchrist had watched the movie *Jerry Maguire* and promised himself that if the Australians happened to win from nowhere, he'd dance like Rod Tidwell after he'd scored a touchdown!

There had been some overnight rain and initial hopes of a wash-out, given Australia's dire situation. But come the morning, the skies were a brilliant blue and with 10 overs before the next new ball was due, Pakistan opened with second-stringer Azhar Mahmood and Saqlain.

'They played into our hands,' said Langer. 'With Waqar, Wasim and Shoaib at their disposal, the last thing I expected were some "sighters" from Azhar. Even though he was whippy and reverse-swung the ball, his slightly slower pace allowed us to play ourselves in. By the time the quicker men came on, we were set.'

At 75, Langer nicked Akram through to keeper Moin Khan, but umpire Peter Parker turned down the concerted, extended appeal. At 5–237 another 132 were still required. It was a huge moment in the game. The Pakistanis were beside themselves and Shoaib, the fastest bowler in the game, produced a searing spell, striking Langer on the chin with a bouncer. Rather than showing any distress, Langer bounced up and started grinning at the Pakistanis.

'Mate, you're crazy!' said Gilchrist.

'Bring it on,' said Langer. 'I bloody love it.'

By lunch just 92 were needed. The game was stopping a nation, Parliamentary debate being interrupted for the score. Langer and Gilchrist were encouraging each other after virtually every ball.

'Thiss ball,' they'd say, 'thisss ball.'

Both left-handers reached their centuries, Gilchrist first, having given Langer 35 runs head start. Pakistan was panicking and despite their fast-bowling riches and a wearing fifth day wicket, they were leaking runs everywhere. With 20 to go, Langer did a Lleyton Hewitt fist-up and a 'Come-oonnnn' in the direction of the dressing room. It

**FIVE OTHER FAMOUS FOURTH INNINGS RUN CHASES**

| | | |
|---|---|---|
| 7–418 | West Indies | v Australia, St John's, 2002–03 |
| 4–406 | India | v West Indies, Port-of-Spain, 1975–76 |
| 3–404 | Australia | v England, Headingley, 1948 |
| 4–387 | India | v England, Chidambaram Stadium, 2008–09 |
| 7–362 | Australia | v West Indies, Bourda, 1977–78 |

was his mightiest Test innings and while he was out within a six-hit of the victory, Gilchrist soon ensured a famous four-wicket win.

The win had reminded the old Invincibles of Headingley, 1948. It had been the third highest fourth innings run chase in history.

Gilchrist (149 not out) and Langer (127) had shared a stand of 238 against an opposing attack with almost 1000 Test wickets to their credit. It was one of Australia's greatest wins and the second in a streak of 16 wins in a row, justifying the team's tag of being 'modern-day Invincibles'.

That night's celebrations at an Irish pub in the heart of Hobart included a Gilchrist soft-shoe shuffle *à la* Tidwell, before the players, many still in their whites and baggy greens, headed off to a nearby McDonald's for a Big Mac and a couple of impromptu key lines from *Underneath the Southern Cross I Stand. . .* 'Australia you #@^&ing beauty!'

## WINNING THE UNWINNABLE

One thousand and one Test wickets together! Never has there been a more potent bowling pair. It's little wonder Australian teams featuring Glenn McGrath and Shane Warne won an unprecedented 16 Tests in a row and were undisputed champions of the world for a decade and a half.

It was the ultimate luxury to have two of the finest and most celebrated bowlers in the same XI operating in tandem. Thanks to them, Australia won Test matches it had no right to.

While one was a fast bowler and the other a leg-spinner, they complemented each other superbly, McGrath with his seam, kicking bounce and unerring accuracy, and Warne with his astonishing side-spin, variations and attitude which made him the game's quintessential matchwinner.

They were the first graduates from the Australian Cricket Academy to make international ranks, Warne's ride rockier than McGrath's after he was suspended for ill-discipline and was bussed back from Darwin to Adelaide. Fast-tracked into international cricket before he had served any meaningful apprenticeship, Warne had one focus: to change the course of games with a big wicket or two. The Richie Richardson flipper, the Mike Gatting 'Ball of the Century', the Shiv Chanderpaul back-break in Sydney. . . the memories of Warne's very best from his early days are still vivid. Later he became the grand master of spin, his decorations including *Wisden* Cricketer of the Century status. About the only accolade the Victorian missed was taking a 'five-for' at Lord's and having his name on the most famous of all cricketing honour boards.

McGrath, from Narromine in country New South Wales, had been 'discovered' after dismissing a mature-aged Doug Walters in an exhibition match. Tall and committed, he hated conceding even singles. Behind the easy-going country boy's smile was a coiled tiger who clinically bailed up batsmen before delivering withering knockout punches.

It mattered little if Australia was attacking or defending, McGrath and Warne were the ultimate pairing, who stymied and shut down opponents before dismissing them one by one from the biggest names down. In a star-studded era for Australian cricket, they were durable, determined and more dynamic than any of Australia's other champions – Ricky Ponting, Matthew Hayden, Adam Gilchrist. . . even the Waugh twins.

'I used to love bowling in tandem with Pigeon [McGrath],' said Warne. 'We would wear down batsmen into making a mistake and challenge their patience and techniques. Glenn had the uncanny knack of being able to change gear and take an important wicket when it really mattered.'

Combining for the first time against the New Zealanders in Perth in 1993–94, the pair survived injury, suspension, selection rebuff and family crisis to be on the frontline for 15 years. Australia did not lose even one home Test for 10 years while *both* McGrath and Warne were present. And it never lost even one home Ashes Test in their time together.

'We just knew if I was bowling at one end and he was at the other, something would happen,' said Warne. 'I put a lot of my wickets down to having Glenn bowl at the other end. I was very lucky to have someone with such accuracy and high concentration levels.'

Few top batsmen could play either with comfort, Indian Sachin Tendulkar (average 85) an exception against Warne, and the New Zealander Nathan Astle (70) batting above his fighting weight against McGrath.

Both embarrassed a host of cricket's biggest names. In Tests from 1999 to 2007:

- England's Mike Atherton averaged under 7 in direct one-on-ones against Warne and 14 against McGrath. His overall career average was 37.
- South Africa's AB de Villiers averaged 8 against Warne and Sri Lanka's Sanath Jayasuriya 7 against McGrath.
- England's Andrew Strauss fell eight times to Warne and averaged just 17, while another captain, Nasser Hussain, averaged 9 against McGrath.

Thriving on the challenge of competition and relishing the responsibility of so often being pivotal to Australia's Test and one day international fortunes, the pair dominated in the 1990s and into the new millennium. On the rare occasions where one was quiet, the other would invariably step up.

In 1999 in the Caribbean when Warne returned too quickly from a shoulder operation, bowled poorly and was controversially dropped from the deciding fourth Test in St John's, McGrath relished the extra responsibility, taking 30 wickets to be Australia's pivotal player in the squaring of one of the great series of all. Few were as enveloped by white line fever, and in the deciding Test at St John's, so hard did he kick a boundary wall in frustration at what he considered to be a poor umpiring decision, he all but broke his foot.

When McGrath stepped on a ball during the warm-ups at Edgbaston in 2005 and was carried out from the back of the Old Pavilion on a stretcher and ferried to the nearby Priory Hospital – his Test over before it had even started – Warne took 10 wickets in the greatest solos of his career, despite vicious taunts from the crowd about his private life being in tatters. The more the rowdies jeered and hooted, the more he bowed in their direction. Even in adversity, he was the grand showman. Coach John Buchanan and teammates marvelled at how Warne could switch on and be such a powerful and influential player despite the arguments and off-field acrimony which were to result in his much-publicised divorce. McGrath struggled with injuries throughout that 2005 summer, Warne taking a Test-best 40 wickets in the greatest Ashes series of all.

The pair were integral to Australia's finest win in Ricky Ponting's time, against the 2006–07 Englishmen in Adelaide. Having started the match with 6–551 declared, England simply froze on the final day, handing Australia an extraordinary win, every bit as good as Headingley 1948 and Bourda 1978.

Only 17 wickets had fallen on the first four days. Warne was one of the few who truly believed a result was possible. England started the fifth and final day at 1–59 and an overall lead of 97. Just 10 runs came in the first 10 overs, Strauss and Ian Bell playing with exaggerated caution. The collapse began after Strauss was unlucky to be given out caught off his front pad. But his defensive mindset swept through the entire team and they capitulated meekly under the fieriest of Australian attacks. Bowling unchanged from the northern end, Warne was irresistible, taking four for 29 from 27 overs on a wicket still good for batting. Ponting alternated his pacemen from the river end, McGrath's 10 overs producing the final two wickets as the Englishmen were bowled out for 129. First innings hero Kevin Pietersen was a key wicket in the collapse, bowled off-stump attempting an ill-advised sweep shot before he was set. Warne claimed later that Pietersen's ego had got in the way of common sense.

England's No. 4 Paul Collingwood was marooned on 22, having batted 198 minutes in an Ashes go-slow which made England's 1950s snail Trevor Bailey look audacious.

**Celebration Time Again:** Australian teams of the late 1990s and early 2000s won a record 16 games on end thanks to the combined menace of Glenn McGrath and Shane Warne, cricket's finest ever bowling combination.

The Australians made the required 168 runs with three overs remaining and the entire team swept onto the field, hugging each other and completing a joyous lap of honour, arms raised in jubilation, hardly believing their good fortune. A still-stunned Ponting declared it the finest victory he'd ever been associated with – his 'go to' bowlers McGrath and particularly Warne having produced their best yet again when it counted most.

Later that summer, on Warne's Test retirement, Ponting said Warne 'was probably the greatest cricketer there has ever been'. Certainly he was the greatest team man of his time who inspired and encouraged those around him like no-one else. His amazing impact on the game was truly Bradman-like and he rightly stands with the Don in the pantheon of all-time Australian cricket icons.

McGrath may not have had Warne's array of party tricks, or profile, but he was equally effective and just as discomforting. Paul Reiffel loves to tell the story of the day he and McGrath bowled England out at Lord's in 1997:

'Pigeon took eight mind you – and I got just the two. . . but we did bowl 'em out!'

## McGRATH AND WARNE'S BEST TESTS TOGETHER

| Wickets | |
|---|---|
| 18 | v England, The Oval, 2001 (McGrath 2–67 and 5–43, Warne 7–165 and 4–64) |
| 17 | v England, The Oval, 2005 (McGrath 2–72 and 3–85, Warne 6–122 and 6–124) |
| 16 | v England, Old Trafford, 1997 (McGrath 3–40 and 4–46, Warne 6–48 and 3–63) |
| 15 | v Pakistan, Sara Stadium, Colombo, 2002–03 (McGrath 1–48 and 3–38, Warne 7–94 and 4–94) |
| 15 | v Pakistan, Sharjah, 2002–03 (McGrath 4–41 and 3–18, Warne 5–74 and 3–56) |
| 15 | v England, Lord's, 2005 (McGrath 5–53 and 4–29, Warne 2–19 and 4–64 |

## MOST CAREER WINS

| Player | Tests | Wins | Percentage |
|---|---|---|---|
| Ricky Ponting (Australia) | 165 | 108 | 65.45 |
| Shane Warne (Australia) | 145 | 92 | 63.45 |
| Steve Waugh (Australia) | 168 | 86 | 51.19 |
| Glenn McGrath (Australia) | 124 | 84 | 67.74 |
| Mark Boucher (South Africa) | 144 | 73 | 50.69 |
| Adam Gilchrist (Australia) | 96 | 73 | 76.04 |

Table: Ross Dundas

McGrath's hat-trick in the extraordinary first hour of the 2000–01 Perth Test guaranteed Australia a record twelfth consecutive victory. It was a handy threesome: Sherwin Campbell, Brian Lara and Jimmy Adams. A week earlier in the first Test at the Gabba he'd taken six for 17 and four for 10. The West Indies were beaten 5–0 and never again accorded a five-Test series.

'Glenn was two bowlers in one,' his long-time captain Steve Waugh said. 'He could keep it tight when you wanted him to, but

**Personality of the Tour:** A very blond Shane Warne was the life of the party during the 1990 Australian Youth team tour of the Caribbean. Seven of the team were to play Tests, two with England. The team from the back row, left to right: Jason Young, Damien Fleming, Stuart Oliver, Brendon Julian, Chris Mack, David Castle, Jason Gallian, Shane George, Craig White Front: Damien Martyn, Warne, Brian Taber (manager), Jamie Cox (captain), Steve Bernard (coach), Michael Bevan and Darren Berry.

he could also be aggressive and take wickets.' Waugh said it was the ultimate luxury to have both McGrath and Warne in the same XI, as it allowed Australia to consistently field four specialist bowlers and bat Adam Gilchrist at No. 7.

David Gower said McGrath was 'a genius at putting the ball in the right place with immense consistency and then keeping the batsman guessing whether the ball would then continue on the same line or take another tack'.

McGrath's secrets of success revolved around his momentum through the crease, an upright seam position and pinpoint accuracy – allied with an off-cutter good enough to dismiss anyone in the game, including long-time world No. 1 Lara. His committed fitness work off the field in the gymnasium and general management allowed him to maintain peak fitness longer than most. He never wanted to rest. While he didn't possess the sheer pace of a Lillee, Thomson or his contemporary Brett Lee, his strike rate was just as impressive.

He loved bowling alongside Warne as the challenges for the batsmen were so different: McGrath with his seam and bounce, Warne with his curve and side-spin. Occasionally, like in the first innings of that famous Adelaide Test, they could be mastered. McGrath's figures blew out to none for 107 from 30 and Warne's one for 167 from 53. But that was a rare blimp in their fabulous record, which is unlikely ever to be equalled, let alone surpassed.

In 104 Tests together, they captured 50.5 per cent of Australia's wickets, McGrath 488 and Warne 513. They were directly responsible for winning more Test matches than anyone else ahead of the Don, Wasim Akram and Muthiah Muralidaran.

In their final decade, they played together 38 times at home for 32 wins and six draws, McGrath claiming that outside Bradman, Warne had the biggest impact of any cricketer to wear Australia's baggy green cap.

Ashley Mallett, Australia's champion spinner of the 1970s, said Warne changed spin bowling forever with his arc, spin, energy and dipping flight. He estimated Warne's 'danger area' as the width of a dinner table. Others like Anil Kumble had a danger area of just a dinner plate!

Ian Chappell reckoned Warne had so many ways he could beat you: spin, curve, subtle variations and flight.

'Very few bowlers can say they won the unwinnable match: but Warne did in Adelaide in 2006–07,' he said.

Abans
Abans
Abans

# X

**‘Reassuringly, his defence was solid and he instinctively flowed into several pull shots like the Ponting of old. The battle was compelling, the crowd totally absorbed. . .’**

## X-FACTORS

Few deny Ricky Ponting's standing as Australia's finest batsman since Don Bradman. Talented, passionate and prolific, he has been a champion of his generation. But age catches up with even the mighty, and with an average of 25 in Australia's first seven Tests of 2011–12, Ponting's right to his place at No. 3 was questioned like never before. He was 37, no longer captain and batting with little of the command or authority of yesteryear. An embarrassing lbw against the New Zealanders, when he lost balance at the crease and walked even before being given out in home town Hobart, could easily have been the cue for Australia's revamped selection panel to immediately promote one of the younger ones.

Further fuelling the debate, selection supremo John Inverarity insisted that no player, no matter how distinguished, had an ongoing right to Test selection.

Ponting was among those told to spend Christmas week at coach Mickey Arthur's batting school in Melbourne. And with a pair of 60s in the first Test of the summer against the Indians at the MCG, Ponting survived for Sydney and the second of the summer's feature Tests. His career, however, was still very much on the precipice.

---

**Exhilarating:** A feature of Michael Clarke's brilliant 2011–12 summer was two stellar stands with the man he replaced as Australia's captain, Ricky Ponting. *Australian Cricket Summer Guide*

Meanwhile, his successor as captain, Michael Clarke, had been outstandingly dominant, making three centuries in four Tests, one in Sri Lanka, one in South Africa and another back in Australia. His leadership was decisive and positive – as was his admiration and support for the beleaguered Ponting.

'I know his game backwards. He's working hard. He'll come good,' he said in the lead-up to the Boxing Day Test.

After an even first three days against the much-vaunted Indians in Melbourne, the Australians won the final day comprehensively and were 1–0 ahead approaching the New Year Test in Sydney.

Bowled out for under 200 on an action-packed opening day, India hit back with veteran swing specialist Zaheer Khan taking the first three wickets for just 23. At 2–8, Ponting entered on a hat-trick. When Ed Cowan succumbed, Australia was 3–37 and teetering. Clarke was averaging just 26 in Sydney. An early play-and-miss against bouncy Ishant Sharma added to the early tension. The Australians were being seriously challenged.

Ponting was playing only when he had to. Reassuringly, his defence was solid and he instinctively flowed into several pull shots like the Ponting of old. The battle was compelling, the crowd totally absorbed. A signature Clarke cover drive or two eased the pressure and by stumps the pair had advanced Australia's score to 3–115, Clarke the aggressor on 47 and Ponting 44, their unconquered stand already worth 79.

The Indians had remained competitive, young expresses Umesh Yadav and Ishant bowling with genuine heat and the 33-year-old Zaheer bending the ball around menacingly, if not at the speed of old.

It had been two years and 32 innings since Ponting's thirty-ninth Test century. Could he turn a promising start into his fortieth hundred and again shape Australia's destiny?

Despite their outstanding solo careers and having batting's 'x' factor, he and Clarke had so often underachieved as a pair. Only twice before in 27 partnerships had they shared in three-figure stands, the triple-century against Pakistan in Hobart two years earlier the only one which could truly be termed decisive in the winning of the match.

Ponting seemed calm and his footwork assured on resumption, and within minutes of play starting on the second morning, he reached his half-century. The reception was generous and long-lasting, most of the 30,000-plus crowd standing to cheer. Clearly they were buoyed and wanted more. Ponting was defending the good ones and taking full advantage of those over-pitched or short. Every single was enthusiastically applauded as India's modest first innings score was approached and then passed.

Other than a play and a miss at Zaheer, who went around the wicket in the opening over, Clarke was also comfortable and the pair scored at a run a minute against a ball rapidly losing its sheen.

A classic Clarke cover drive on the eve of lunch saw him register three figures, Ponting being 97 at the interval. During the final over the pair had run two leg byes, the crowd groaning in disappointment when the runs weren't given to Ponting.

Immediately after the break, with his score on 99, he struck a ball firmly just slightly wide of mid-on, called for a single which wasn't there and made a desperate dive for the crease. Zaheer Khan's high-speed throw from close range only just missed the stumps. Had it hit, Ponting would have been out. He slowly picked himself up, dirt all down his shirt. The reception for his hundred was even louder than for local hero Clarke. In half a day's batting, Ponting had reminded everyone of his class, especially those who had already written his obituary.

His matchwinning fightback with Clarke was ultimately to be worth 288 at almost four an over, Clarke's contribution 154 and Ponting's 122. An even bigger stand (334) was to follow that afternoon and into the fourth day between Clarke and next-man-in Michael Hussey, Clarke declaring with his own score on 329 and Hussey's 150, the Australians winning Sydney's one hundredth Test match by an innings.

At a packed press conference, Ponting told of the frustration he and Clarke had both felt in not being able to bat together for as long as they'd wished.

'Through our careers, even in the dominant teams, we haven't actually spent a lot of time together out in the middle,' he said. 'We

**CENTURY STANDS IN TESTS BETWEEN RICKY PONTING AND MICHAEL CLARKE**

| | |
|---|---|
| 386 | v India, Adelaide, 2011–12 |
| 358 | v Pakistan, Hobart 2009–10 |
| 288 | v India, Sydney, 2011–12 |
| 210 | v India, Adelaide, 2007–08 |

had a great partnership in Hobart, and we know how important we are to the team and probably over-emphasised that a bit too much last summer [against England] and put a little too much pressure on ourselves to be the men that were going to hold the hopes of the team up.'

With their different techniques, Ponting felt the pair should have prospered more often.

'Michael tends to use his feet against the spinners a bit more than I do and we both probably play fast bowling a little bit differently as well. So if you sat back and looked at it that way you'd think we'd be a very successful partnership together, but so far it hasn't been as productive as we would've liked. Hopefully that can continue to change.'

Perth was to be a quieter Test for them both before they finished the summer in Adelaide with imperious double-centuries, Ponting 221 and Clarke 210 as Australia completed a 4–0 thrashing of a fast-fading, directionless India. Their stand this time was worth a massive 386 and came at better than a run a minute, the pair batting three full sessions. From the time he started his innings with a straight drive against Yadav, to the longest boundary in the country, Ponting was in supreme command, Bill Lawry saying he hadn't seen him play as well for years.

For the second time in three Tests the pair had shown themselves to be Australia's most outstanding batsmen. For Ponting, it kept alive his dream of one last Ashes tilt in England in 2013.

**Prolific:** Michael Clarke with Ricky Ponting during their epic 386 run fourth wicket stand against the Indians in Adelaide, 2012. Both made double-centuries. *Peter Argent*

**Flat-Out:** Rick Darling dives for his crease after yet another misunderstanding with opening partner Graeme Wood, Melbourne, 1978–79. Cricketer *magazine*

# Y

**‘It got too much for young Johnny who yelled: “Jessssus #@&%ing Christ!”. . .’**

## ‘YOU BASSTARDDDD!’

The Rev. Garry Jacobs had been a notable first-grade player in Perth before matters of the cloth took precedence and he became the Presbyterian minister at my old home town of Beaumaris, 30 minutes south of Melbourne.

Sunny-natured, skilful and smart, he involved himself in the local cricket club, wanting to meet as many of the locals as possible. Telling them that he'd played a bit of cricket, he was immediately included in the first XI.

A 17-year-old John Ward, destined for Victorian honours, was the local express and they formed quite a combo: ‘c Jacobs, b Ward’.

One day an opening batsman from Cheltenham played and missed at Ward three times in a row. On the third it got too much for young Johnny who yelled: ‘Jessssus #@&%ing Christ!’

‘No, noo, NOOO John,’ called the Reverend in admonishment. ‘Never use Christ's name in vain.’

Next over the opener got an edge. It flew to the Reverend's right. . . a bread-and-butter catch that he somehow managed to drop. Seething with rage he pointed to the sky and yelled: ‘You basstardddd!’

## YES, NO... SORRY

Adelaide Riverlander Rick Darling is another old cricketer who thanks billionaire businessman Kerry Packer for helping to change the game in the late 1970s.

Without Mr Packer's considerable investment into the game from 1977, Darling could well have stayed in the backwater of Sheffield Shield cricket.

Apart from the emerging Kim Hughes, who was never offered a contract, Packer was to claim the very best two dozen Australian

**Shotmaker:** Riverlander Rick Darling at the Sydney Cricket Ground, 1978–79. Cricketer *magazine*

cricketers for his rebel World Series Cricket movement and thus in the next two years, 23 newcomers were introduced into traditional Test cricket ranks. Darling was one of those to be promoted, and with his attractive strokeplay he was an immediate favourite.

In 14 Tests he was to average only 26, and when Mr Packer brokered a compromise with Sir Donald Bradman, Darling was among a dozen to return permanently to lesser grades.

He made an impression, however, all but swallowing his tongue after being hit by English express Bob Willis in home town Adelaide, and developing an opening combination with West Australian Graeme Wood which was so helter-skelter that they soon became known as the Kamikaze Kids, their full-length dives at the crease a common occurrence after a 'Yes, no. . . sorry' call.

They ran each other out in two of their last three Tests together, their average of just over 25 including just three half-century stands in 16 innings. Running in unison was not their forte. . .

**Shooting Star:** Injury stopped World Cup representative Andrew Zesers in the late 1980s just as his career was blossoming. Zesers is one of only two cricketers with a surname beginning with 'Z' to represent Australia.
Cricketer *magazine*

# Z

**'They caused a sensation by all but winning in Melbourne, and in the following Test defeating the might of the Australians. . .'**

## ZULCH AND FAULKNER

When the South African Springboks toured Australia for the first time in 1910–11, opposing a galaxy of revered Golden Age legends from Victor Trumper and Clem Hill to Warren Bardsley and Bill Whitty, they caused a sensation by all but winning in Melbourne, and in the following Test defeating the might of the Australians in Adelaide.

Two of the most pivotal in the strong showings were opener Billy Zulch and the team's champion all-rounder Aubrey Faulkner, among 11 from the Transvaal in the touring XV. Both made two centuries each, including tons in Adelaide, where South Africa won for the first time against the Australians in an exciting finish.

Sharing a 135-run stand in the first innings, Zulch made 105 and Faulkner 56. In the last Test of the summer in Sydney, they added 143, with Zulch scoring a career-best 150 and Faulkner 92, forcing Australia to bat a second time. For the Test summer Zulch made 354 runs at almost 40, and Faulkner made 732 runs at 73, a record aggregate at the time.

Faulkner is one of South Africa's ultimate Hall of Famers, while Zulch is among just eight Test players to have a surname beginning with 'Z' – and the only one to make a Test century.

Just two Australians with a surname starting with 'Z' have played at international level: Tim Zoehrer, who played 10 Tests and 22 One-Day Internationals; and Andrew Zesers, who had two ODIs during the 1987 World Cup campaign.

## BILLY ZULCH IN TEST CRICKET

**Debut:** 1909–10

**Tests:** 16

**Runs:** 985

**Average:** 32.83

**Highest score:** 150 v Australia, Sydney, 1910–11

**100s:** 2

## AUBREY FAULKNER IN TEST CRICKET

**Debut:** 1905–06

**Tests:** 25

**Runs:** 1754

**Average:** 40.79

**Highest score:** 204 v Australia, Melbourne, 1910–11

**100s:** 4

* Faulkner also took 82 wickets at 26.59 with 3 5wl

**Teaming Up:** Members of the Australian and South African Test teams in Sydney 1910–11. Jack Zulch is pictured in the very front row on the extreme right and his champion Springbok teammate Aubrey Faulkner seated behind him on the extreme right. The teams: back row, left to right: Warren Bardsley (A), Sid Pegler, Charlie Kelleway (A), Charles Llewellyn, Vernon Ransford (A), Orm. Pearse. Middle: Warwick Armstrong (A), Dave Nourse, H. V. 'Ranji' Hordern (A), Lou Stricker, Algy Gehrs (A), A. 'Tibby' Cotter (A). Seated: Jimmy Sinclair, Victor Trumper (A), Percy Sherwell, Clem Hill (A), Reggie Schwarz, Bill Whitty (A), Faulkner. Front: S. J. 'Tip' Snooke, Charlie Macartney (A), J. M. M. 'Mick' Commaille, H. 'Sammy' Carter (A), Zulch. Insets: Tom Campbell and A. E. 'Bert' Vogler.

# Bibliography


## ANNUALS

Beecher, Eric (editor), *Cricket Close-Up 1978* (Newspress Pty Ltd, Melbourne), 1978

Chettle, Geoff (editor), *South African Cricket Annual 1959* (Hayne and Gibson, Durban), 1959

Compton, Leslie (editor), *The Denis Compton Annual* (Mandeville Publications, London), 1952

*Cricketer Annual*, various issues 1974–77 (Newspress Pty Ltd, Melbourne)

Finlay, Ric (editor), *Cricket Tasmania 1997–98* (Sportsnews Tasmania, Kingston), 1998

Piesse, Ken (editor), *Cricket Digest 1979* (Newspress Pty Ltd, Melbourne), 1979

*Wisden Cricketers' Almanack,* various issues

## BOOKS

Amiss, Dennis, *In Search of Runs* (Stanley Paul and Co., London), 1976

Armstrong, Geoff, *A Century of Summers, 100 years of Sheffield Shield Cricket* (Ironbark Press, Sydney), 1992

Astle, Nathan, *Astle* (Hachette Livre NZ Ltd, Auckland), 2007

Barnes, Sid, *It Isn't Cricket* (Williams Collins Overseas Ltd, Sydney), 1953

Brayshaw, Ian, *Caught Marsh, Bowled Lillee* (ABC Books, Sydney), 1983

Chalke, Stephen, *Five Five Five, Holmes and Sutcliffe in 1932* (Fairfield Books, Bath), 2007

Chappell, Greg, *Fierce Focus* (Hardie Grant Books, Richmond, Melbourne), 2011

Coward, Mike, *Calypso Summer* (ABC Books, Sydney), 2000

Crace, John, *Wasim and Waqar* (Boxtree Limited, London), 1992

Fletcher, Keith, *Captain's Innings, an Autobiography* (Stanley Paul and Co., London), 1976

Frindall, Bill, *The Wisden Book of Test Cricket,* various vols (MacDonald and Jane's, London)

Frith, David, *The Fast Men, a 200-year cavalcade of speed bowlers* (Van Nostrand Reinhold Company Ltd, London), 1975

Frith, David, *The Slow Men* (Richard Smart Publishing, Sydney), 1984

Harris, Norman, *What Are You Doing Out Here? Heroism and Distress at a Cricket Test* (Last Side Publishing, Hamilton, NZ), 2010

Healy, Ian, *Playing for Keeps, the Ian Healy Story* (Swan Publishing, Dalkeith, Perth), 1996

Hill, Alan, *Tony Lock, Aggressive Master of Spin* (The History Press, Gloucestershire), 2008

Hookes, David (with Alan Shiell), *Hookesy* (ABC, Sydney), 2001

Johnson, Ian, *Cricket at the Crossroads* (Cassell and Company Limited, London), 1957

Knight, James, *Mark Waugh: the Biography* (HarperSports, Sydney), 2002

Kumar, Vijay P, *Cricket Lovely Cricket, West Indies v England 1950* (self published, Jamaica), 2000

Lawry, Bill, *Run-Digger, Bill Lawry's Own Story* (Souvenir Press, London), 1966

Lawson, Geoff, *Henry: The Geoff Lawson Story* (Ironbark Press, Randwick, Sydney), 1993

Lee, Frank, *Cricket Lovely Cricket* (Stanley Paul, London), 1960

Lloyd, Clive, *Living for Cricket* (Stanley Paul and Co., London), 1980

Lloyd, David *David Lloyd: The Autobiography (*CollinsWillow, London), 2001

Lloyd, David, *G'day Ya Pommie B. . ..! and Other Cricket Memories* (Weidenfeld and Nicholson, London), 1992

Lock, Tony, *For Surrey and England* (Hodder and Stoughton, London), 1957

Luckhurst, Brian, *From Boot Boy to President* (KOS Media Publishing Ltd, Kent), 2004

Malcolm, Devon, *You Guys Are History* (CollinsWillow, London), 1998

Mallett, Ashley, *Grimmett, the Bradman of Spin* (University of Queensland Press, St Lucia, Brisbane), 1993

Marsh, Rod (as told to Ian Brayshaw), *You'll Keep* (Hutchinson Group (Australia), Melbourne), 1975

Martin-Jenkins, Christopher, *Oxford World Cricketers* (Oxford University Press, New York), 1996

McCool, Colin, *Cricket is a Game* (Stanley Paul, London), 1961

Menzies, Sir Robert, *The Measure of the Years* (Cassell and Company, London), 1970

Midwinter, Eric, *Brylcreem Summer, the 1947 Cricket Season* (Kingswood Press, London), 1991

Miller, Keith, *Cricket Crossfire* (Oldbourne Press, London), 1956

Morrison, Danny, *Mad As I Wanna Be* (Hodder Moa Beckett, Auckland), 1997

Piesse, Ken and Hansen, Brian, *Wild Men of Cricket Vol. 1* (Brian Hansen Publications, Moorabbin, Melbourne), 1997

Piesse, Ken, *Down at the Junction* (St Kilda Cricket Club, St Kilda, Melbourne), 2006

Richardson, Vic (with RS Whitington), *The Vic Richardson Story* (Rigby Limited, Adelaide), 1967

Riley, John, *Tenth Wicket First Class Cricket Record Partnership, 307 Runs* (self published, Melbourne), 1997

Roebuck, Peter, *Great Innings,* (Pan Books Australia, Pty Ltd, Sydney), 1990

Romanos, Joseph, *John Reid, a Cricketing Life* (Hodder Moa Becket, Auckland, 2000)

Smith, Ian (with Roger Brittenden), *Just a Drummer in the Band* (Moa Publications, Auckland), 1991

Smith, Nigel, *Kiwis Declare: Players Tell the Story of New Zealand Cricket* (Random House NZ, Auckland), 1994

Smith, Rick, *Cricket's Enigma, the Sid Barnes Story* (ABC Books, Sydney), 1999

Smith, Terry, *Bedside Book of Cricket Centuries* (CollinsAngus and Robertson, North Ryde, NSW), 1991

Taylor, Mark (with Ian Heads), *Time to Declare, an Autobiography* (Pan Macmillan Australia, Sydney), 1999

Thomson, AA, *Hirst & Rhodes* (Epworth Press, London), 1959

Thomson, AA, *Hutton & Washbrook* (The Epworth Press, London), 1963

Van Ryneveld, Clive, *Twentieth Century All-rounder* (Pretext Publishers, Cape Town), 2011

Washbrook, Cyril, *Cricket the Silver Lining* (Sportsguide Publications, London), 1950

Waugh, Steve, *Out of my Comfort Zone, the Autobiography* (Penguin/ Viking, Melbourne), 2005

Wilde, Geoff, *Ernest Tyldesley: His Record Innings by Innings* (ACS Publications, West Bridgford, Nottingham), 2001

Wright, John, *John Wright's Indian Summers* (Souvenir Press, London), 2007

Wright, Wally, *It's Your Wally Grout* (Ken Piesse Cricket Books, Mt Eliza), 2011

Yardley, Bruce, *Roo's Book* (self published, Perth), 2011

## E-MAGAZINES AND NEWSLETTERS

*Break o' Day* (Australian Cricket Society, Tasmanian branch, Hobart)

## MAGAZINES

*Cricketer* (Australia)

*Great Triumphs in Test Cricket,* edited by Ken Piesse (CP Publishing, Woollahra, Sydney), 1978

*Magic Moments in Australian Cricket,* edited by Ken Piesse (Emap Australia, Sydney), 2002

*The Cricketer* (UK)

*Wasim Akram Benefit Year, 1998*

## PAMPHLETS

Campbell, RH (editor), *Cricket Casualties* (ABC, Sydney), 1933

Miller, SG, *Ball by Ball Record, Together with Averages and Summary of 1946–47 Series, Test Matches, England v Australia in Australia* (self published, Ryde, Sydney), 1947

## RADIO

The ABC Test broadcasts, 2011–12

## WEBSITES

Cricinfo.com

cricketbooks.com.au

# THE AUSTRALIAN

## Souvenir edition

# WORLD'S BEST

Courtesy of Jane and Gerry Dorset

# Index

**SCOREBOARDS**



**STATISTICAL TABLES**